BC

musical performance: learning theory and pedagogy

Daniel L. Kohut
School of Music
University of Illinois
at Urbana-Champaign

Prentice-Hall, Inc., Englewood Cliffs, New Jersey 07632

Library of Congress Cataloging in Publication Data

Kohut, Daniel L., 1935–
    Musical performance.

    Includes bibliographical references and index.
    1. Music—Instruction and study.   2. Music—
Performance.   3. Learning, Psychology of.   4. Teaching.
I. Title.
MT1.K624   1985   780'.7   84-1729
ISBN 0-13-607862-1

Editorial/production supervision
and interior design: Virginia Cavanagh Neri
Cover design: Diane Saxe
Manufacturing buyer: Ray Keating

To Arnold Jacobs:
artist-musician, gifted teacher
and superior human being

Printed in the United States of America

10   9   8   7   6   5   4   3   2   1

ISBN 0-13-607862-1   01

Prentice-Hall International, Inc., *London*
Prentice-Hall of Australia Pty. Limited, *Sydney*
Editora Prentice-Hall do Brasil, Ltda., *Rio de Janeiro*
Prentice-Hall Canada Inc., *Toronto*
Prentice-Hall of India Private Limited, *New Delhi*
Prentice-Hall of Japan, Inc., *Tokyo*
Prentice-Hall of Southeast Asia Pte. Ltd., *Singapore*
Whitehall Books Limited, *Wellington, New Zealand*

CONTENTS

CAT Oct 21 '85

two

Neuromuscular Physiology 19

three

Foundations of Human Psychology 35

four

Psychophysiological Principles and Techniques of Learning 58

PART II PRINCIPLES AND METHODS OF TEACHING

five

Introduction to Teaching 73

preface

The purpose of this textbook is to provide you, the teacher of singers and/or instrumentalists, with specific practical methods for teaching performance skills to music students. The main focus will be on perceptual-motor learning because I believe that this is where the greatest confusion in music methodology exists today. Discussions with physical education and dance instructors indicate that a similar problem also exists in their fields. It is my hope, therefore, that several chapters of this text will be useful to these instructors as well as teachers of singers and instrumentalists.

Why still another book on teaching methods? With the advancement of Western civilization since the Renaissance, and especially the scientific discoveries and technological progress during this century, one would reasonably expect that teaching methodology would also be at a relatively high level of advancement. After all, teaching is not a new profession; teachers have been around since the time of Socrates at the very least and probably long before that. And yet in the area of musical performance, we still find considerable confusion, controversy and diversity regarding what is valid methodology and what is inaccurate and charlatanism. In the area of breathing, for example, Hutton—in a survey dating as far back as 1951—cites 428 different concepts of breathing related to singing alone, with twenty-five of them being documented studies based upon x-ray research techniques.[1] In the era of brass instrument embouchure, Reinhardt reviews his personal experiences in studying with numerous teachers, all of whom tried to teach him a different type of embouchure.[2] These are only two examples that illustrate the basic problem. Together you and I could easily identify many others ranging from proper use of the glottis in singing to how one should teach efficient bow control in string playing. Clearly, then, we need to find ways to determine what is valid methodology and what is not. Learning to sing and/or play an instrument is challenging enough even when proper methods are used. Why make it harder by using erroneous methods of teaching and learning?

This textbook is divided into three main parts. Part I focuses on learning theory while Part II is devoted to various aspects of teaching theory. This theoretical background information then leads us to Part III, which deals specifically with the principles, methods and theories of musical tone production. The key to good tone production is efficient perceptual-motor coordination. Without it, good tone production is impossible.

More specifically, the main purpose of Part I is to provide a psycho-physiological basis for teaching perceptual-motor skills. First I will provide a general overview of learning theory in Chapter One. Then, I will cover neuromuscular physiology with special emphasis given to body feedback and the importance of posture and body balance as a means toward avoiding excessive muscular tension. Other major topics will include a discussion of both Eastern and Western psychology and related concepts including self-image and self-esteem, mental imagery and the development of good concentration.

The underlying purpose of Part II, Teaching Theory, is to establish basic principles and methods of teaching based upon the principles of learning outlined in Part I. Major topics to be covered include motivation, competition, a review and evaluation of selected methods of teaching including imitation plus techniques of developmental and remedial teaching and a special section on teaching students how to practice.

In Part III, Tone Production, the initial focus will be on the anatomical and physiological aspects of tone production with a special section on muscular physiology related directly toward breathing. Following a review and evaluation of selected theories of breathing, I will discuss specific tone production problems—their causes and solutions—with a special section on the use of audiovisual-kinesthetic teaching aids. The text ends with the Epilogue.

---

[1]Charles L. Hutton, Jr., *A Survey of Research Pertaining to the Singing Voice* (Unpublished Master's Thesis, Dept. of Speech, University of Pittsburgh, 1951), p. 19.

[2]Donald S. Reinhardt, *The Encyclopedia of the Pivot System* (New York: Charles Colin, 1964), p. 19.

AUTHOR'S BACKGROUND
AND EXPERIENCE

I am a musician, music teacher and teacher of music teachers. I am not a physiologist, psychologist or learning theorist in the professional sense. However, I have devoted considerable time and effort to the study of these nonmusical disciplines over the past ten years, including full-time study and research in 1977 in the Motor Learning and Development Laboratory, College of Applied Life Studies, University of Illinois. Two sabbatical leaves, in 1973 and 1980, were also devoted to study in these areas, including interviews with several teachers with specialized knowledge in these fields.

I feel very fortunate to have had, during this time, both my summers in Vermont, where I could read and think in some depth about the subjects in this text, and my work during the academic year, when I could discuss them at length with many very enthusiastic, intelligent students and professional colleagues. Specific colleagues at the University of Illinois include professors Richard Colwell, Mary Hoffman, Charles Leonhard, Daniel Perantoni, David Peters, the late Paul Rolland, and Thomas Wisniewski. I also wish to thank my wife, Maryann Kohut, Coordinator of the Learning Laboratory at Parkland College. To all of these distinguished persons and treasured friends I owe a great debt for the time, interest, stimulation and feedback that they gave to me, much of it in informal discussions over coffee and extended lunch periods. Although I take full responsibility for any errors or inconsistencies that may appear in this text, I am certain that many of the ideas and analogies proposed here belong either directly or indirectly to these persons. While I would like to give credit to specific individuals where it is due, it is difficult to identify exactly where and with whom certain concepts originated when one actually gets around to writing them down on paper.

There is one person, however, to whom I feel I owe a special debt: Arnold Jacobs, principal tubaist of the Chicago Symphony and internationally recognized wind-instrument teacher, who first activated my interest in the physiological and psychological aspects of wind instrument performance, and who was also a major influence in helping me choose the specific directions my study should take and the sources I should read. What I am and believe as a teacher today is due in significant measure to his untiring and unselfish efforts in helping me learn new ways of viewing the teaching-learning process. This text is therefore respectfully dedicated to this distinguished gentleman.

Finally, I would like to express appreciation to Mrs. Elisabeth Carlin, of Middlebury, Vermont, for the sincere care and attention she gave in deciphering and typing what originally was almost an illegible manuscript.

Daniel L. Kohut

iNTROd∪CTiON

Dear Reader:

    Much of what is to be discussed in this section is normally included as part of
a Preface. In my experience, however, I find that very few people read a Preface
seriously and I did not want that to happen in this instance. In an attempt to
circumvent this problem I have labeled this section an introduction in hopes that you
will be more likely to read the contents herein. The purpose of the Introduction is to
show you how to read, comprehend and really learn the material in the body of the
text. You are therefore strongly urged to read and study it carefully. If you have not
as yet read the actual Preface, I urge you to go back and do so. It, too, is important
and should be read.

WHY I WROTE THIS BOOK

As stated in the Preface, the purpose of this textbook is to provide you with specific
practical methods for teaching performance skills to music students. The main
reason why another book on performance pedagogy is needed is because of the great
confusion, controversy and diversity which exist. Most musicians do not understand
how the musical performance process operates from a perceptual-motor standpoint.
In the following paragraphs I will explain how I arrived at these conclusions. I will

do this via a brief chronicle of my own study and research during the past twenty-three years.

As a public school teacher I looked forward to the day when I might be in charge of training prospective music teachers at the college/university level. Little did I realize at the time the immensity of the challenge I would later face. I began preparation for my first methods course with a review of all instrumental-methods texts published through the late 1960s. From this review I became aware for the first time that most texts failed to deal with important subjects like tone quality, intonation and articulation in any real depth; the tendency instead was to cover a large number of diverse subjects in survey form. I also found that some critical topics like the teaching of music reading were often omitted entirely. This motivated me to prepare supplementary handouts for my teacher-trainees, which became the nucleus of my first text, *Instrumental Music Pedagogy,* published by Prentice-Hall, Inc., in 1973.

An even greater, more complex problem I discovered during the above investigation was the large number and diversity of methods recommended by various authors for the teaching of basic performance skills as cited in the Preface. The more I became aware of the immensity of the problem, the more I could not help wondering if there was not some way to solve it, to eliminate the inconsistency and confusion through development of some kind of basic guidelines or principles which would apply to everyone. And if there was a way, how might someone like me go about trying to accomplish this task? Eventually I decided that the logical place to begin was with the study of breathing. The main reason I selected breathing was because it is the primary basis for good vocal and wind instrument tone production. I also found myself unable to answer adequately many questions about breathing function which my teacher trainees asked me. This was frustrating; I felt viable answers to these questions were needed.

During my sabbatical leave in 1973 I began an intensive study of breathing. However, I soon decided that I could not really reach any definite conclusions about breathing pedagogy without first knowing something about breathing anatomy and physiology. But the more I learned about breathing function, the more I sensed that *real* understanding was impossible until I learned something about the basics of perceptual-motor function. Yet this was still not enough. My continued study eventually expanded to include the larger area of total mind-body function. This in turn led me to related areas such as anthropology, evolution, biochemistry and psychology, including Eastern psychology and its focus on mind-body integration and meditation. As a result I felt that for the first time I was beginning to understand what I had read earlier in the writings of Buckminster Fuller, Alfred North Whitehead and other philosopher-scientists—that human knowledge cannot be effectively dissected and compartmentalized into isolated specializations and still be accurately understood. In-depth understanding comes only after information from all related disciplines is integrated into a single, unified whole. In the case of musical performance I found that this requires knowledge of philosophy and aesthetics as well as of the biological and behavioral sciences.

Finally I felt I was getting somewhere. I began to feel a degree of confidence in knowing and understanding my subject in some depth. But knowledge of subject matter alone is not enough for someone whose ultimate goal is to teach it to others. One must also develop practical strategies for communicating this information logically and systematically. Accomplishing this first requires understanding of how people learn. Milhollan and Forisha illustrate this concept beautifully with the following statement: "Teaching is an activity which emerges from some conception about how learning occurs."[1] Teaching, therefore, is largely a deductive process rather than an inductive one. Teaching methods should be based on established principles of learning, not vice versa.

Being convinced that this above approach was a logical one, I began investigating various books on learning theory, four of which are listed below. I strongly recommend that all four of these be read before studying the body of this text, preferably in the order listed. All of them are easy to read, relatively short and are, in my opinion, the best books currently available on the subject of perceptual-motor skill development.

GALLWEY, W. TIMOTHY. *The Inner Game of Tennis.* New York: Random House, 1974.
SUZUKI, SHINICHI. *Nurtured By Love.* New York: Exposition Press, 1969.
GALLWEY, W. TIMOTHY. *Inner Tennis: Playing the Game.* New York: Random House, 1976.
MALTZ, MAXWELL T. *Psycho-Cybernetics.* New York: Pocket Books, 1960.

While I am currently a strong advocate of the learning theories of Gallwey, Suzuki and Maltz, this was not the case when I first read their books. The use of imitation, repetition and mere trial and error practice as *primary* methods of learning seemed too simplistic at first. A number of my colleagues and students shared this view. Still other concepts, particularly those related to Eastern psychology, were confusing to me. But my continued study of anatomy, physiology and both Eastern and Western psychology eventually proved that the above learning theories were essentially very valid ones. There really was research evidence to support these theories and concepts. In addition, I also found documented support for some of the other, more traditional methods used by music teachers. At the same time I discovered that music methodology is also fraught with considerable misinformation, error and confusion as well. These facts convinced me that such information needed to be disseminated to the entire profession. This is the main reason I wrote this text.

Why did I tell you about all of this in this Introduction? I wanted you to know the various directions I took in my study and why I chose them. I see this as an important preliminary step to your understanding my line of reasoning and why I chose to cover the specific topics found in the body of this text.

---

[1]Frank Milhollan and Bill E. Forisha, *From Skinner to Rogers: Contrasting Approaches to Education* (Lincoln, Neb.: Professional Educators Publications, Inc., 1972), p. 8.

CHApTER ONE

bAsic CONCEPTs
of pERCEpTUAL-MOTOR lEARNiNG

As stated in the Introduction, "teaching is an activity which emerges from some conception about how learning occurs."[1] In other words, before we can know *what* and *how* to teach, we first need to know how people learn. This seems logical enough, but the answer is not necessarily a simple one. No two people are exactly the same physiologically or psychologically; thus no two people learn in exactly the same ways. Two people striving to achieve the same performance goal may well accomplish it in strikingly different ways. Who is to say which procedure is superior? Like two children in the same family whose behavior is very different, who can honestly say that one child is appreciably "better" than the other? And yet there are certain basic concepts of learning that can be broadly applied to almost everyone. Discussion of these basic concepts is the main purpose of this chapter.

THE NATURAL LEARNING
PROCESS

The Natural Learning Process (hereafter referred to as NLP) is the same process we used in first learning how to walk and talk. It involves use of mental imagery, imitation and trial-and-error practice as primary methods of learning. It also in-

[1]F. Milhollan and B. E. Forisha, *From Skinner to Rogers: Contrasting Approaches to Education* (Lincoln, Nebraska: Professional Educators Publications, Inc., 1972), p. 8. Reprinted by permission.

volves the use of body feedback for detection and correction of performance errors.

Even though the label NLP originated with Gallwey, Suzuki's philosophy seems to be in basic agreement with the NLP concept. Suzuki recommends, for example, that children should learn to perform music in essentially the same way they learn to talk: by developing musical conception (mental imagery) through listening, followed by imitation and trial-and-error practice. These procedures represent the essence of what he calls the Mother Tongue Approach to musical learning.[2]

Have you noticed that the term "student" has not been used thus far in this discussion? This term automatically implies the existence of a teacher, and NLP does not require a teacher in the formal sense. All that is really needed is a good performance model and an interested person with a sincere desire to learn. This is why NLP is truly a *natural* process of learning.

Does NLP really work? Certainly it does; children use it all of the time. In the case of musical performance, there is ample evidence that it has worked exceedingly well, particularly in the case of many jazz and country-western musicians who were largely self-taught. And yet some musicians are quick to argue that the ability to learn on one's own, like jazz improvisation, is a rare talent possessed by only a few unique individuals. I cannot accept this line of thinking. Having had extensive personal experience performing with both jazz and country-western musicians, I am convinced that almost anyone can learn via NLP and improvise so long as he or she is highly motivated, starts early enough in life and practices sufficiently. True, such performers often lack some of the technical skills possessed by so-called "schooled musicians"; but most of them are still quite capable of expressing themselves *musically,* which to me is still *the* most important aspect of musical performance. On the other hand, I am sure we have all known some "schooled musicians" who studied with several teachers for many years and still could not perform with musical feeling. Obviously, then, formal musical training in itself does not insure genuine musical success. In some cases it appears to have resulted in just the opposite.

Mental Imagery

Mental imagery involves using our imagination to create "mental pictures."[3] In regard to perceptual-motor performance, it means creating "mental blueprints" of specific performance goals or tasks.

To acquire specific mental images we use our sense organs of sight, hearing, touch, taste and smell. In the case of walking, for example, we as babies acquired pertinent mental images through watching and observing our parents and significant others. We acquired mental images of talking mainly through repetitive listening to these same persons. In each case these images were recorded automatically by our

[2]*Nurtured By Love* © 1969 by Shinichi Suzuki. Reprinted by permission of Exposition Press, Smithtown, N.Y., pp. 9–17.

[3]From the book, *Psycho-Cybernetics* by Maxwell Maltz © 1960 by Prentice-Hall, Inc. Published by Prentice-Hall, Inc., Englewood Cliffs, NJ 07632, p. 13.

brain and became a part of our stored mental film library. Later, when it came time for us to learn how to walk and talk, we simply retrieved them and used them as our performance goals. This same basic process is one we use in learning to sing, play musical instruments, play sports and in other perceptual-motor activities. We use mental imagery as the model of the goal we hope to achieve.

Imitation

Imitation involves trying to reproduce the mental images stored in our brain through live performance. In simplest terms it means mimicking the actions of another person. With regard to musical performance it means trying to duplicate the performance of another musician through trial-and-error practice.

How do we acquire the ability to imitate? We don't have to acquire it. We already have it, we were born with it. Without it we would never have learned how to walk and talk. We also use it unconsciously in numerous other ways all of the time. Like mental imagery, imitation is a principal means through which we learn to interact with and adapt to our environment. Without this ability as young children, we probably would not have survived.

In order to imitate, we need a performance model. Can you imagine trying to learn to ride a bicycle if you had never seen anyone else do it? In time you would no doubt figure it out, but why do it the hard way? The same applies even more to complex skills, such as learning to play a violin. Nature provided us with eyes and ears, which possess incredible potential. We should use them fully for learning, as nature intended.

Trial-and-Error Practice

Trial-and-error practice means making proper adjustments through repetition until you finally achieve your goal (reproduce your mental image). It is like an artillery crew firing a cannon at a target and making adjustments until eventually the target is hit. Practice makes perfect, as we all know, and trial and error is an integral part of the process. Without sufficient high-quality practice, however, there is no way you can learn to "hit the target" consistently.

Directly related to trial-and-error practice is the concept of repetition, one of the major elements of Suzuki's Talent Education philosophy. "We simply have to train and educate our ability, that is to say to do the thing over and over again until it feels natural, simple and easy. That is the secret."[4] The question, then, is not whether repetition is important to learning; rather it is a question of *how* to use repetition to our best advantage in practice. The answer to this question holds the key to all high-quality learning.

[4]*Nurtured by Love* © 1969 by Shinichi Suzuki. Reprinted by permission of Exposition Press, Smithtown, N.Y., p. 51.

Body Feedback

Body feedback involves sensory information that we use to monitor and evaluate our performance. Our sense organs of sight, hearing, touch, taste and smell gather information from our external environment and let us know how we did. Our kinesthetic sense and body-balance mechanism monitor our internal environment and keep us apprised of our physical disposition in space. Together these various forms of feedback provide us with the means for error detection and correction during trial-and-error practice.

In summary, then, NLP is nothing more than our body's inherent ability to interact with and adapt to our environment through the use of its sensory mechanisms. All of us possess these marvelous mechanisms, barring any genetic defects or permanent injuries sustained after birth. All we have to do is allow them to function naturally and efficiently, as nature intended.

HOW WE LOST OUR
NATURAL ABILITY TO LEARN

When we were young children, learning was a relatively easy, natural and simple process for most of us. In learning how to walk and talk, for example, we didn't need a psychophysiological lecture from our parents in order to learn these skills. We simply did what seemed perfectly natural at the time and proceeded in a calm, relaxed manner without any fear, judgments, pressure or anxiety. Nor was it necessary for our parents to understand learning theory in order to help us. Our parents also did what seemed most natural at the time: they praised us for every improvement and encouraged us to keep trying. And try we did continuously, until we finally achieved our goal.

Initial Influences of Verbal
Cognition

But once we learned to talk and communicate verbally, we also began to lose some of our natural learning ability from a perceptual-motor standpoint. Our parents, and later our teachers, made us aware of performance technique. They told us that if we practiced various components of a complex skill in a specified manner, this would help us learn much faster and more efficiently. Later we were also told that if we really understood what we should be doing physiologically, this too would help us. Ultimately we were misled into thinking that perceptual-motor learning required mastery of highly complex skills that could only be acquired through intense mental and physical effort. There was no simple, direct, natural way to learn to play the clarinet, for example, or throw a baseball.

But instead of these attitudes and approaches really helping us, they usually made things worse. Now there was so much to think about; we became confused.

The harder we tried, the more awkward and clumsy we seemed to be. It was all so terribly frustrating.

Involvement of the Ego

As if all of this weren't bad enough, the worst was yet to come: when we learned the meaning of concepts such as good and bad, fast and slow, smart and dumb. Suddenly our ego and emotions became directly involved. We experienced anxiety and nervousness, which led to excessive muscular tension. This caused breakdowns in neuromuscular coordination, which resulted in our performances being even worse than before. But the final blow probably was when we became involved in individual competitive sports. This is when our egos really became fully involved; our self-images and feelings of general worth as people were now at stake. The goal was to win, not lose. Winning was synonymous with success; losing meant failure. This served to increase our anxiety, through added pressure and tension. Now the cycle was complete.

Reasons Why We Rejected NLP

Why did we, as intelligent human beings, allow ourselves to be led so far astray? Why have so many of us as teachers largely rejected the basic methods of NLP, particularly in regard to perceptual-motor learning? I suspect one reason is that we have tended to view imitation, repetition and trial and error as being appropriate mainly for lower animals, as in teaching dogs to do "circus" tricks. Since human beings are far more intelligent than animals, they should use much more sophisticated, and thus more efficient, learning methods. But this line of reasoning needs to be seriously questioned, particularly as it relates to perceptual-motor learning. We have a great deal more in common with lower animals than many of us realize.

Of all animals the human baby is the least able to take care of itself after birth. It is, for all practical purposes, totally dependent on its mother and/or father. A major reason for this is that it takes somewhere between eighteen months to two years before a human baby can walk and seek its own food. The same is obviously not true of lower animals. Their development is much more rapid. They learn to walk, fly or swim and obtain their food fairly soon after birth.

Nature has also provided lower animals with numerous instincts, which they further use for their physical survival. The human baby, on the other hand, possesses very few instincts in comparison and thus must learn to survive mainly through imitating its parents. For these reasons human beings rely on and need imitative learning far more than any other living creature.

Another reason why we have ignored NLP is that ours is essentially a visual, scientific, verbal and cognitive society. Most of our training in school is therefore focused in these directions. But musical performance involves very little of any of these concepts. It is essentially an aural, aesthetic, nonverbal, perceptual-motor skill. It has relatively little in common with the scientific-verbal-cognitive disciplines, and our methods of training musicians should reflect that. Perhaps most important is the need to teach it primarily through nonverbal means (specifically demonstration and imitation) rather than using verbal-cognitive approaches. In musical performance training, one aural picture is worth millions of words!

RELEARNING HOW TO USE
NLP

Unfortunately, many of us tend to teach and learn music largely through verbal, analytical and cognitive means. To reverse this tendency requires that we unlearn all of those habits that prevent normal function of NLP. This means finding a way to eliminate the barriers that we and others have imposed upon our way of thinking and doing things, which interfere with our body's natural ability to learn. Specifically it means applying the basic techniques of remedial learning.

The first technique of remedial learning is to stop using all of our old methods of learning. Allow them to become nonfunctional through total lack of usage. The second technique is to replace the old methods with the methods of NLP. This means relearning what it feels like to function in a childlike manner, to trust our bodies and their inherent ability to learn on their own without continual interference from the mind (conscious analytical brain). It means a complete change in our attitude about how we function during performance and how we learn to perform.

The Conscious Versus
the Unconscious Brain

The human brain operates at two levels: conscious and unconscious. The conscious brain has to do with the thinking, perceiving aspects of performance. The unconscious brain has to do with the body's automatic operations, including those involved with perceptual-motor function and learning as used in NLP. Gallwey uses the terms "Self 1" to identify the conscious brain and "Self 2" to identify the unconscious brain. Self 1 is the "teller," who specifies the performance goal, while Self 2 is the "doer," who is responsible for executing the performance act.[5]

When we were young children, Self 1 and Self 2 worked in perfect harmony with each other. Self 1 gave the commands and Self 2 carried them out. We were thus able to remain calm and interested in what we were doing, two qualities that Gallwey says "make it so easy for a child to learn."[6] But as we grew older, Self 1 became increasingly more dissatisfied with its limited function; it wanted to get involved in the more intricate and complex operations assigned to Self 2. Self 1 wanted control not only over *what* was to be done but also over *how* to do it, and that is when our

---

[5]Timothy Gallwey, *The Inner Game of Tennis* (New York: Random House, Inc., 1974), p. 25. Reprinted by permission.

[6]W. Timothy Gallwey, *Inner Tennis: Playing the Game* (New York: Random House, Inc., 1976), p. 22. Reprinted by permission.

problems in learning really started. Instead of learning becoming more efficient, it became increasingly more inefficient. Self 1's ego began creating static interference in the nervous system, causing the nerve signals to the muscles to be garbled and unclear. Eventually it caused the entire system to become "jammed." To solve this problem, we need to relearn the method we used as young children; we need to learn how to focus on the performance goal, not the process involved in achieving it.

Focusing on the Goal, Not the Process

"Focus on the goal" is a directive we give to Self 1 to remind it of its proper role in perceptual-motor activities. It means Self 1 must tell Self 2 *what* it wants done, not *how* to do it. Total responsibility for executing the performance goal belongs to Self 2. In other words, we should avoid doing consciously what nature already does automatically.

Let me give you a specific example of what I mean. Learning to ride a bicycle does not require understanding verbal concepts, nor does it require cerebral analysis. It requires instead a good sense of balance and efficient neuromuscular coordination, abilities which can be developed best through trial-and-error practice. But what happens when most youngsters first get on a bicycle and fall down? Parents, brothers, sisters and/or friends try to provide all kinds of detailed verbal instructions on how to ride a bicycle correctly. But do these instructions really help? In most cases they only confuse the youngster and make things worse. They cause the child's Self 1 to lose sight of the performance goal and become involved in the process that is the function of Self 2.

We need to be reminded, however, that most young children already know how to focus on the goal if we only let them do it. Animals also know how to focus on the goal. They too learn to achieve superior performance without knowledge of technique and conscious control. As Gallwey points out, "You don't see many uncoordinated birds flying across the sky. The leopard isn't thinking about technique at the moment he's about to jump upon his prey."[7] In both of these cases, it is simply a matter of deciding on a specific goal and then doing it without giving the matter any further conscious thought.

To put it in another way, focusing on the goal means concentrating on the performance result we want to achieve rather than the *means* through which we achieve it. In musical performance it means concentrating on the so-called finished musical product, which includes all of the expressive, artistic qualities as well as the technical aspects of performance. Too often we direct too much of our attention to the means (breath, embouchure, fingers) or the process (supporting the tone, keeping the embouchure firm and the fingers relaxed) in making music. In so doing we lose sight of the musical goal, and our performance then becomes sterile and mechanistic rather than musical and artistic. Instead we should always begin with a

[7]Ibid., p. 16.

clear mental image of the "big musical picture" and then concentrate on trying to reproduce it.

In closing, I wish to point out that focusing on the goal is not a new concept to music teaching. Fillebrown, a nineteenth-century voice teacher, recommends a similar concept: "Think of the effect desired rather than the process."[8] This remains valid today.

Focusing on the process should be avoided for the following reasons:

1. Regarding perceptual-motor activities, focusing on the process in essence means trying to focus on neuromuscular function. This is not only impractical; it is essentially impossible. Even those scientists who specialize in neurophysiology are among the first to admit this. Our current knowledge of human physiology only allows us to generalize about some of the body's most basic, elementary functions. We are still a long way off from fully understanding its more complex operations.

2. No two people are exactly the same physiologically or psychologically. Thus no two people function or learn in exactly the same ways. Consequently there is no single process or mode of function that is ideal for all of us to use beyond the general principles inherent in NLP. The precise means through which each of us achieves a given performance goal will always be somewhat different.

3. Even if it were possible to identify *the* ideal process, we could not exert any conscious control over it no matter how hard we might try. Our neuromuscular mechanism (Self 2) was designed to operate on an unconscious level, not a conscious one (Self 1).

On first thought the foregoing ideas may strike some readers as being a bit dogmatic and unorthodox. After all, isn't musical performance basically a voluntary act, directly controlled by the performer? If one doesn't exert some control over muscular action at least, then how is it possible to achieve consistently good performance results? As a first step in answering these questions we need to realize that everyone who inhabits a human body possesses an absolutely marvelous piece of mechanical, chemical and electrical equipment. Contrary to what most people seem to believe, it is quite capable of executing many complex functions on its own without any conscious direction from us. It was designed to operate this way. When we give it too many instructions, we only interfere with its superior capability, confuse, confound and jam up its intricate mechanisms and thus cause it to perform poorly. The fewer instructions we give it, the better. The primary instruction our body needs from us (Self 1) is specification of the general musical goal, not a detailed set of instructions on how to achieve that goal.

To further illustrate this concept, let us use the analogy of a construction company and how it functions. We have a chief executive (president, boss or owner) who gives orders (general goals) to his foreman or work supervisor. The chief executive's goals will usually be of a general nature, such as "go build a house, based on these architectural specifications, at this address." The foreman is then responsible for translating the chief executive's orders into more specific goals,

[8]Thomas Fillebrown, *Resonance in Singing and Speaking* © 1911 Oliver Ditson Company. Reproduced by permission of the publisher.

organizing the work schedule and assigning specific jobs to individual specialized workmen. The good chief executive normally is not involved beyond stating the general goal. If he continually looks over the shoulder of his foreman, criticizes his way of doing things and, worst of all, moves right in and takes over the job of telling each worker what to do and how to do it, then major problems become inevitable. Confusion, frustration, anxiety, paranoia, internal conflict and general chaos are the usual result.

At the most basic level, human mind-body function is similar to this process. The stimulus for action originates in our conscious brain, which functions as the chief executive, who specifies the general goal, such as "open that door." Our unconscious brain then takes over and functions as the foreman, who is responsible for translating the conscious brain's command into specific goals, organizing the work schedule and assigning specific jobs to individual specialized workers (body muscles). Beyond specifying the general goal, the conscious brain is not normally involved, nor should it be. If it continually monitors the work of its foreman (the unconscious brain), criticizes its mode of operation and, worst of all, tries to exert direct control over the individual workers (muscles) themselves, mental confusion and eventual chaos are the result. As stated before, we should avoid doing consciously what nature already does automatically. Unconscious brain function is essentially automatic in its operation.

Closely related to focusing on the goal is the concept of mental imagery, as described briefly earlier and as discussed in detail in Maltz's *Psycho-Cybernetics* (see the introduction to this text). Before we can focus on a goal, we need to have a clear image (mental picture) of the performance result we hope to achieve. If our mental image is unclear, the performance result will likewise be unclear. But if there is a performance model available for us to observe and imitate, this allows us to develop a mental film library of pictures or images for future use. This, then, is the major purpose of imitative learning, to be discussed in the next section.

THE ROLE OF IMITATION IN TEACHING AND LEARNING

Unlike some of the other aspects of NLP, the ability to imitate is something we never lose. We still have it and use it frequently, albeit on an unconscious level for the most part. But the problem exists mainly in the negative attitude many teachers have toward it. They simply refuse to accept it as a viable, effective and efficient method of learning.

A Historical Overview

When imitation is mentioned nowadays around music teachers, most of them immediately think of Shinichi Suzuki. True, Suzuki is greatly responsible for the current popularity of this method, but he certainly did not create it. Pestalozzi used it in the early 1800s. Porpora and other voice teachers of the "Old Italian School" reportedly used it extensively, long before that. In 1908 Taylor wrote: "Singers are trained today exactly as they were two hundred years ago, through a reliance on the imitative faculty."[9]

But in a world so drastically changed by scientific advancement and technology, especially during the current century, one has to wonder seriously if the imitation method isn't outdated. Some would have us believe that musicians are much too conservative, and even foolhardy, in ignoring the rapid changes being made in the teaching of other disciplines, while theirs remains essentially the same. They further argue that improved methods of teaching music surely exist within the discoveries of science if only we would take the time to search them out.

Science has, without a doubt, changed the performance of music in very significant ways. Witness its impact in the areas of recording, electronic instruments, and even electronic music itself. The invention of the metronome, stroboscope, tape recorder and other mechanical and electronic aids has also provided us with useful teaching aids, and few will deny that the science of musical acoustics has also benefited us in very significant ways. But the basic way through which human beings learn to perform music has not really changed. According to Arnold Jacobs, currently tubaist with the Chicago Symphony and internationally known wind-instrument teacher: "Imitation was, is and always will be the best method we have."[10] Add to this persons such as Gallwey, Nideffer and others involved with sports training, as well as psychologists such as Bandura, and we find considerable support for the use of imitation as a viable, highly effective and efficient method of teaching and learning.

Does Imitation Stifle Creativity?

A specific criticism leveled against imitation by some persons is that it stifles creativity. But empirical evidence does not necessarily bear this out. Take the case of some of our leading jazz musicians of the past, persons who created significant new concepts in jazz style. How did they initially learn to perform? They learned to perform in the same way other creative musicians did: through lots of concentrated listening combined with imitation. Creation of their own original style of performance came much later. The same holds true for master composers like Beethoven. How else do we explain the fact that his first symphony sounds so much like Mozart? And doesn't early Mozart sound a good deal like Haydn and others who came before? The natural sequence, therefore, is to listen and imitate first, and create in the fullest sense during a later, more mature period of life.

Musical creativity is an intense struggle with musical problems and their solution, rethinking and reorganizing them until a new concept or style is finally realized. Some believe that the end result is achieved via inspiration emanating from the unconscious brain. In any case, creativity in its first stages can be defined

---

[9]David C. Taylor, *The Psychology of Singing* (New York: The Macmillan Co., 1908), p. 134.
[10]Based on a personal conversation with Arnold Jacobs.

simply as lots of hard work in the form of mental effort. In this context, the writing of this text was a creative effort. Using the old definition of talent, I can personally verify that this text is a result of 99 percent perspiration and 1 percent inspiration.

Ways in Which Imitation Directly Influences Our Lives

Have you ever closely observed the walk of a young boy and then observed the way his father walks? In most cases the walking style of both will be very similar; that is, like father, like son. In the case of regional language accents, a similar situation exists. Children from New York talk like New Yorkers, and those from Mississippi talk like Mississippians. They do this because they learn to talk via the imitative process. But these two examples represent only the most basic things we learn via imitation from our parents. An in-depth study of human psychology will reveal that children's imitation of parents includes practically every aspect of human behavior. And yet the main problem with imitative teaching today is that too few teachers actually teach this way. Music teachers, for example, rely mainly on verbal description and physiological analysis as the primary means toward teaching musical-performance skills as well as musical expression. If repeated verbal description and analysis fail to achieve results, one is then likely to see the teacher in exasperation either sing or play the passage, as if singing or playing it for the student were the last resort! But since music is a nonverbal form of artistic expression, trying to teach it *primarily* through verbal description and analysis goes against all sense of reasonable logic. We should be doing just the opposite—teaching nonverbal concepts through nonverbal means. To reinforce this idea, a quote from Gallwey seems appropriate here: "Images are better than words, showing better than telling, too much instruction worse than none, and conscious trying often produces negative results."[11]

Imitative learning, therefore, is an obvious fact of our existence. Human beings learn automatically, naturally, easily and, in my view, most efficiently through imitation. So instead of refusing to accept it or trying to pretend it doesn't exist, why not capitalize on it? We don't have to teach it; everyone already knows how to use it. All we need to do is accept it as a viable technique of learning and then learn to use it properly to achieve high-quality performance. To better understand how to apply it directly to the teaching of musical performance, see Figure 1-1.

Imitative Teaching and Learning for Adults

The value of imitation is not limited only to children; it also works well with adults. Barring major physical handicaps and significant body degeneration in later life, there is also no reason why elderly people cannot learn to sing and play musical

---

[11]W. Timothy Gallwey, *The Inner Game of Tennis* (New York: Random House, Inc., 1974), p. 19. Reprinted by permission.

FIGURE 1-1   Teaching via Imitation

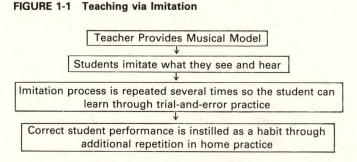

instruments using the imitation method. Basically it requires motivation, being convinced that learning is still possible and the ability to develop a childlike attitude toward perceptual-motor learning. This means being able to focus on the performance goal rather than the process, and being able to use imitation, repetition and trial-and-error practice as the primary methods of learning.

The Purpose of Trial-and-Error Practice

Trial-and-error practice is an integral part of imitative learning and, like imitation, is something we never lose the ability to do. The problem is mainly one of some people's negative attitude regarding its efficiency as a method of learning. And yet most of us will agree that in many things we learn, experience is the best teacher. With regard to perceptual-motor learning, trial-and-error practice is *the* means through which we acquire experience.

In the cognitive domain there are several different approaches to learning, and some are indeed better than simple trial and error. But even in the cognitive domain there are some things that, it seems, are best learned through experience. Experience is sometimes not only the best teacher, but it may be the only teacher. Anyone who doubts this fact has never dealt with teenagers in a direct way as a parent, teacher or employer. No matter how reasonable, rational and logical one may be in dealing with a teenager, the only way some teenagers can learn some things is through personal experience; that is, trial and error. And if we are willing to be completely objective about it, the same continues to be true for most of us as adults, although to a lesser degree, of course! But the fact remains that experience is vital to all types of learning, and trial and error is the means through which we are able to acquire direct personal experience.

OBSERVING CHILDREN LEARN

Three major elements of Suzuki's Mother Tongue Approach are listening, imitation and repetition. How did he go about identifying these major elements? I suspect he did what most good teachers have always done: observing and studying the learning behaviors of young children.

To put it another way, we can say that the cornerstone of scientific research is the scientific method. The first and most important phase of this method is observation. Before doing anything else the astute scientist first devotes considerable time to observing the object or behavior he or she is studying. Actual experimentation comes much later. This same concept applies equally to teaching. Observation of how children learn should be an essential requisite to becoming a teacher. Like a scientist who spends hours observing specimens under a microscope, teacher trainees should spend equivalent time observing children. This should also be the first step in learning how to teach. Application and experimentation (practice teaching) should definitely come later.

The kinds of things a prospective teacher can learn through observation are—

1. that children learn to walk, talk and even ride a bicycle by watching and listening to others and then trying to imitate them. They also accomplish these complex tasks without any need for formalized instruction.

2. that young children enjoy imitating others and are quite good at it. They also do it spontaneously and without inhibition.

3. that children learn to do by doing, through constant repetition; unlike most adults, they enjoy repetitive activities. Anyone who has observed children at play or has driven across the country with them in an automobile knows this all too well. Repeating the same words or singing the same motif over and over, for example, does not bore them, as it does most adults.

4. that children improve their ability to walk, talk and ride bicycles through trial-and-error practice. In so doing they concentrate on the goal they wish to achieve, not on the details of how to achieve it. Fortunately they are not yet capable of analyzing "how." Their focus is on the end product, the performance goal.

5. that children need love as much as they need food in order to survive. (Studies in hospital nurseries have shown this to be true.) Accordingly, when parents give encouragement, praise and personal attention to children who are learning how to walk, for example, this motivates them to learn and probably helps them to learn faster.

6. that children have lots of physical energy; thus they enjoy physical activities, not just mental ones. If you have ever watched schoolchildren during recess in a playground or observed them after their being turned loose in an open meadow after several hours of riding in a car, this fact will be obvious to you.

7. that children do not like to sit and listen patiently for long periods of time. They seem to learn best through doing, not through verbal analysis or extended lectures. Their attention spans are also relatively short, which requires the teacher to offer a variety of activities in addition to careful attention to good pacing.

8. that children enjoy bright colors and respond favorably to objects and books that exemplify these.

9. that children learn as a result of experience; for instance, tasting sweet candy, smelling fragrant flowers and also by getting burned when touching a hot stove.

10. that in the context of experience, children also learn through punishment and fear, which are forms of negative motivation.

SUMMARY

The Natural Learning Process involves the use of mental imagery, imitation and trial-and-error practice as our primary methods of learning. It also involves the use of body feedback as a means for detection and correction of performance errors.

Mental imagery involves using our imagination to create "mental pictures." In regard to perceptual-motor performance, it means creating "mental blueprints" of specific performance goals or tasks.

Imitation involves trying to reproduce the mental images stored in our brains through live performance. In regard to musical performance it simply means trying to duplicate the performance results of another musician through trial-and-error practice. Trial-and-error practice means making proper adjustments through repetition until you finally achieve your goal.

To detect and correct performance errors we use our senses of sight, hearing, touch, taste and smell, as well as kinesthesia and our body-balance mechanism. These various forms of body feedback provide us with a means of monitoring and evaluating our performance and keep us apprised of our physical disposition in space.

While the Natural Learning Process is something we were all born with, most of us lost some of it in the process of "growing up." Our parents, and later our teachers, taught us to concentrate on performance technique rather than the performance goal. We were also given lengthy verbal descriptions about the correct way to perform, including an analysis of physiological function. Still later we were encouraged to enter competitions to "test" our skills. The resulting anxiety we felt created nervousness and excessive muscular tension, which in turn caused our performance to become worse in most cases instead of better. Performance had now become a psychological trauma rather than a natural routine physiological process.

In order to relearn how to use NLP, we need to relearn how to focus on the performance goal, not the process. This in turn requires that we understand the two levels of brain operation: conscious and unconscious. Gallwey uses the term Self 1 to identify the conscious brain, Self 2 to identify the unconscious brain. The function of Self 1 is to give commands (specify performance goals) to Self 2. Self 2's function is to execute these commands (carry out the process). But if Self 1 tries to get involved in the execution or process function of Self 2, it only creates interference in the neuromuscular mechanism, eventually causing the entire mechanism to jam up. The solution, therefore, is to remind Self 1 repeatedly that its proper role in perceptual-motor function is to tell Self 2 *what* it wants done, not *how* to do it.

Unlike some of the other aspects of NLP, the ability to imitate is something we never lose. But the problem is that many teachers simply refuse to accept it as a viable, effective and efficient method of learning. This attitude is indeed unfortunate, since a careful study will reveal that imitative learning permeates practically every aspect of our lives, whether we realize it or not. In regard to musical learning, it was, is and probably always will be the best method that we have.

Trial-and-error practice, like imitation, is also something we never forgot how to do. But again the problem exists mainly in many people's attitudes toward it. We learn through action (experience). Experience is not only the best teacher in some situations; there are times when it is the *only* true teacher—and trial and error is the *only means* through which we are able to acquire direct, personal experience.

One of the best ways to learn about how children learn is to observe them. In fact this should be an integral part of teacher preparation. What does one learn from observing children learning? Among the most obvious things one discovers is that they use imitation, repetition and other aspects of NLP almost instinctively. They also focus on the goal, not the process.

For a brief synopsis on relearning how to use NLP, see Figure 1-2.

FIGURE 1-2   Relearning How to Use NLP

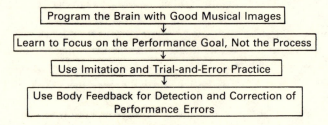

CHAPTER TWO

NEUROMUSCULAR physiology

The main purpose of this chapter and the two that follow is to provide a scientific basis for the learning theories discussed in Chapter One. Through this means I intend to supplement the writings of Gallwey, Suzuki and Maltz with pertinent information drawn from the disciplines of physiology and Western and Eastern psychology. Other purposes of these chapters related to parts II and III of this text are—

1. to provide a scientific basis for analysis and evaluation of selected theories of teaching and learning;
2. to establish principles of learning from which reliable teaching methods can be developed.

In viewing the human body as whole, we find it to be an exceedingly intricate, complex organism, comprised of eleven different systems, all of which influence perceptual-motor performance to some degree. For this reason, knowledge of at least the basic principles of human mind-body function is highly desirable if not essential. Due to space limitations, however, only three body systems most directly involved with neuromuscular function will be discussed in this chapter. A comprehensive study of human mind-body function can be obtained by consulting the recommended physiology texts in the bibliography.

INTRODUCTION

Through its ingenuity and creative ability the human race has uncovered many secrets of nature and the universe, and continues to do so at an increasingly rapid rate. It has also created many complex machines and sophisticated computers, which have radically changed our personal lives as well as the environment in which we live. Yet, despite all of these major advances, we still know relatively little about our own machine, the human body. Physiologists are among the first to admit this, particularly as regards understanding the operation of the brain. Neurophysiologists are just beginning to understand some of the brain's most basic, elementary functions.

Concerning perceptual-motor learning, however, these facts are not necessarily matters of serious concern. Musicians, dancers and athletes throughout recorded history have been able to function without having any such knowledge, and they will surely continue to do so in the future. We don't need to understand the structure and function of our bodies in order to perform. The main thing we need to know is how to operate our body's controls properly. Our situation is, in a sense, like that of an automobile driver. To drive an automobile you don't need to understand the structure and function of every part under the hood. What you need, first of all, is a mental image or conception of what you want to do (driving goal or destination). Beyond that all you need to learn is how to operate the controls properly and then be constantly alert to avoid accidents in reaching your destination. If a major malfunction does occur under the hood, the driver normally takes the automobile to a mechanic trained to diagnose and solve such problems.

As performing musicians we function (or at least should function) in much the same way as does the driver of an automobile. We use our driver, the brain, to create a mental image of our musical performance goal. Then we simply tell our brain what we want done, not how to do it. We do not normally concern ourselves with all of the intricate details of what is going on under our "human hood." We can't really do it even when we try. When we do try we only create additional problems for ourselves. The best solution, therefore, is simply to focus on the musical performance goal and let physiological function take care of itself. If this proves to be unsuccessful, then we would be well advised to seek the help of a competent teacher specifically trained to diagnose and solve such problems.

If musicians do not need to understand mind-body function in order to perform, then why should you read this chapter and why did I write it? I remind you that this text is intended primarily for teachers who need to know how to diagnose and solve performance problems accurately. Basic knowledge of neuromuscular physiology can be very helpful, if not essential, in developing these skills.

As a final statement on this topic I include another reason, advanced by Kofler: Would you trust a physician who you knew had no training in anatomy or physiology? Of course not. Why then should you put your faith in a voice teacher who boasts of his ignorance of vocal anatomy and physiology? Knowledge of the natural laws that govern the function of the vocal organs is essential if one is ever to be a conscientious vocal trainer.[1]

If for no other reason, this knowledge is important to voice teachers so that they can avoid causing physical damage to students' voices through improper training. Certainly this is no small consideration, since the extent of such damage caused by vocal charlatans of the past is a fact generally well known. The same no doubt applies to wind- and string-instrument teaching as well, even though this has not been as widely discussed in written form. A specific case in point has to do with hernias and other physical problems caused by improper use of the breathing apparatus in high-register brass playing. With regard to string playing, there are also potential problems with pinched nerves and tendonitus, which sometimes can be quite serious. (For a specific case study involving partial dislocation of spinal vertebrae caused by incorrect performance habits, see Robert Dawley's article in *Dialogue in Instrumental Music Education,* Vol. 5, No. 2, pp. 36–44.)

THE MUSCULAR SYSTEM

The three body systems most directly involved in neuromuscular function are the sensory, nervous and muscular systems. Of these three, the muscular system is often the one which seems to receive the most pedagogical attention. But such an approach is misguided at best and totally wrong at worst, as I will explain in the following discussion.

Basic Structure and Function

The muscular system includes three types of muscles: skeletal, smooth and cardiac. This discussion will be limited to skeletal muscles, since these are the ones most directly involved in musical performance. As the name implies, skeletal muscles are those directly attached to various parts of the body skeleton.

Muscles are the primary agents that respond to movement commands from our brain. They can perhaps best be described as organs that produce motion through contraction. Muscle contraction is made possible as a result of food or energy in the form of various proteins, acids and enzymes that are delivered to each muscle via the bloodstream. When skeletal muscles contract, they initiate a system of levers and pulleys in the form of bones, tendons and ligaments. Our muscular system, therefore, can be viewed as a machine that converts chemical energy into mechanical energy. As such it represents what Fulton calls the most impressive example of living machinery in existence.[2]

---

[1]Leo Kofler, *The Art of Breathing as a Basis for Tone Production,* 7th rev. ed. (New York: E.S. Werner, 1897), p. 21.

[2]John F. Fulton, *A Textbook of Physiology,* 17th ed. (Philadelphia: W.B. Saunders Co., 1955), p. 123. Reprinted by permission.

Muscles do not function independently. They are totally controlled by the brain. Like the wheels on an automobile, they cannot initiate movement, nor can they control it. Having no mind of their own, they function like highly obedient servants to the commands of their master, the brain. If the brain's commands in the form of nerve signals are ill-conceived, muscular action will likewise be ill-conceived. Muscles cannot improve or alter their function in any direct way without first receiving specific instructions from the brain.

Neuromuscular Coordination

Coordination means harmonious working together; operating in a smooth, integrated way. Neuromuscular coordination has to do with harmonious or integrated function between the nervous and muscular systems as used in musical performance, dance and sports. When a given type of neuromuscular coordination becomes highly developed, we call it a skill.

Good musical performance, of course, requires an extremely high level of neuromuscular coordination. To illustrate this within a music-ensemble context I shall use the following analogy. Most teachers of typing would consider the idea of eighty to one hundred typists actually staying together from start to finish while typing the *same letters* at the *same speed* for more than one minute to be quite a feat. But music-ensemble players are expected to stay together while playing *different pitches* and *different rhythms* at the same tempo (speed) for considerably longer than one minute and with exact precision. Obviously this requires mental concentration and neuromuscular coordination of the highest order. Few activities and/or professions require this degree of precision.

If our body fails to respond properly during musical performance, we judge coordination as being poor or at least below average. Conversely, if body function appears to be excellent, we say the person is well coordinated. It is easy enough to explain poor coordination in those cases where an individual has congenital defects or since birth has sustained physical injuries that render normal functioning impossible. But what about those persons judged to be physically normal and healthy? Is poor coordination, particularly in the young, due to inheritance, poor training or something else?

Unfortunately, the tendency of some teachers is to blame the muscles for their alleged poor performance. The problem is then referred to as one of poor *physical* coordination. But the real source of most coordination problems is mental, not physical. Errors in neuromuscular coordination are caused by brain dysfunction, not nerve or muscle dysfunction. In using the term "brain dysfunction" I do not mean brain damage or mental retardation. Instead I am referring to neuromuscular problems we create for ourselves because of anxiety, poor posture or improper methods of training.

Probably the biggest problem we face is the interference of our conscious brain (Self 1) in the performance process. When we "try too hard" or try consciously to control muscle action, we only create tension within the system. Teachers, however well intentioned, are often the prime instigators of this problem, when they ask us, for example, to concentrate on "supporting the tone with the diaphragm." Such instructions should be avoided, since they ask the student to focus on the wrong things. According to Arnold Jacobs, "the focus of our teaching should be on training the performer's brain. We can't really train the muscles; we train the brain, which controls the muscles. To accomplish this we need to study nervous stimuli more so than the body mechanism itself."[3]

THE HUMAN BRAIN

Of all the body systems, the nervous system is of greatest importance to us. It is comprised of two basic sections: (1) the central nervous system, which includes the brain, brainstem and the spinal cord, and (2) the peripheral nervous system, which consists of all the nerve cells and parts of nerve cells that enter or leave the brainstem and the spinal cord and connect them to the rest of the body. Of all of these, the brain is the most intriguing and the most complex. John C. Eccles, Nobel laureate in neurophysiology, even goes as far as to say that the human brain "is without any qualification the most highly organized and most complexly organized matter in the universe."[4] Because it is so complex, it is also the body organ that we know the least about. Nevertheless, let's take a brief glimpse at what we do know as it pertains to perceptual-motor function.

Basic Structure

Viewing the brain externally, it is divided into two major parts: (1) the upper brain, which consists of the cerebrum and cerebral cortex, and (2) the lower brain, which contains the medulla, pons and other parts of the brain stem (see Figure 2-1).

Viewed internally, at a microscopic level, the brain contains about ten billion cells called neurons, with each neuron functioning as a minute electrical communication system. Each of these neurons is capable of producing hundreds of electrical charges per second, which can travel several hundred feet per second. When a signal is sent from the brain to the foot in one second, for example, this amounts to a speed of several hundred miles per hour.

Our brain also contains a complex mixture of chemicals, and in recent years this has been the focus of considerable research. Some biochemists believe that the most important secrets regarding the brain concern its chemical rather than its electrical functions. In any case we can be reasonably sure that future research will provide some interesting and valuable information in this area.

[3]Based on a personal conversation with Arnold Jacobs.

[4]John C. Eccles, *The Understanding of the Brain* (New York: McGraw-Hill Book Co., 1973), p. 1. Reprinted by permission.

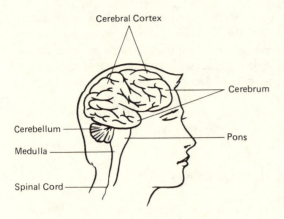

Cerebral Cortex

Cerebrum

Cerebellum

Medulla

Pons

Spinal Cord

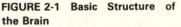

FIGURE 2-1   Basic   Structure   of the Brain

The Three Stages of Brain Function

Brain operation can be divided into three separate stages of functioning: (1) information processing, (2) the decisional-executive stage and (3) the motor-output stage, where neural commands are organized into sets of instructions and then released, via the spinal cord, to the muscles. Since the motor-output stage was essentially covered in the section dealing with the muscular system, only the first two stages will be discussed here.

Information processing.   Before the brain can function at all, it must receive a stimulus. Stimuli reach us via our sensory system, which provides us with various types of information. But before we can use any kind of sensory information, it must first be processed by the upper levels of the brain. We call this process "perception." Perception, therefore, is the processing of information by the brain, which reaches our senses in the form of sights, sounds, tastes, smells, aches and pains. These items of information are known as perceptual cues or stimuli.

The foregoing, of course, is not simple. Processing intricately detailed information from a single receptor such as the eye is difficult enough. But if we consider the huge amount of information received by the brain from the other senses, in addition to the body-feedback mechanisms, the task of the brain becomes even more overwhelming.

Logically one might assume that the brain accepts and uses all of the information provided by the sensory system, but normally it cannot and does not. In order to function efficiently it automatically filters out useless, irrelevant information and uses only that which it needs to achieve the performance goal immediately desired.

How does the brain know which information to accept and which to reject? Some of this ability is inherited; the rest is acquired through experience in adapting to the environment. After conception we have no real control over inherited ability, of course, but the variety, quality and quantity of our environmental experiences have a direct effect upon our perception. The more experienced we are, the better we are able to process the sensory information we receive.

In the case of driving an automobile, for example, the quality and appropriateness of the driver's perceptual ability is directly proportionate to one's knowledge, learned skill and innate ability. Inexperienced drivers, for example, have trouble at first because they do not know how to interpret properly the stimuli they receive, nor do they understand how to operate the automobile's controls properly. The automobile may be in good operating condition, but the signals it receives from its driver are ill-conceived, perhaps given in the wrong sequence and, therefore, inappropriate for achieving the desired goal. But through experience involving trial-and-error practice, the driver's ability to interpret external stimuli and make good driving decisions gradually improves. The more experienced one is, the less one needs to concentrate on every specific detail of what one is doing. Eventually, the majority of the driver's actions become relatively automatic, in that they require minimal conscious effort or attention.

In applying this concept directly to human mind-body function, let us use the example of young children learning to walk. At first young children have difficulty maintaining their balance, and their movements are very awkward. Through trial-and-error practice, however, their ability improves, and they have fewer falls and show increasing evidence of improved coordination. Finally, walking becomes a natural aspect of their routine functioning, requiring minimal if any conscious thought. Psychologists refer to this as operant conditioning; Gallwey calls it the Natural Learning Process.

In more complex types of perceptual-motor learning, including musical performance, this same basic principle also applies. When we try to produce our first musical tone, for example, a good deal of conscious thought is required. With practice, less and less conscious thought is needed, until finally we are able to produce a good tone and execute other complex performance tasks with what appear to be automatic or involuntary functions. We don't have to concentrate so much any more; we just do. The speed at which we learn and the quality of our performance is directly proportional to the innate ability and experiences of our driver, or control center, the brain.

Let us assume, however, that the brain was incapable of automatically filtering irrelevant sensory information and that we found it necessary to do this ourselves on a conscious level. The result would be mental chaos and confusion. We simply couldn't function. It is therefore indeed fortunate that this process is taken care of for us automatically.

The decision-executive stage.   In the decision-executive stage, processed information is translated into neural decisions or commands and then organized into sets of neural instructions to be relayed to the muscles. Because of the immense complexity of this stage, it is the one we know the least about. In an effort to explain the brain's function in this stage, many persons have compared the brain to a computer. Such an analogy is satisfactory so long as we realize that the human brain is infinitely more complex and efficient than any computer yet devised. Perhaps Gallwey explains it best when he states that if it were possible to build a computer equivalent to the human brain using the smallest, most sophisticated hardware available, that computer would be more than three times the size of the Empire State Building.[5] Even then it would probably still require a human brain to program and operate it. For this reason I find it more beneficial to compare the human brain to that of lower animals, at least as a starting point.

A Comparison of Human and Lower-Animal Brains

Human beings are the most intelligent of all living animals. The reason is that our upper brain is much larger, relatively speaking, and much more highly developed. This provides us with the ability to think, reason and make decisions based on a variety of choices. In contrast, the upper brains of lower animals are much smaller; thus their conscious thinking ability is very limited in comparison. Because of this, Nature has provided lower animals with many reflex and instinctive powers (lower-brain functions) to help them function and survive in their respective environments.

As human beings we are also superior to lower animals because our higher intelligence allows us to exercise significant control over our environment including many of the animals themselves. Because of this, some of us assume then that we can control almost anything, including our own neuromuscular function. We also tend to assume that we have nothing in common with animals. Animals operate largely on reflex and instinct; we operate mainly via conscious control or acts of the will. Both of these assumptions are essentially wrong. First of all, we cannot consciously control all of our bodily functions; many are involuntary and essentially beyond our conscious control. Secondly, we possess over 100 known reflexes, which means that we have a great deal more in common with lower animals than some people might like to admit. It also means that a great deal can be learned about human behavior through careful observation and study of animals, particularly in terms of neuromuscular function.

Nevertheless, human beings do possess a much higher level of intelligence than lower animals. In the past this intelligence was said to be due to our having a mind, something that lower animals do not have. For humans the term "brain" was used simply to identify the physical structures inside the head. In terms of this discussion, at least, such a distinction seems unnecessary and somewhat misleading. The main distinction of immediate practical value is to view the brain in terms of its voluntary and involuntary functions.

---

[5]W. Timothy Gallwey, *The Inner Game of Tennis* (New York: Random House, Inc., 1974), p. 50. Reprinted by permission.

Voluntary and Involuntary Functions

The human brain functions on two different levels: (1) the voluntary conscious level, which Gallwey calls Self 1, and (2) the involuntary unconscious level, labeled Self 2 by Gallwey. Self 1 controls all voluntary acts of the will, which are learned as a result of our continuing adaptation and readaptation to the environment. It is also responsible for all mental functions related to intellect and intelligence. Self 2 serves as a memory-storage center for all involuntary body functions. These include inherited reflexes, along with other functions such as breathing, blood circulation and digestion. Self 2 also controls conditioned reflexes, those learned after birth. Self 1, therefore, appears to exist in the upper-brain area, while Self 2 is located mainly in the lower-brain area.

In discussing involuntary function, scientists refer to it as the body's "automatic servo-mechanism." To explain this concept they compare it to the operation of a home furnace thermostat. To maintain a specific temperature range in our homes, we set the thermostat to the desired temperature level. When the temperature drops below that level, this information is processed by the thermostat, and a command or signal is sent to an electrical switch, which automatically turns on the furnace. Once the temperature reaches the desired level, the thermostat again reacts by sending another command or signal to the electrical switch, this time causing the furnace to shut off. In other words, the furnace operates on a self-regulated or involuntary basis, once it has been properly programmed, through a system of input and output signals processed by its control center, or brain, the thermostat. In its predominant automatic or involuntary functions, the human body operates in much the same way. For example, if one is engaged in running or some other strenuous physical activity, the body sends signals to the brain to increase the rates of respiration and heartbeat so as to provide additional energy for executing the physical task. When the physical task is completed and the need for additional energy ceases, the body again sends signals continuously to the brain to decrease respiration and heartbeat gradually back to normal rates of operation.

Despite the clear distinctions made in this discussion, we need to understand that voluntary and involuntary functions are by no means mutually exclusive. Highly developed voluntary actions often take on the image of involuntary function, as in the case of a highly skilled concert artist who seems to perform complex musical feats automatically, with no conscious effort. At the other extreme are documented examples of Yoga masters who are able to bring involuntary functions such as blood circulation and body temperature under conscious (voluntary) control. Nevertheless, it is helpful to use these two types of physiological function as general starting points. Later, exceptions to these generalizations will be dealt with individually.

Reflex Actions

Another type of involuntary function exists in the form of reflex actions. Reflexes are unconsciously controlled actions or movements that are believed to be genetically preprogrammed (inherited). Probably the most commonly known reflex is the knee jerk we experience during physical examinations in a doctor's office. Other examples of reflex actions include coughing, sneezing, body balance, perspiration, tears, salivating, ''goose pimples'' and dilation and contraction of the pupil of the eye in response to the available light. Altogether we possess some 100 reflex actions which are inherited and believed to be controlled within the spinal cord area rather than in the brain itself, according to some physiologists.

In addition to inherited reflexes, most persons also possess conditioned reflexes, acquired after birth as a result of intensive, repetitive learning. The experienced driver of an automobile, for example, who sees another car crossing over into his lane automatically turns his wheel in the opposite direction to avoid an accident. Likewise the artist singer or wind player faced with a long musical phrase responds almost automatically by taking bigger, deeper breaths. Unlike novices, they need not do this through direct conscious control. Rather they tend to respond unconsciously in such situations. Since the action is controlled at lower levels of the brain rather than the cerebral cortex, this is why such responses seem so automatic and effortless.

While conscious actions can become unconscious in their function through learning, there is evidence that inherited reflexes can also be brought under conscious control. An example of this is the fall in dance. Normal reflexes associated with body balance try to prevent the fall. Through intensive and correct training, however, this reflex can be inhibited.

The brain, therefore, is the master control center for all communication between our body and its environment. It controls every aspect of our physiological and psychological behavior. It receives information from the external environment via the sense organs of sight, hearing, taste, touch and smell. It processes this information and organizes it into nerve commands, which are relayed to the muscular system via the spinal cord and peripheral nerves connected directly to the muscles themselves. The muscular system simply responds to the brain's nerve commands in the form of specific physical movements.

THE SENSORY SYSTEM

Basic to our ability to survive on this earth is our potential for interacting with and adapting to our environment. Our sensory system is our primary means for achieving this potential. It gathers information from our environment and sends it to the brain for processing and decision making. In perceptual-motor function and learning specifically, the sensory system provides the stimuli for starting and stopping movement along with making adjustments in between. As such it serves as the primary basis for our ability to function and learn.

Sensory information reaches the brain via specialized nerve cells called receptors, of which there are two types: external and internal. Our eyes, ears, sense of taste, touch and smell serve as our external receptors, which keep us apprised of conditions in our external environment. Our internal receptors include physical sensations such as those associated with pain and sensitivity to hot and cold. Regarding perceptual-motor function specifically, our "kinesthetic sense" and vestibular mechanism serve as our primary internal receptors, which constantly and automatically provide us with information about our physical disposition within the environment.

External Feedback—Knowledge of Results

In adapting to their environment, most people rely mainly on information received through their senses of sight and hearing. Someone who is vision-impaired, on the other hand, must learn to compensate by developing the sense of hearing on a higher level and also by utilizing the sense of touch and internal receptors to a much greater extent. A person who is hearing-impaired, of course, must learn to use the sense of sight as the primary source of external sensory input.

In the case of musicians, the primary external receptor used is the ear. When we perform a musical passage or even a single tone, our ear provides us with feedback on "how we did." Not only does the ear evaluate the various properties of musical sound (pitch, timbre, intensity and duration), but it monitors the expressive musical qualities as well. Scientists refer to this kind of feedback as KR (knowledge of results).

KR is the primary type of feedback we consciously use during trial-and-error practice. It is particularly important to us in the early stages of learning. When all KR is eliminated, as has been done in some experiments, the subjects soon become frustrated, since they have no knowledge of how they are doing on the task assigned to them. (Imagine yourself trying to improve your tone, intonation or phrasing with earplugs in your ears.) In the advanced stages of learning, KR is not quite as critical, so long as kinesthetic memory is fairly well established. Knowing "how it should feel," based upon numerous accurate repetitions in the past, can still guide us through the process with a reasonable degree of accuracy.

KR can be used in two ways: during the performance or afterward. When used during the performance, it is referred to as "action feedback." When used after the performance, it is called "terminal feedback." Whether we use action or terminal feedback is determined by the amount of time it takes to complete a given response. In very rapid movements or responses, terminal KR is usually our only source of information, while in slower movements we are able to use action feedback to good advantage.

In addition to providing information, KR can also serve as a reinforcer or source of motivation for us. For example, if we hear ourselves improving during successive trials, this encourages us to keep practicing for longer periods. Hearing someone else who performs better than we do can also become a motivational kind of KR when it activates our desire to improve. Elementary-school teachers often use KR when they place gold stars on a classroom performance chart. In this context, however, it is often called KP (knowledge of progress), which is simply accumulated KR.

A specific type of motivational KR related to musical learning has to do with what I call getting beginners "over the hump." This idea is based on the fact that most people, regardless of training, can differentiate between extremely poor and good performance. Even young children are aware when their performance doesn't sound good, when the tone is poor and the intonation painful. This can be, and often is, a negative factor in terms of motivation for continued practice after the first two or three months of study. Good students in particular become frustrated if the tonal results they achieve are poor. But once tone and intonation improve sufficiently, practice comes easier, because it is more fun when one sounds better. The time period for getting "over the hump" will vary with the individual, of course, but in my experience it takes an average of two years for most students. Parents in particular should be made aware of this problem from the start, so that they can be prepared to give added encouragement during this difficult early period of instrumental music study.

In addition to the ear, the eye also serves as an external receptor for musicians. String-instrument students involved with imitative learning in particular use it constantly. The performer in a large ensemble, of course, relies heavily on visual cues when trying to interpret the conductor's musical sign language. But the ensemble performer must never forget that listening to the other ensemble players is equally as important as watching the conductor. If you don't listen, how is it possible to achieve good intonation, balance and blend, as well as rhythmic precision? Music is first and foremost an aural art, which requires constant and careful listening at all times during performance.

In connection with this, I am reminded of the days when I was a member of the Eastman Wind Ensemble, under the direction of Dr. Frederick Fennell. Our rehearsal room had two signs in it: a No Smoking sign, which was required by the fire marshall, and another, hung there by Dr. Fennell, with the word "Listen" spelled out in large capital letters. Whenever we forgot to listen in rehearsal, he would immediately turn around and point to the sign. One of the major keys to being a good ensemble player, therefore, is to learn how to *listen!*

Internal Feedback—Proprioception

In perceptual-motor function and learning we rely on two types of internal feedback: kinesthesia and vestibular function. The term "proprioception" is used when referring to both of these feedback types collectively.

Kinesthesis.   When we perform, certain physical sensations are generated within our body that are automatically monitored by the brain. Normally we are not consciously aware of these sensations unless someone like a teacher points them out to us. They are involuntary responses, which contribute significantly to what Gallwey calls the Natural Learning Process. In more scientific terms, these sensations represent a type of internal feedback called kinesthesis.

If we repeat a specific movement or performance act enough times in a similar way, these physical sensations eventually establish themselves as a memory pattern or "groove" in the brain. Once established, such a memory pattern helps us to recall and duplicate a specific movement at will during future performances. I call this "programming the brain" with images of feeling (kinesthetic memory) to meet the goals of the performer's "musical ear."

Where do these physical sensations originate, and how do they operate in the body? The problem is that we don't know the answer to either of these questions for certain. "In spite of years of study and research, kinesthesis is [still] not fully understood either physiologically or psychologically."[6] Because of this it is difficult to define in specific terms. Some refer to it as an awareness of movement sensation. Others refer to it simply as "muscle sense" or even "muscle memory." Yet we are all reasonably certain that it exists. Even the ancient Greeks, by setting it clearly apart from the sense of touch, obviously believed it to exist. Perhaps kinesthesis can best be defined as internal sensory information about our movements in terms of position, speed, tension and force.

Traditionally we have assumed that the primary source of kinesthetic sensation was in the muscle spindle; hence the use of a term like "muscle memory" to describe it. There has also been speculation that the skeletal bone joints and tendons function as kinesthetic receptors. Recent research indicates with a fair degree of certainty that the bone joints are definitely involved, but we are no longer so sure about the muscles and tendons. More research is needed on this subject.

The vestibular mechanism.   The vestibular mechanism is an internal sensory organ that regulates body balance through recording the position of the head in space. As such it provides us with information about body equilibrium and serves as our orientation to gravity. It is located in the semicircular canals of the inner ear, which contain a liquid called endolymph. As long as the head is in an upright position, the mechanism remains basically passive. But once the head is tilted in any direction, the eyes dilate and the fluid in the inner ear moves back and forth in much the same way as the fluid in a carpenter's level. This causes nerve signals to be relayed immediately to the brain, which in turn automatically triggers certain body muscles, particularly those in the neck and shoulders, to contract reflexively in order to maintain body balance. While it is necessary for maintaining body balance, this process also creates excessive muscular tension, which in turn can inhibit good neuromuscular function.

From this description it should be obvious that body balance and posture are related. But the big difference between the two is that while body balance is controlled through reflex action in the brain, posture is not. Good posture is something that has to be learned after birth. No one knows for sure why this is so. Some scientists suggest, however, that this may be still another example of the body's

---

[6]George Harvey Sage, *Introduction to Motor Behavior: A Neuropsychological Approach,* © 1977. Addison-Wesley, Reading, MA. p. 296. Reprinted with permission.

slowness in adapting to its environment; that is, that it still hasn't fully adapted to walking and standing on only two feet. In any case, body balance and posture are, without a doubt, vitally important to good neuromuscular function. In fact, they are basic to good performance.

SUMMARY

Despite rapid advances in human knowledge and technology, especially in recent times, we still know relatively little about our own machine, the human body. And yet this need not give us cause for serious concern since we have been able to function effectively without this knowledge in the past and will surely continue to do so in the future. We don't need to understand the structure and function of our bodies in order to perform. The main thing we need to know is how to properly operate our body's controls. We do this by creating a mental image of the performance goal desired and then simply telling the brain what we want done, not how to do it.

The three body systems most directly involved in perceptual-motor function and learning are the sensory, nervous and muscular systems. Of these, the only one that is clear to us visually is the muscular system. Perhaps for this reason, it is the area where many teachers have focused the bulk of their teaching efforts. But such an approach is misguided at best and totally wrong at worst. We can't really train the muscles. Instead we should direct our efforts toward training the brain which controls the muscles.

The brain is the master control center for all body functions. It receives various types of sensory information, which it processes and organizes into neural commands, which in turn are relayed to the muscles. This includes involuntary body functions such as breathing as well as sensory feedback in the form of proprioception.

Contrary to the opinion of some, human beings rely on the use of reflex actions and involuntary function to a relatively large degree. We do not function exclusively or even primarily in a voluntary way. In this context our brain operates at two basic levels: a voluntary (conscious) level and an involuntary (unconscious) level. The conscious brain controls all voluntary acts of the will. The unconscious brain serves as a memory storage center for all involuntary body functions, including both inherited reflexes and those acquired after birth (conditioned reflexes).

In terms of monitoring and regulating performance, the body possesses as part of its sensory system two types of feedback: (1) external feedback, involving the sense organs of sight, hearing, taste, touch and smell, and (2) internal feedback, or proprioception, which includes kinesthesis and the vestibular mechanism.

Kinesthesis involves physical sensations generated inside the body, which are automatically monitored by the brain. This information keeps us aware of our physical disposition within the environment. The vestibular mechanism is located in the inner ear and is responsible for regulating body balance. If the head is tilted downward, for example, the vestibular mechanism automatically sends appropriate messages to the brain that trigger specific body muscles to respond in a reflex fashion to the task of maintaining body balance. Thus, vestibular function and posture are directly related.

CONCLUSION

If we use the Natural Learning Process discussed in Chapter One as a learning model and add the feedback systems discussed in this chapter, then we are able to construct a schematic applied to musical performance as seen in Figure 2-1.

To explain Figure 2-1 in more detail, we begin by listening to a performance model and then try to imitate it. During the process of imitation we receive both external and internal feedback from our body's sensory system. Our ear serves as our main source of external feedback, or KR (knowledge of results). Internal feedback comes to us in the form of kinesthetic and vestibular information. Together these two types of feedback allow us to evaluate our performance and detect errors. We identify errors by comparing our live performance to the performance model stored in our brain (recall memory). Through continued imitation in the form of trial-and-error practice, we are able to improve performance through continued use of body feedback.

Let us now apply all this to a more specific learning situation. For example, each time we repeat something like picking up a pencil, our body-feedback mechanisms send messages to the brain on how well we did. The memory-storage center in the brain automatically records for future use (retrieval) the movements that we perceive as being correct. It ignores and forgets our incorrect movements. The more information we have in our memory-storage center, the more refined our movements become. In explaining this concept Maltz uses the term "automatic mecha-

FIGURE 2-2   The Function of Performance Feedback

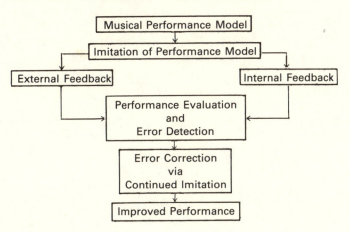

nism'' in lieu of body feedback. He says, "It 'remembers' its successes, forgets its failures, and eventually repeats the successful action without any further conscious 'thought'—or as a habit."[7]

Our body-feedback mechanisms, therefore, serve as important sources of error detection and correction for each of us, but they are not the most important key to good performance. Most important is the mental picture or image we have of what the correct response or movement should be. If the mental image we have is vague or incorrect, this means that the information recorded in our brain's memory-storage center will likewise be incorrect. Continued repetition of the same eventually results in the establishment of a bad habit, something each of us hopes to avoid. The focus of our teaching, therefore, should be on training the brain, especially the conscious brain, which is responsible for creating mental images for us. In the next two chapters I will review Eastern and Western psychological approaches intended to deal with this issue.

chapter three

foundations
of human psychology

The purpose of this chapter is to provide a psychophysiological basis for the principles and techniques of learning to be presented in the next chapter. To accomplish this I will discuss various Eastern and Western concepts that have influenced our beliefs regarding teaching-learning theory. Among these are Western behaviorism and humanism, Eastern meditation and mind-body integration. The chapter ends with a summary.

A HISTORICAL OVERVIEW

Human beings have probably always been curious about their existence on this earth. "Why am I here? How did I get here? What happens when I die?" Today, various answers to these questions are found within the doctrines of the world's religions. But serious concern about such matters has not been limited to theologians alone. Anthropologists, philosophers and others have also wrestled with these questions since the dawn of recorded history. We know, for example, that Socrates, Plato and Aristotle were specifically interested in the relationship of the human body and its soul. In fact the word "psyche" is a Greek word meaning "soul," from which psychology derives its name.

Is human behavior predictable, or is it essentially unpredictable? Is perceptual-motor performance under the direct control of the performer or is it essentially an unconscious, involuntary function? And what about superior ability and intelligence? Are these inherited traits or are they acquired through training after birth? These are other questions that human beings have raised about their psychological and physiological nature over the centuries and for which they are still seeking definitive answers today.

Psychology is the study of the mind and the mental processes related to it. Physiology is the study of how the various parts of the body function. In the perceptual-motor domain the traditional focus of the psychologist has been on the stimulus (input) and the response (output) aspects of performance and learning. The physiologist, on the other hand, has been concerned mainly with the neuromuscular operations occurring in between the stimulus and the response.

Considering the rapid advances in Western civilization since the Renaissance and especially during the current century, one would expect that by now psychologists and physiologists together would have discovered answers to some of the above questions. Unfortunately this has yet to happen. This is due in part to the fact that Western physiologists and others in the past tended to view the field of psychology with suspicion and, in some cases, a degree of disdain. Some psychologists, on the other hand, failed to see any real practical value in neurophysiological study. To understand why these attitudes existed we first need to realize that Western psychology as we know it today is still a relatively new science. It did not become a discrete discipline until well into the nineteenth century. The early psychologists were academically trained philosophers in most cases, and were members of university philosophy departments. The first "scientific" psychologists were trained physiologists and physicists, who did not emerge until the 1860s.[1]

Animal physiology, on the other hand, had its first known beginnings in the early seventeenth century, but modern physiology as we know it today did not really begin to flourish until the eighteenth century. Although one might expect that we would have a fairly good understanding of human physiology by now, we do not. Other than knowing some of the most elementary aspects of body function, we still do not fully understand human physiology, particularly as it pertains to the brain.

Even though psychology is still a relatively new discipline and our knowledge of brain function is limited, significant progress is being made in both fields all the time. As stated earlier, the field of biochemistry shows promise of uncovering major secrets of brain function. Also, recent studies of Eastern psychology by Western psychologists have already provided us with an entirely new perspective on perceptual-motor learning and performance potential, as I will explain in this chapter.

Unlike Western psychology, Eastern psychology has a very long history. It has also remained relatively close to its religious, philosophical and cultural origins, while Western psychology has become increasingly more scientific in its method

[1]George Harvey Sage, *Introduction to Motor Behavior: A Neurophysiological Approach.* © 1977. Addison-Wesley, Reading, MA. pp. 1, 2. Reprinted by permission.

and orientation. Because of this basic difference, most Westerners have traditionally viewed Eastern psychology with askance. Since its basic concepts are quite foreign to our culture, we have tended to look upon Eastern psychology as being illogical, unscientific and, thus, unworthy of serious consideration. Fortunately, some of these narrow-minded attitudes are beginning to change.

Another positive factor in the acceptance of Eastern psychology is the relatively recent emergence of a new group of Western researchers with dual backgrounds in psychology and physiology. Referred to as specialists in motor control, these researchers' energies are directed almost exclusively toward the study of perceptual-motor function. Many of them are associated with university departments of physical education. Others with a strong interest in motor control are members of psychology, special education and physical therapy departments. More recently, expert musician-pedagogues, such as the late Paul Rolland of the University of Illinois, have also shown a renewed interest in the area of motor control. (See Chapter 2 of Rolland's *The Teaching of Action in String Playing*.) It is my hope that this trend will continue, and that one of the by-products of this text will be to stimulate still more interest in this area.

BASIC WESTERN
PSYCHOLOGICAL SCHOOLS

Despite the numerous schools of thought in Western psychology today, Milhollan and Forisha have categorized them all into what they call the two general models or images of man: the behaviorist and the phenomenological (humanistic) models.[2] In the behavioristic model, human beings are viewed as passive organisms responding essentially in an unconscious way to external forces within their environment. In the phenomenological model, human beings are considered to be active participants in the control of their own behavior. They possess conscious control over their behavior through their ability to think, reason and make their own decisions. These two models are best exemplified today in the form of two major psychological schools: behaviorism and humanism.

Behaviorism

To understand behaviorism we first need to understand the stimulus-response theory associated with the Russian physiologist Pavlov. Pavlov understood involuntary reflex action, of course, and noted that his dog began salivating whenever he saw food. So each time food was presented to the animal, Pavlov would ring a bell. Eventually the dog would salivate in response to the sound of the bell alone, even before he saw or smelled the food. Scientists later discovered that human beings

---

[2]F. Milhollan and B. E. Forisha, *From Skinner to Rogers: Contrasting Approaches to Education* (Lincoln, Nebraska: Professional Educators Publications, Inc., 1972). Reprinted by permission.

could also be conditioned (taught) to respond to specific stimuli in a similar manner. We know this process today as "reflex conditioning."

In the United States, B. F. Skinner and others were greatly influenced by the work of Pavlov and those who followed him. But Skinner demonstrated that reflex conditioning, focused mainly upon controlling the stimulus, explained only one part of human behavior. In his view the real answer was to find ways to control the behavioral response. This led to the establishment of what we now know as behavior modification.

Humanism

The humanistic school of psychology, currently headed by Carl Rogers, is the major school based on the phenomenological model of man. The humanists believe that all people are different, often unpredictable, and that they function psychologically in numerous diverse ways, depending on heredity, environmental influences and training since birth. They further believe that most human behavior cannot be analyzed realistically through the use of traditional scientific methods because the uniqueness of each human being defies such analysis. People as a whole do not necessarily function according to predetermined laws and patterns unless they have been brainwashed. Our free will gives us the capacity for making various choices and decisions, and the diverse experiences from our differing backgrounds directly influence those choices and decisions.

The recent surge of interest in humanistic psychology has fostered several new concepts such as self-esteem, self-image, self-actualization, the power of positive thinking and psycho-cybernetics. All of these will be discussed later in this chapter. But first let us summarize the basic concepts of behaviorism and humanism by relating them to the two types of brain function discussed in Chapter Two: voluntary and involuntary function. Applied to these physiological types of function, behaviorism can be said to represent the involuntary mode and humanism the voluntary mode. Based on this comparison it seems obvious to me that human behavior, rather than being totally involuntary or voluntary, is instead a combination of both. Our past experiences, learned habits and system of values and beliefs tend to make all of us function in involuntary and predictable ways to a great degree. When confronted with new situations, however, we tend to function in voluntary and unpredictable ways. Human behavior, therefore, appears to be both behavioristic and humanistic, not exclusively one or the other.

BEHAVIOR MODIFICATION

Behavior modification, which comes to us from the behavioristic school of Western psychology, is based upon the premise that behavioral responses can be controlled primarily through techniques of reward and punishment. For example, if a dog does a trick and you immediately reward him with food, the dog will remember this and be anxious to do the trick again in order to be given more food. In other words, control the consequences related to the response and you eventually gain control over the behavior itself. As the behavioral response becomes more conditioned, the need for continuous reward becomes less and less strong. Once the response becomes fully conditioned (habitual), the reward can be withdrawn entirely.

Behavior modification obviously works with lower animals. It also works with babies and young children. Parents and teachers have used it almost instinctively for ages, by rewarding children for good behavior (positive reinforcement) while expressing displeasure and even punishing children for unacceptable behavior. In so doing they have to be able to modify (some say manipulate) children's behavior to the point of actually controlling it.

There is also evidence that behavior modification works with older children and adults in school, in the military and in work situations. The older the person, however, the less effective it tends to be. As we grow older, our responses to new situations become less passive and more reasoned and thought out. In other words, we respond on the basis of certain beliefs or attitudes, which we have developed over a period of time. Therefore, in order to modify or change the behavioral response, we must first change the attitude. Focusing on the behavioral response alone will not automatically solve the problem. It is here that humanists find major fault with the general concept of behavior modification.

Behavior Defined

Behavior is the observable response to an environmental stimulus. It is the external manifestation of human function. In the context of behavior modification, behavior is viewed essentially as an involuntary or unconscious response, because there is minimal, if any, conscious thinking involved. Those who function in this manner do not use logical reasoning to determine what their response should be; they simply react to the stimulus, and do so in essentially the same way each time that the same stimulus is presented. In other words, the response is consistent, automatic and habitual.

Theoretically at least, behavior is derived from two types of stimuli: (1) genetically based, internal stimuli, which affect cardiovascular and glandular function, including the emotional reactions resulting therefrom, and (2) external, psychological, environmental stimuli, which trigger specific responses acquired as a result of repetitive conditioning after birth. Based on this distinction one would logically assume that genetically based behavior is preprogrammed before birth and cannot be changed, but this is not true. Recent research with a Yoga master has proved that cardiovascular behavior, as one example, can be consciously controlled through self mind control. Others assume that conditioned behavior learned after birth can be rather easily changed, but this assumption is also incorrect. Conditioned behavior, once it has been deeply ingrained in the unconscious mind, is usually very difficult to change. It requires remedial teaching and learning, which can involve several months and sometimes years of concentrated effort. In these respects the foregoing theoretical classification is basically an artificial, superficial one, and should be viewed as such. Instead it makes more sense to believe that all behavior potentially is subject to modification and/or change, but extreme effort may be required to bring it about.

For a better understanding of all this, let us use the example of a young child who is afraid of dogs. Each time the child sees or hears a dog, its response is one of fear, manifested by a frightened look and crying. The response is basically automatic, and it is the same each time. In the past we have assumed the cause to be some traumatic experience with a dog very early in life. Recent research suggests, however, that such behavior may be inherited. In any case the child's response usually operates like a genetically based reflex. It also seems almost impossible to change and often continues into adult life.

Attitude Defined

Attitude is the mental posture or position we take concerning a specific issue, person, place or thing. It is based upon a previously determined theory, opinion or value judgment that a person holds. Unlike behavior itself, which is essentially an unconscious response that can be observed externally, attitude is established internally and consciously for the most part. It is the intermediary between the stimulus and the response, which influences and often directly controls what our behavioral response will be. It is the result of our free will to choose and decide. The only exception to this is brainwashing (external mind control), which is a topic beyond the scope of this discussion.

To illustrate the concept of attitude let us use the example of a student who is habitually late to ensemble rehearsal. In dealing with this problem one solution is to threaten the student with expulsion from the ensemble if his tardy behavior continues. We might call this the "old school" disciplinary approach, which also requires that the threat be carried out if necessary. Another approach would be to recognize the possibility that the student doesn't really understand *why* his punctuality is so vital to the proper functioning of the total ensemble. Accordingly, the director needs to spend some time explaining the situation to the student, in the hope of changing his attitude. If the student is capable of understanding the consequences of his tardiness, this could change his attitude and cause him to be punctual, without the need for negative threats and possible punishment.

Current belief in some quarters is that the "old school" disciplinary approach is only a temporary solution to behavioral problems, since it does not consider attitude as an integral part of permanent behavioral change. While I agree with this to a large extent, there is no assurance that a young child or student is fully capable of comprehending the need for change in the same way that an adult perceives it. If the student fails to understand the need after it has been explained to him, then threats of punishment may be the only alternative. For example, if after a calm explanation your children continue to run out into the street without looking to see if cars are coming, then you threaten to punish them. You have no other alternative except "learning through experience," which might well result in the child's death—hardly a viable alternative for loving, reasonable parents!

Despite this extreme example, approaching behavioral change through working first on attitude is still the most ideal, preferred solution. But much depends upon the maturity of the person involved and the ability to comprehend the need for behavioral change. For a better understanding of this process let us take a look at how behaviors and attitudes are developed, beginning with infancy.

Behavior and Attitude Development

When an infant is born, most of its behavior, like that of lower animals, is instinctive (genetically based). It has minimal experience in its new environment; thus it has no real notion of how to control it. Consequently, the significant adults in its environment are the ones who largely control and shape its behavior. Let us apply this to a specific situation. We are told, for example, that a young infant often cries because it needs to exercise its lungs and related body organs. This is a normal function and should not be cause for serious concern. But if the parents consistently rush to the infant, hold and comfort it *each time* it cries, the infant learns very quickly that all it has to do is cry and the parents will respond immediately. In this context the infant has learned to control its parents' behavior. But if the parents learn to distinguish between normal crying and crying due to pain or other problems, then they are able to exert control over the infant's behavior.

The younger the child, the more malleable and controllable he or she is. As one gets older and reaches the age of reason, one begins to acquire certain attitudes that make one less prone to behavioral control. Behavior is no longer an end in itself. It becomes increasingly more related to internally based attitudes. Thus, to change the behavior to any significant degree, one needs to focus on changing the attitude first. Let's apply this principle to a specific situation. Most parents and teachers frequently try to change children. The impetus for such change usually comes from a negative reaction to a child's behavior, as when a child continually fights and argues with his parents. The parents may choose to punish or threaten to punish the child, but this solves the problem only to a limited degree, since the child has a previously established attitude about fighting and arguing, which he learned in his own home. Having seen his parents fighting and arguing with each other many times and observed the same thing in their dealings with his own brothers and sisters, he has formed the attitude that this is the way to solve problems. His own behaviors, therefore, are simply an external manifestation of that attitude.

To solve this problem, we need to understand that the child is not the real source of the problem. The real problem lies with the parents and the environmental model they have provided. In order to change the child's attitude and behavior, the parents' attitude and accompanying behavior must change first, in order to establish a new environment for the child. This will then allow the parents to be able to reason with the child—if he is old enough to understand reason—and work on changing his attitude. Eventually this should bring about a change in the child's behavior, assuming prior success in actually changing his attitude.

Such a situation becomes more pronounced during adolescence, and even more so in adult life. For example, most of us know at least one person—a friend, relative or coworker—whom we would like to change if we could. Let's say this person displays some negative behavior that we simply can't tolerate. If we are in a position of power over her, we can perhaps effect behavioral change, either through direct punishment or through the fear of punishment. But the person whose behavior we have tried to change will probably resent our heavy-handed manner and do as she pleases when we are not around. Consequently, all we have succeeded in doing is bringing about a superficial, temporary, and external behavioral change in that person. The reason for this is that our focus for change was directed at the wrong thing. We should have been trying to change the person's attitude, which serves as the underlying basis for her behavior. Try to change the attitude first, and then work on the behavior. If the attitudinal change is sufficient, those concerned will take charge of changing their own negative behavior.

Conscious and unconscious use of behavior modification, therefore, has always been at least moderately successful in controlling the behavior of infants and young children. Its value in changing adult behavior, however, is much more limited. Yet, as a psychological method of studying human behavior, Skinner and others argue that it is the only reliable method we have. Behavior modification specialists also point out its scientific validity; they are able to demonstrate results based on objective data. Other psychological methodologies presumably cannot and do not do this.

With the behaviorists' emphasis on scientific data, one might logically expect them to be interested in the physiological study of brain function in which experiments with animals, involving brain lesions and other surgical procedures, have been performed. Strict behaviorists, however, are generally opposed to neurophysiological study. They believe that since we still do not understand how the brain really functions, we should stop trying to base learning theory on physiological data. Rather we should direct our energies toward studying behavior itself.

Behavior is something that can be easily observed and described. We also have workable techniques through which we can develop and change it. But since behavior modification has been used successfully in prisons, mental institutions and prisoner-of-war camps, many have come to view it as a form of brainwashing and mind control. This in turn has caused them to be very fearful of it and, therefore, bitterly opposed to its widespread use. What would happen, they ask, if a small group of specialists decided to establish mind control over a large population?

Even though we should certainly be concerned about inappropriate use of behavior-modification techniques, I see no reason for extreme anxiety about the issue. As noted earlier, parents and teachers have always used behavior modification in its most basic form in controlling the behavior of infants and young children and will no doubt continue to do so in the future. In the case of older children and adults, behavior modification as we know it becomes increasingly less effective, especially with people who have learned to think for themselves. The ability to think for oneself and act on those thoughts is directly related to self-esteem and self-image.

SELF-ESTEEM
AND SELF-IMAGE

What do you want out of life more than anything else? Typical answers to this question are: I want to feel loved, recognized, and respected by others; I want to feel important, to be appreciated for what I am and what I do; I want to be happy, to be emotionally secure, to have peace of mind. It would appear, then, that there are many answers, and that no single answer will meet the needs of everyone. However, there is one term that I feel incorporates and integrates all of the above. That term is "self-esteem." The more self-esteem we have, the more loved, recognized, respected, important and appreciated we feel. This in turn allows us to be happy, to be emotionally secure and have peace of mind. Self-esteem allows us to like and trust ourselves. It allows us to think for ourselves and be confident about the validity of our thoughts and decisions.

Self-Esteem Defined

According to Branden, "Self-esteem . . . is the integrated sum of self-confidence and self-respect."[3] It is an *integrated* sum of these two qualities because they are inseparable. They directly influence each other; you can't have one without the other.

Self-esteem is based largely upon evaluations of our past performances and/or experiences by significant others in our environment. If those evaluations are essentially positive, this enhances our self-confidence and self-respect, which in turn bring about high self-esteem. If those same evaluations tend to be largely negative, this leads to a lack of self-confidence and self-respect, resulting in low self-esteem.

In order for human beings to survive physically, they must learn to adapt to their physical environment. In a sense, self-esteem fulfills a similar function in the psychological domain of human existence. The degree to which we possess self-esteem or lack it directly affects our ability to live life. While lack of self-esteem does not automatically result in physiological death—although it sometimes does, in the form of suicide and other forms of self-destruction—it has a direct and primary influence on our psychological survival. A person who lacks self-esteem is psychologically dead, in my opinion. Those who are psychologically dead have nothing to contribute, to themselves or to others. Without psychological life, mere physical existence then becomes meaningless.

At this point I would like to go back and answer personally the question posed at the beginning of this section. What do I want out of life more than anything else? I want to be able to live life to its fullest. As a major part of that goal I want to make a *contribution* to society within my sphere of influence as a teacher. I recognize that my own self-esteem must be high in order to meet this goal effectively. In this context Branden states: "There is no value-judgment more important to man—no

---

[3]From *The Psychology of Self-Esteem* by Nathaniel Branden. By permission of Bantam Books Inc. Copyright © 1969 by Nathaniel Branden. All Rights Reserved.

factor more decisive in his psychological development and motivation—than the estimate he passes on himself."[4] (The estimate man passes on himself is based on his self-confidence and self-respect, which form the basis for self-esteem.) If we accept this statement as being true, then the importance of self-esteem needs no further explanation or justification. It *is* the key to human psychological development and motivation.

If self-esteem is so important, then through what means are we able to acquire it if we have little of it? Through what means are we able to get more of it? The basic answer lies in the development of a positive self-image.

Self-Image Defined

Maltz says that self-image is the mental blueprint or picture that we have of ourselves.[5] He also states:

> The "self-image" is the key to human personality and behavior. Change the self-image and you change the personality and the behavior. But more than this. The "self-image" sets the boundaries of individual accomplishment. It defines what you can and cannot do. Expand the self-image and you expand the "area of the possible."[6]

Self-image, therefore, is our perception of who and what we are. It also controls our perception of who and what we can become and thereby sets the limits of our potential. In so doing, it directly affects our capacity for learning. For this reason it is possibly the most basic and most important topic we as teachers can study in our quest for knowledge relative to teaching-learning theory. It has a direct impact upon the quality of our nervous stimuli.

Some people, unfortunately, have a negative image of themselves, which is reflected in their performance results. Worst of all, they believe that "we are who we are" and that this cannot be changed. Maltz disagrees. He says that each of us can change who we believe we are, through using what he calls "creative imagination," which is the ability to use our imagination in a positive, constructive way, as opposed to using it negatively and destructively. Human beings always act, feel and perform in accordance with what they *imagine to be true* about themselves and their environment. If they imagine themselves to be stupid, they will act, feel and perform in a stupid manner. If they imagine themselves to be brilliant, they can function brilliantly.[7]

Self-image is crucial to good perceptual-motor function, in that it directly affects the quality of our mental images. In musical performance, for example, being able to reproduce one's musical image alone is not enough. One also must be able to "see oneself" reproducing it accurately and consistently. In other words,

[4]Ibid., p. 109.

[5]From the book *Psycho-Cybernetics* by Maxwell Maltz. © 1960 by Prentice-Hall, Inc. Published by Prentice-Hall, Inc., Englewood Cliffs, N.J. 07632.

[6]Ibid., p. ix.

[7]Ibid., p. 31.

self-image has a direct influence on our potential for performance success, based on whether or not we view ourselves as good performers or poor ones.

While it is easy to become careless after a time and use the terms self-image and self-esteem interchangeably, they are not really synonymous. Self-image has to do with how people view themselves, the image they have of themselves. That image may be inaccurate, but it is real to you until something happens that causes you to change it. Self-esteem, on the other hand, represents how people "feel" and respond to how they view themselves (their self-image). Self-confidence and self-respect, the key ingredients of self-esteem, are thus the outgrowth of one's self-image.

Even though self-esteem and self-image are not synonymous, it should be obvious that they are very closely related. In fact they are so closely related from the standpoint of human performance as to be almost inseparable, so highly integrated that it is difficult to achieve one without directly affecting the other. For this reason they will be discussed concurrently to a large extent in the following pages.

If the answer to improving self-esteem lies in the development of a positive self-image, then how do we go about developing it? According to Maltz, self-image is changed by "experiencing," not by intellectual knowledge alone. "It is not the child who is taught *about* love but the child who has experienced love that grows into a healthy, happy, well-adjusted adult."[8] This indicates that past experience, particularly during the earliest years of life, forms the basis of both our self-esteem and our self-image.

How Self-Image and Self-Esteem Are Developed

First of all, we are products of our environment. We are also products of our parents' genes and, more specifically, the DNA formula within those genes; but we are also who and what we are psychologically as a result of the environment in which we grew up and the environment in which we currently exist. With regard to personality factors such as self-image and self-esteem, it seems reasonable to believe that environment is the dominant influence in their development and establishment.

It is a generally accepted fact today that the first three to five years of a person's life are the most critical in establishing potential for future growth and development. I believe this to be especially true with regard to self-image and self-esteem. During children's earliest years, their evaluations of themselves are largely a direct reflection of their parents' evaluations of them, such as "good child," "bad child," "pretty little girl," "tough little guy." Children also identify with their parents by imitating them in numerous ways. They usually walk and talk like their parents. They also learn to act, respond and eventually think the way their parents do. Consequently it seems reasonable to assume that concepts of self-image

[8]Ibid., pp. x, xi.

and self-esteem are at least partially acquired through similar means—through the example or model of self-image and self-esteem that their parents provide.

Later, as children enter school, their teachers, classmates and friends become additional influences on both their self-image and self-esteem as well as on their values, attitudes and general view of life itself and their role and function within it. Here again the early years of school, especially the first year, are critical to the child's later success (or failure) in school. (Astute elementary-school principals demonstrate awareness of this important fact when they assign their most competent and experienced teachers to the kindergarten level and their youngest, least experienced teachers to the upper grades.) Teachers, therefore, can and usually do have a major impact on students' development of self-image and self-esteem. In some cases, perhaps a significant number, teacher influence can be so strong that it eventually becomes *the* major influence in a child's life, even stronger than that of the parents. In this sense, the role a teacher plays in the lives of students is a highly significant one indeed. It therefore behooves us as prospective and practicing teachers to understand this important aspect of our professional function as thoroughly as we can.

Self-Actualization

Earlier I said that attitude is the posture or position we take concerning a given issue, person, place or thing, based upon a previously established theory, belief or value judgment that we have. Perhaps the most important attitude we possess is that concerning our self-image. It directly influences almost everything that we think and do. Therefore, to change our self-image we have to change the basic attitude we possess about who and what we are. We must convince ourselves that who and what we are right now is not necessarily a fate to which we are forever destined. We have to be convinced that it is possible to change, and that we have the power to exert at least some control over our own destiny. The humanistic psychologist Maslow used the term ''self-actualization'' to define this process.

For many people self-actualization is difficult, even next to impossible. The older one is, the more defined our concepts of self-image and self-esteem become. The more clearly defined they are, the more difficult they are to change. Consequently some people believe that changing them after a certain age, say thirty or forty, is next to impossible, remarking, for instance, ''He's too old to change'' or ''It's in her genes.'' I do not deny that change, particularly attitudinal change, becomes increasingly difficult as we grow older. At some point certain basic attitudes no doubt become so deeply entrenched that they might as well be ''in the genes''; changing them is extremely difficult at best. Religious beliefs based on the concept of predestination also make attitudinal change in this area equally difficult. Still others view self-actualization as a form of self-centeredness and self-worship, which they believe is antithetical to the basic reason for our existence on this earth.

It is not my purpose to try to change anyone's basic religious belief or to tell you what your goal in life should be. These are major personal decisions, which each individual must ultimately make for oneself. Instead my intention is to try to convince you of two basic things: (1) that the key to the development of human potential often lies in changing a person's self-image and (2) that self-image is best altered by changing one's basic attitudes about oneself. Related to the second notion is the concept that it is possible to change both one's attitudes and behaviors, even in later life.

Positive Thinking

In the 1950s Norman Vincent Peale first wrote about what he called "the power of positive thinking." More recently, similar concepts, such as "the power of suggestion," "auto-suggestion" and "self mind control" have been used by some psychologists. The basic premise underlying all of these is that all of us have the ability to take charge of our lives and control them from within. In line with basic beliefs emanating from the humanistic school, we can choose to be the masters of our fate or we can simply allow ourselves to become victims of it.

Let me give an example of how this concept works. In the field of medicine, there are numerous documented cases of physicians prescribing placebos (sugar pills) to patients, which resulted in the cure of certain minor ailments. One explanation for this is that the patients didn't need any type of medication in the first place in order to get well. Another possible explanation is that the patients' complete confidence (faith) in their physician allowed their minds to take control of the healing process; hence, the power of positive thinking or self mind control combined with faith.

Another example exists in the form of upset victories in competitive athletics where mediocre teams soundly defeat top-ranked teams. I believe such phenomena are the result of faith in positive thinking (mental attitude) in addition to superior preparation through proper practice, mental as well as physical.

At the other extreme, we have all heard about psychosomatic illness; that is, illness presumably mentally suggested by the patients themselves. This infers at least that the human brain has far greater control over our lives, both physiologically and psychologically, than most of us realize. We are just beginning to comprehend the immense potential for power and control that exists within each of us. We have to learn how to unleash all of this potential so we can use it for our own benefit and that of others. In trying to do this, some people erroneously assume that all you have to do is simply replace negative, restrictive thinking with positive, constructive thought. But mere positive thinking is not enough; wishful thinking will not make a dream come true. Instead, major changes in mental attitude must precede everything else.

First of all, you must be convinced that change in general is possible, regardless of age, past experience, background and heredity. Secondly, you must be convinced that the specific goal aimed for is within the realm of possibility for you and that it is a desirable goal. Then you must act upon it, realizing that all learning (change) requires trial-and-error practice, time and patience. Ultimately, you have to have what theologians call "faith," not only in the desirability of the concept but in the belief that it can and will work for you.

Psycho-Cybernetics

The term "cybernetics" is derived from a Greek word that means "steersman." Physicists and mathematicians first used it to describe goal-striving, goal-oriented behavior of mechanical systems. In other words, "cybernetics explains 'what happens' and 'what is necessary' in the purposeful behavior of machines."[9] Maltz simply coined the term "psycho-cybernetics" to denote goal-oriented behavior of human beings.

Maltz believes that the key to human personality and behavior lies within one's own self-image. If you view yourself in a certain way—as happy, confident, shy or awkward—this is the image you will also present to others. You are what you think you are. In terms of the future, you will also be what you believe you are or think you will be. We control our personalities and thus our lives largely from within, based upon our self-image, or our concept of ourselves.

I find it particularly interesting that Maltz, who died in 1975, was a plastic surgeon rather than a psychologist. And yet he discovered that if one's face is altered through plastic surgery, the personality and behavior are often also altered as a result. In some cases he found that plastic surgery can affect a person's self-image to such an extent that even one's basic talents and abilities seem to improve.[10] On the other hand, he also explained that some patients didn't change at all. Despite the acquisition of a new face, they "went right on wearing the same old personality."[11] How can this be? We need to be reminded that the center for all thought and action of human beings resides in the brain and the rest of the central nervous system, which constitutes the source of our "goal-striving mechanism." We are able to exert control over this mechanism through the use of mental imagery, as described in Chapter One. We have a definite choice in how we decide to use it. We can use it as a "success mechanism" or as a "failure mechanism," depending on the goals we set for it. Thus, we can use it to increase or limit our potential.[12]

The Upper Limits of Human Potential

What are the upper limits of human potential? Actually, we have no real way of knowing. Whatever they may be, it is doubtful that we are anywhere close to reaching them. If past history is a valid indicator, the promise of future human advancement is at least equal to that of the recent past. In the area of science, for

[9]Ibid., p. viii.
[10]Ibid., pp. v, vi.
[11]Ibid., pp. 7, 8.
[12]Ibid., p. x.

example, there are more scientists alive today than have existed in all of history. In the area of self-regulation of involuntary body functions as practiced by Yoga masters, human potential also shows equally great promise. It is therefore probable that the extension of human potential in the future will greatly surpass anything we have known in the past. But we must keep in mind that we are the ones directly responsible for limiting the potential of ourselves and others. We have preconceived notions and deeply rooted attitudes about what we believe to be possible and impossible. These notions and attitudes then govern (in most cases limit) our potential accordingly.

Ornstein provides us with an excellent example of how we do this. There was a time when most people believed that it was humanly impossible to run a mile in less than four minutes. Then one person "broke" the four-minute mile, and this seemed to make it automatically possible for several others to do the same thing.[13] Factors such as improved methods of training and better nourishment, health habits and techniques of body development were no doubt responsible for this to some degree. But I believe that the primary factor that allowed this to happen was the runner's faith that he in fact *could* do it. He had a strong belief in himself (a strong positive self-image, if you will), a belief that he could accomplish what others had considered to be impossible.

Let me now relate this idea to musical performance. There was a time when percussionists viewed the percussion part to Stravinsky's *The Soldier's Tale* as being next to impossible to play. Eventually a few performers were able to transcend this defeatist attitude and master the challenge. Today most percussionists still consider this music quite difficult, but other literature composed since that time requires even greater performance facility. Most importantly, there is no reason to believe that we are anywhere near to reaching the end of all this.

Preconceived notions or attitudes can, therefore, severely limit our potential. Unfortunately, we as teachers are frequently guilty of this in dealing with our students. We establish certain levels of performance achievement for specific grade levels and follow them with excessive rigidity regardless of individual potential. For instance, we say, "She is too young to start the oboe"; "He shouldn't be trying to sing that difficult solo." Obviously, common sense must prevail in such matters, but we also need to maintain a flexible attitude as well. Human beings are not all the same, and this includes mental potential and learning ability as well as physical characteristics. Let those occasional student "superstars" grow and flourish; don't limit them unnecessarily!

In closing, I wish to use one last example of a general nature cited by Maltz. By the time people in our society reach at least the age of seventy, we usually label them "old." But some people begin to look, think and act old at the age of forty and fifty. Still others still look, think and act young at seventy, while others, such as

---

[13]Robert E. Ornstein, *The Psychology of Consciousness*, 2nd ed. (New York: Harcourt Brace Jovanovich, Inc., 1977), p. 4. Reprinted by permission.

the conductor Stokowski, continue to be alert, vibrant and excitingly alive in their eighties and even into their nineties.[14] The explanation for this lies in the fact that we are what we think we are. We become what we expect to become. The attitudes, mental images and expectations we have tend to be self-fulfilling prophecies. With regard to perceptual-motor learning, Gallwey states: "I know of no single factor that more greatly affects our ability to learn and perform than the image we have of ourselves."[15]

BASIC EASTERN
PSYCHOLOGICAL CONCEPTS

As stated earlier, Eastern psychology is not a new field of knowledge; it has been around for thousands of years. Yet most Westerners know relatively little about it. Perhaps the main reason for this lies in our inability to accept some of the unbelievable reports we have heard. The idea of Yoga masters being able to exercise voluntary control over their body temperatures and pulse rates, for example, strikes most of us as being impossible and therefore ridiculous. We normally consider such body functions to be involuntary, and thus beyond our conscious control. Being unable to explain them in rational, scientific terms, our tendency has been to relegate Eastern psychology to the realm of "mysticism" and the "occult."

But British medical people knew about self-regulation of so-called involuntary bodily functions as long as 250 years ago. In their study of Yogis in India, they found that these persons had the phenomenal ability to self-regulate both the mind and the body.[16] In March 1970, at the Menninger Foundation, in Lawrence, Kansas, an Indian Swami was tested in the laboratory under scientifically controlled conditions. The results proved that not only could he speed up and slow down his heart rate at will; he could also stop his heart entirely.[17] Thus we can no longer deny or ignore the existence of such phenomena.

I suspect, however, that the real source of our difficulty in relating to Eastern psychology is that we don't really understand it. Trying to understand such basic concepts as meditation and mind-body integration is difficult enough, but even more difficult is to try to understand the various philosophies, religions and cultures from which these concepts come. They are so different from anything we know; they are particularly foreign to the Western scientific mind. And yet recent study and research by a few Western psychologists is beginning to change some of our

---

[14]From the book *Psycho-Cybernetics,* by Maxwell Maltz © 1960 by Prentice-Hall, Inc. Published by Prentice-Hall, Inc., Englewood Cliffs, N.J. 07632.

[15]W. Timothy Gallwey, *Inner Tennis: Playing the Game* (New York: Random House, Inc., 1976), p. 111. Reprinted by permission.

[16]*Biofeedback and Self-Control 1972: An Aldine Annual of the Regulation of Bodily Processes and Consciousness* (Chicago: Aldine Publishing Co., 1973), p. 152.

[17]Ibid., pp. 160–163.

earlier biases. In this context, the following quote seems particularly appropriate:

> In the days when an idea could be silenced by showing that it was contrary to religion, theology was the greatest single source of fallacies. Today, when any thought can be discredited by branding it unscientific, the power previously exercised by theology has passed over to science; hence science has become the greatest single source of error.[18]

In my opinion the time has come to cast aside some of our negative attitudes and beliefs concerning Eastern psychology. We can learn a great deal from studying it, particularly as it relates to perceptual-motor learning and performance. In fact the learning theories of Gallwey, Maltz and Suzuki appear to have their basic roots in Zen and Yoga.

The Two Modes of Consciousness

The upper brain (cerebrum and cerebral cortex) is divided into two sides, or hemispheres. The left side (connected to the right side of the body) is predominantly involved with verbal, analytical, objective and sequential functions, as, for example, in reading and mathematics. The right side (connected to the left side of the body) is concerned mainly with nonverbal, intuitive, holistic and spatial-orientation functions, which include performing-arts activities as well as sports.

But before going any further, I must qualify these generalizations. The two sides of the brain do not function in total isolation of each other. There is definitely some interplay between the two; both sides participate to some extent in most activities. This interplay is made possible by the corpus callosum, a large bundle of nerve fibers, which connects the two sides in normal people. Nevertheless, each side does specialize in certain specific functions despite the interplay between the two. We know this to be true because of studies done with those having a "split brain," where the corpus callosum was completely severed, either from surgery or a serious accident. Therefore, it can be said that each of us has two modes of consciousness available to us: one that is mainly verbal and analytic, the other being largely nonverbal and intuitive.[19]

In our Western, scientific culture the main focus of our educational methods and training has been on the verbal, analytic mode (the left brain). When we learn to play ball, dance or play a musical instrument in school, for example, the teacher analyzes our performance and gives us verbal feedback. Some of this kind of feedback can be quite helpful when it is given in the context of identifying a specific performance goal to work toward. When teacher feedback involves detailed analysis of physiological function, however, much harm can be done. Carried to an extreme, this type of teacher feedback can result in what some physical-education

[18]Rollo May, *Psychology and the Human Dilemma* (Belmont, CA.: Brooks-Cole Publishing Co., 1967), p. 111. Reprinted by permission.

[19]Robert E. Ornstein, *The Psychology of Consciousness*, 2nd ed. (New York: Harcourt Brace Jovanovich, Inc., 1977), p. 14. Reprinted by permission.

teachers refer to as "paralysis through analysis." This means simply that when students are asked to concentrate on several minute details of physiological function and performance technique simultaneously, they get so confused that they cannot do anything correctly, resulting in paralysis through analysis.

In contrast, the main purpose of Eastern psychology is to open up or develop the nonverbal, intuitive mode of consciousness—the right brain.[20] Concepts of quieting the mind, shutting out the external environment in order to concentrate on the internal one, are stressed by means of meditation. Training the verbal, analytic mode (left brain) tends to be slighted. If this is true, then aren't both the East and West negligent in favoring one type of training at the expense of the other? Shouldn't both modes of consciousness receive more balanced attention? I believe that both modes of consciousness are important and that each should be properly trained so that we can realize our full potential. Within the context of this book, a major reason for training the right brain is to improve perceptual-motor learning and performance. Other, more general reasons include learning to control hypertension and experiencing the full range of consciousness and reality.

Meditation

The underlying basis for Eastern psychology lies in the concept of meditation. According to Ornstein, meditation refers to a set of "techniques designed to cultivate a certain mode of operation of the nervous system, at a certain time, within a certain context."[21] It is "designed to produce an alteration in consciousness . . . often a shift from an external focus of attention [left brain] to an internal one [right brain]."[22] Still more detailed explanations are found in the following quotes from Naranjo:

> . . . all meditation is a *dwelling upon* something . . . meditation practices generally involve an effort to . . . set our attention upon a single object, sensation, utterance, issue, mental state, or activity . . . the importance of dwelling upon something is not so much in the *something* but in the *dwelling upon*.[23]

> We can [also] consider the process of meditation as similar to that of taking a vacation—leaving the situation, "turning off" our routine way of dealing with the external world for a period, later returning to find it "fresh," "new," "different," our awareness "deautomatized."[24]

Ornstein further points out that there are two types of meditation, concentrative meditation and "opening up" meditation. Each is designed to accomplish

---

[20]Ibid., p. 125.

[21]Ibid., p. 157.

[22]Ibid., p. 158.

[23]From *On the Psychology of Meditation* by Claudio Naranjo and Robert E. Ornstein, p. 10. Copyright © 1971 by Claudio Naranjo and Robert Ornstein. Reprinted by permission of Viking Penguin Inc.

[24]Ibid., p. 194.

different goals. The purpose of concentrative meditation is to restrict one's aware-ness to a single, narrow focus of attention, such as playing a musical instrument. This process is sometimes referred to as one-point concentration. Transcendental meditation (TM), which has become fairly well known in the United States, can be classified as one form of concentrative meditation. But the average Westerner can perhaps best relate to concentrative meditation through the concept of prayer, when one temporarily closes off the external world and focuses on the internal, spiritual world of the soul.[25] With regard to perceptual-motor function, Gallwey states, "Meditation is nothing more than pure concentration of the mind."[26]

"Opening up" meditation, on the other hand, is designed to expand our normal awareness above and beyond normal consciousness. It involves self-obser-vation of routine, habitual functions and actions, bringing conditioned reflexes back into our conscious awareness. The analogy of taking a vacation, as quoted earlier, is especially applicable to this type of meditation; that is, we leave the routine situa-tion temporarily and return later to find it "fresh" and "new." In the most extreme sense, opening up meditation involves intense concentration on involuntary body functions so that they can eventually be brought under conscious control. This is a specific goal in certain Yoga traditions.[27]

To view the topic in still another way, let's review some of the physiological aspects of perceptual-motor function discussed in Chapter Two. First of all, our sensory systems gather information from the environment and send it to the brain. The brain then automatically selects and retains certain information and filters out or rejects all the rest. We called this process "perception." In Eastern psychology this kind of perception is viewed as being unnecessarily limiting, an obstacle to full perception and awareness, which we should try to overcome through meditation. The purpose of "opening up" meditation, therefore, is to lift our perception out of its basic involuntary or automatic mode and bring it under direct conscious con-trol.[28]

Another way to look at meditation and its role in opening up our perception is to relate it to the stars in our universe. Most of us think of the stars "being out" only at night, not during the daytime. But they are always there, and they are always shining, however faintly. The main reason we don't see them during the day is because of the overpowering brightness of the sun.

In our internal physical environment there are many faint signals (stars) that exist, but our sense organs and brain (bright sun) have learned to filter out these

[25]Robert E. Ornstein, *The Psychology of Consciousness,* 2nd ed. (New York: Harcourt Brace Jovanovich, Inc., 1977), p. 160ff. Reprinted by permission.

[26]W. Timothy Gallwey, *Inner Tennis: Playing the Game* (New York: Random House, Inc., 1976), p. 65. Reprinted by permission.

[27]Robert E. Ornstein, *The Psychology of Consciousness,* 2nd ed. (New York: Harcourt Brace Jovanovich, Inc., 1977), p. 176ff. Reprinted by permission.

[28]*On The Psychology of Meditation* by Claudio Naranjo and Robert E. Ornstein, p. 191. Copyright © 1971 by Claudio Naranjo and Robert Ornstein. Reprinted by permission of Viking Penguin Inc.

signals almost automatically. One faint signal that is sometimes filtered out is that of kinesthetic sensation. In order to improve the quality of our learning in this area we need to increase our awareness of kinesthetic sensation. We need to search for the shining stars, which are always there even during the brightest daylight. But first we must temporarily "block out" the sun's excessive brightness so that we can see (perceive) the stars. We are able to accomplish this through meditation.

Ironically, all of us were born with the ability to perceive faint signals like kinesthetic sensation, and we used them instinctively in order to roll over, crawl, stand up and walk as youngsters. As we began to talk, think and reason (left-brain development), our reliance on the nonverbal, right brain progressively decreased, thus allowing the left brain to become increasingly dominant. The left brain's dominance caused the right brain to become passive. This passivity allowed the left brain's interference (bright sunlight) to become so strong that eventually it completely blocked out the faint signals (stars) trying to reach the right brain, leaving the right brain nonfunctional to a great degree.

The purpose of meditation, therefore, is to alter our normal state of consciousness so that we can increase the outer limits of our perception, perception not only of the internal environment but of the external one as well. We do this by "tuning out" the verbal, analytical left brain so that the nonverbal, intuitive right brain can be free to operate at peak efficiency. This allows the right brain and sensory systems to perceive the faint signals we need to monitor more efficiently kinesthetic sensation and help us detect performance errors. Once we arrive at this state of consciousness, we have achieved what Easterners refer to as mind-body integration.

Mind-Body Integration

Mind-body integration involves the mind and body working together as an integrated unit to achieve a specific motoric goal. The Japanese martial art, Ki Aikido, and its Chinese counterpart, Tai Chi, both rely on this concept, as does Karate. When a Western athletic coach speaks of "getting it all together" for the game, he is presumably speaking about much the same thing.

Mind-body integration is achieved occasionally in a random, accidental way, as when someone says that she played that solo "way above her head," or he played "out of his mind" today. But such occasional "superperformances" are of little real value unless they can be repeated at will with some degree of reasonable consistency. We are able to achieve this kind of control and consistency only through increasing our powers of concentration to a very high level. Orientals increase their powers of concentration through the practice of various meditation exercises.

More specifically, mind-body integration involves focusing all of one's thoughts directly on the performance goal. No external thoughts or feelings can be allowed to interfere with one's concentration. In a competitive sport, for example, one must avoid all thoughts about winning. Such thoughts allow for emotional states, such as anxiety, which interfere with concentration. Anxiety brings about nervousness and excessive muscular tension, which then causes performance to become stiff and awkward. Instead, one must learn to "quiet the mind" and not let any external influences enter one's consciousness. The mind and body must be allowed to "function as one" in the way that nature supposedly intended. We have to develop a childlike view of the world, to become totally immersed in our performance without analyzing it or even consciously thinking about it.

Probably all of us have heard about, if not actually seen, a karate expert breaking a board or brick with his fist or the side of his hand. Nideffer says that psychologically this is accomplished by "the maintenance of an attitude that allows the person to hit *through the board* [italics mine]. He must be able to focus all his attention on a spot a couple inches behind the board."[29] Musicians apply similar psychological concepts in performance. One instance is when a performer learns to project his sound better by mentally aiming his tone toward the last row of the balcony. Another example is when a player thinks of playing *through* a phrase in order to achieve better phrasing instead of playing "up to" each individual note. Masters of the martial art Ki Aikido also think of extending the flow of ki (body energy) through their fingertips to achieve physical dominance and thereby overpower their opponents. What this probably means physiologically is that they avoid tensing the wrong muscles. They learn how to contract only those muscles needed and relax all of the others, thereby achieving maximal efficiency in the use of their muscular system.

We also know that a person who relaxes completely (deadweight) is difficult to pick up. Masters of Ki Aikido think *up* to avoid deadweight, *down* to create it. Thinking down results in a lowering of the body's center of gravity. Thinking up means that the shoulder and neck muscles tense up, allowing the person to get underneath your center of gravity.

To achieve mind-body integration, therefore, the mind and body must be allowed to function as one unit. This becomes possible only when we are able to achieve a high level of concentration. Orientals use various meditation exercises to develop their powers of concentration. The most basic exercise is to focus on one's breathing, simply being aware of it, not trying to control it.

Another basic meditation exercise is that of focusing on the "one point," a spot just behind and below your navel. The "one point" is considered to be one's center of gravity, and if one is properly "centered" this in essence results in good posture, leading to good body balance, as described in Chapter Two. Good body balance allows for efficient control over the use of our bodies without the presence of unnecessary muscular tension.

In addition to the concepts already discussed, Eastern psychology also covers many aspects of normal physiological function and health "which our Western educational process often omits—*how to* breathe, *how to* care for the body, *how to* master bodily functions normally considered 'involuntary.' "[30] Various postures

[29]Robert M. Nideffer, *The Inner Athlete: Mind Plus Muscle for Winning* (New York: Thomas Y. Crowell Publishers, 1976), p. 28.

[30]Robert E. Ornstein, *The Psychology of Consciousness,* 2nd ed. (New York: Harcourt Brace Jovanovich, Inc., 1977), p. 126. Reprinted by permission.

and breathing exercises are also a specific part of the Yoga tradition, along with fasting, which serves as a "technique often used to so upset the balance of ordinary awareness that another mode can develop."[31] Human beings are also viewed as an integral part of the universe, a universe that influences them in terms of internal and external biological rhythms. They are also believed to be affected by microclimatic conditions and ionization of the air. Yet I suspect that to many Westerners the concept of self-regulation of so-called involuntary body functions is perhaps the most intriguing. "Yoga masters, for instance, are said to stop or at least drastically lower their breathing rate and oxygen consumption, to stop blood flowing from a cut, to raise body heat even on cold nights high in the mountains of Tibet."[32] If Yoga masters are able to accomplish such acts, this indicates that we have greatly underestimated our potential for control of so-called involuntary functions. Surely it is time that we "get our heads out of the sand" and take a closer, more open-minded look at this whole area of human function and potential.

SUMMARY

Western psychology as it exists today can be categorized as having two principal schools: behaviorism and humanism. Behavioristic beliefs are perhaps best exemplified in what we know today as behavior modification. Recent theories emanating from the humanistic school include such concepts as self-esteem, self-image and self-actualization.

Behavior modification is based on the premise that behavioral response can be controlled primarily through techniques of reward and punishment. This approach seems to work reasonably well with young children but becomes increasingly limited in its usefulness as a person grows older. Eventually it becomes necessary to focus on a person's attitude first, as the means toward changing individual behaviors.

Among the most influential attitudes we possess are those related to self-image and self-esteem. These hold the key to who we are and what we can become. Since both of these are influenced quite early in life, mainly by parents and teachers, it is important that we learn as much as we can about them.

Self-image (the way we view ourselves) directly influences self-esteem (the way we feel about ourselves). The key to improving (changing) our self-esteem is to concentrate on improving our self-image. We do this by first accepting the fact that all of us have the ability to take charge of our lives and control them from within. This ultimately requires what theologians refer to as faith. Then you must act on this faith, realizing that all learning (change) requires trial-and-error practice, time and patience.

---

[31]Ibid., p. 129.

[32]*On The Psychology of Meditation* by Claudio Naranjo and Robert E. Ornstein. Copyright © 1971 by Claudio Naranjo and Robert E. Ornstein. Reprinted by permission of Viking Penguin, Inc.

To most Westerners Eastern psychology remains essentially a mystery. We tend to relegate it to the realm of "mysticism" and the "occult," because of our inability to comprehend the various philosophies, religions and cultures from which it is derived. But a major key in understanding Eastern psychology lies in understanding the function of the two sides of the brain. In the West the main focus of our training has been directed toward the left brain, which is involved primarily with verbal and analytical thinking. In contrast the main focus of Eastern training has been toward developing the nonverbal, intuitive, right brain.

Training the nonverbal, intuitive, right brain involves understanding the concepts of meditation and mind-body integration. The purpose of meditation is to alter our normal state of consciousness so that we can increase the outer limits of our perception. This increase in perception is achieved through "tuning out" the left brain so that the right brain can function at peak efficiency. A specific value of this kind of "tuning out" as it relates to perceptual-motor function lies in our being able to become more aware of kinesthetic sensation. Mind-body integration, on the other hand, involves the mind and body working together as an integrated unit to achieve a specific motoric goal. This is achieved through developing one's powers of concentration to a very high level. Orientals do it through the practice of various meditation exercises. The most basic one involves focusing on one's own breathing.

chapter four

psychophysiological principles and techniques of learning

Efficient perceptual-motor performance depends upon four prime elements: good mental conception, relaxed concentration, awareness of body feedback and good posture. All of these elements can be learned by musicians, dancers and athletes through self-initiated trial-and-error practice via the Natural Learning Process, of course. But as teachers we can assist students greatly by providing them with ideal environmental conditions in which to learn these elements. Requisite to this is our having a clear understanding of what constitutes good musical conception, concentration and body-feedback awareness ourselves. We also need to understand how and why good posture training can eliminate excessive muscular tension and thus improve neuromuscular coordination. Providing an understanding in these areas is the purpose of this chapter.

CONCENTRATION

Of all the skills required in musical performance, the ability to concentrate is the most important. Not only is it critical to good neuromuscular coordination; it also directly affects the quality of musical conception and the ability to receive and process body feedback.

The importance of concentration is not limited to musical performance alone. As Nideffer and Sharpe point out, "It's really the key to success in almost any situation . . ."[1] Whether we are reading, studying, working or trying to communicate in a business or social situation, our ability to function is directly dependent upon our ability to concentrate.

As discussed in Chapter Three, Eastern psychology provides us with various techniques for the development of concentration and self mind control. But few of us have the time or the motivation to spend years studying and learning to meditate the way Zen and Yoga masters do. Fortunately, this is not necessary. In order to meet our immediate needs, Gallwey, Nideffer and Sharpe provide us with Eastern-based concepts and exercises explained in language that we Westerners can more readily understand and use.

Good Concentration Defined

Concentration is the act of focusing one's attention. Good concentration involves giving one's complete, undivided attention to whatever it is that we are thinking or doing. There can be no outside interference or distraction; otherwise one's attention is interrupted and good mental concentration is lost. In highly skilled performance, which does not allow for even the slightest error, good mental concentration is absolutely essential.

As an illustration, I knew a professional golfer some twenty-five years ago who had also played horn professionally at the major orchestra level. The idea of a dual specialization in golf and horn playing seemed like a curious combination until the gentleman explained to me his philosophy in relation to both fields:

> Keeping your eye on the ball along with accurate contact and follow-through in the golf swing requires the same kind of ability as playing the opening note of a horn solo in a Brahms symphony. Both require intense mental concentration accompanied by flawless coordination.

Good concentration, therefore, means being able to focus completely on a specific goal. Ultimately it means being so absorbed in the area in which our attention is focused that we lose all awareness of other things going on around us. When we reach this level, we have achieved what Gallwey calls a state of relaxed concentration. Relaxed concentration involves a series of four stages, which are outlined below:

1. Paying attention (initially requires some self-discipline)
2. Interested attention (requires motivation)
3. Absorbed attention (being focused to the extent that it requires a strong distraction to change your focus)

[1]Dr. Robert E. Nideffer and Roger C. Sharpe, *Attention Control Training* (New York: Wyden Books, 1978), p. 5. Reprinted by permission.

4. Merging with experience (you have achieved the ideal of mind-body integration. You, the instrument and the music are one. You are now capable of playing "out of your mind"!)[2]

While the first stage—paying attention—does require *some* self-discipline, it does not mean trying hard to concentrate. When we try hard to concentrate, we end up focusing on how well we are concentrating rather than on the performance act itself. This prevents us from ever achieving the third and fourth stages of relaxed concentration.

Understanding the Concentration Process

As young children we found it relatively easy to concentrate, to become totally absorbed by and immersed in a given activity—so long as we were intensely interested in what we were doing! The same is true of adults, the key element being intense interest. Perhaps an even better word is the term "fascination," which implies excitement as well as interest. Gallwey even goes so far as to say that one needs to *love* the object or focus of one's concentration.[3]

To achieve this kind of concentration, we need to develop a childlike state of self-forgetfulness. With regard to playing tennis, Gallwey recommends that we practice focusing on a subtle aspect of the object, such as the ball's seams. In addition we should become personally "attached" to the object in order to bring about "fascination of the mind."[4]

One way to accomplish this in musical performance is to eliminate temporarily our sense of sight. We can do this either by closing our eyes while playing or by turning out the lights in a windowless practice room. In any case the goal is to set up a situation where the ear is not distracted by our visual information receptor, the eye.

This may explain in part why blind musicians often seem to possess exceptionally well-developed ears. Being unable to see, they must rely heavily on the aural sense, which they are thereby forced to develop to a more sensitive level. Thus they become quite sensitive to certain aspects of tone quality, good intervallic connection and phrasing in a way that persons with functioning eyes are not always equally sensitive.

In connection with this, I vividly remember auditioning many years ago for a blind dance-band leader. Since the man was a percussionist and my attitude toward percussionists as musicians at that time was not positive, I approached the audition with less than a positive attitude. To my surprise, however, it turned out to be the

[2]W. Timothy Gallwey, *Inner Tennis: Playing the Game* (New York: Random House, Inc., 1976), pp. 61–63. Reprinted by permission.

[3]W. Timothy Gallwey, *The Inner Game of Tennis* (New York: Random House, Inc., 1974), p. 92. Reprinted by permission.

[4]Ibid., pp. 91, 92.

finest audition experience I had ever had. I learned more about saxophone tone quality, dance-band phrasing and style in about thirty minutes that day than I ever had before or have since. Having been accepted into the band, I also learned later, through real experience, what really good ensemble blend was all about.

MUSICAL CONCEPTION

In Chapter One I quoted Arnold Jacobs as saying that the focus of our teaching should be on training the performer's brain, not the muscles. As a first step in accomplishing this, we need to understand the musical-conception process and how it is developed within the individual performer.

Before a musical performer plays or sings even a single note, he or she must have a mental image or concept of that note in terms of pitch, tone quality and all of the other acoustical and expressive qualities involved. Likewise, when a composer decides to write a piece of music, one must begin with a musical concept, image or idea. Before anything creative can be committed to score paper, it must first be conceived within the composer's brain. We call this process "musical conception."

The Importance of Listening

Traditionally, we define a literate person as someone who can speak, read and write the "King's English." To accomplish this we learn how to speak first and to read and write later, in that order. But the all-important prerequisite to learning how to speak is first to establish a "memory bank" of verbal sounds and concepts through repeatedly listening to others talk. Listening, therefore, is the primary means through which we acquire verbal conception.

These concepts apply equally to musical literacy and learning. A genuinely literate musician is one who can speak, read and write music. To achieve musical literacy one should learn to speak music (perform by ear) via imitation before trying to read or write it. Learning to speak it requires repetitive listening to musical performances. It is through this means that we acquire musical conception.

The quality of our musical conception is directly influenced by the quality of the musical performances we hear, of course. If what we hear is inferior in quality, our musical conception will likewise be inferior. It is therefore critical that the "musical ear" be programmed with superior musical concepts or images acquired through listening to superior performers. The more good performances we hear, the more discriminating our "musical ear" becomes. Without such experience, the musical ear or mind exists as a vacuum.

> The musical mind is concerned predominantly with the mechanism of tonal memory. Before it has absorbed a considerable variety of tonal experiences, it cannot begin to function in a creative way complex enough to be considered art.[5]

[5]Harold Shapero, "The Musical Mind," in *The Creative Process: A Symposium,* ed. Brewster Ghiselin (Berkeley: University of California Press, 1952), p. 41.

The foregoing discussion represents one of the major elements of Suzuki's Mother Tongue Approach. Suzuki specifically recommends that young children be exposed to both recorded and live music from infancy onward, in the same way they are exposed to their Mother Tongue.[6] Through this means, the development of musical conception with the child's "musical ear" is started long before he or she ever picks up an instrument. When one does begin instrumental study, the child already has a reasonably good idea of the musical goals necessary to strive for. In other words, the child's right brain has been programmed with good mental images of musical performance.

An interesting corollary exists in Nature: when a young bird learns how to sing. In research done by Marler and others, it was found that when a young bird listens to the birdsong of its parent, an acoustic memory or "template" of the adult song pattern is formed in the young bird's brain. Later, when the young bird tries to duplicate the song pattern of its parent, it compares its results to the stored reference template and gradually molds its song pattern to it. As evidence of this, it was found that deafened young birds, after exposure to adult birdsong, reproduced the song pattern the following spring. Young birds not exposed to adult birdsong at all prior to deafening failed to develop a copy of the adult birdsong.[7]

Development of musical conception, therefore, involves programming the brain's memory-storage center with musical concepts or images acquired mainly through listening. Development of *good* musical conception requires listening to superior performances by superior musicians. But the quality of the stored musical concepts in our brain depends on one other factor—musical perception.

The Influence of Musical Perception

As stated in Chapter Two part of our perception capacity is probably inherited, like so many other things, but ability in almost all areas must be developed through environmental training. This is where a good teacher can be an invaluable guide. A good teacher is one who exposes the student to good music performed by superior musicians. Such a teacher is also one who teaches specific things the student should listen for.

Musical perception, therefore, is directly related to musical conception, but perception for us in particular involves more than mere response to musical stimuli. Also critically involved are past life experiences and the imaginative or symbolic concepts gleaned therefrom. These additional aspects of perception then form a specific meaning unique to each individual. This explains why no two people necessarily interpret music in exactly the same way. It also explains why one

[6]*Nurtured by Love* © 1969 by Shinichi Suzuki. Reprinted by permission of Exposition Press, Smithtown, N.Y.

[7]George E. Stelmach, ed., *Motor Control: Issues and Trends* (New York: Academic Press, 1976), p. 21. Reprinted by permission.

performer may be able to perform with greater depth of emotional feeling and/or musical maturity than another, less mature person—one whose life experiences have been limited. Our past experiences, therefore, directly influence the quality of our perception and thus directly affect the quality and precise nature of our musical performance. Perception in the form of musical awareness is, therefore, what musicians refer to as musical conception.

The Role of Singing

To reinforce listening as a means of acquiring musical conception, I strongly recommend the use of singing. The human voice is our most natural musical instrument, since it exists within the body. It is, therefore, far more closely connected to the musical ear, where musical conception resides, than any other musical instrument. This makes it the most logical and natural medium for reproduction of musical concepts.

Through singing, the player learns to develop the musical ear more thoroughly and establish good musical conception with greater clarity. But perhaps more importantly, having the student sing before playing helps the teacher determine whether the student's performance problems are due to poor conception or to purely technical problems related to manipulating the instrument. In other words the teacher can read (evaluate) the student's musical mind accurately via listening to the student's voice. One cannot as easily do the same based on the playing performance alone.

The importance of having student instrumentalists learn to sing is of course not new. Many students in Europe, particularly in France, are expected to become reasonably proficient sightsingers long before they are ever allowed to study an instrument. Also, most good conductors rely heavily on singing to communicate their concepts of interpretation and musical style. Audio tapes I have heard of rehearsals by such conductors as Toscanini, Bruno Walter and Pablo Casals clearly demonstrate this. The problem, then, is not whether singing is important; rather it is one of remembering to use it systematically and consistently in our teaching. Particularly in the case of elementary-school children, who tend to be shy about singing in front of their peers, the tendency among young teachers is to give up too soon, until, finally, singing is neglected entirely.

While singing is very important for beginners, it has equal value at all levels of performance development. It doesn't matter if one is an advanced performer or a conducting student, the ability to sing a phrase correctly before playing it is critical. There is no way a performer can reproduce a good musical phrase unless his conception of it is clear in his musical ear. Likewise, a conductor cannot communicate concepts of style and expression effectively unless she can sing it for her players. Music is a nonverbal art form, the expressive qualities of which are best communicated via the instrument most closely connected with the musical ear—the voice.

INNER-GAME
CONCENTRATION
TECHNIQUES

As stated in Chapter One, the key to our relearning how to use the Natural Learning Process again is to relearn how to focus (concentrate) on the goal, not the process. Focusing on the process creates numerous mental problems, which ultimately result in excessive muscular tension, a prime symptom of most neuromuscular-coordination problems. Thus, in order to learn how to focus properly on the goal, we need to begin by relearning how to "trust the body."

Trusting the Body

"Trusting the body" means that the conscious brain (Self 1) has confidence in the body (Self 2) to learn and perform on its own through what Gallwey calls The Natural Learning Process. It means that Self 1 does not try to get involved in trying to control the neuromuscular operations occurring between the stimulus and the response. But, unfortunately, Self 1 does not always trust the body (Self 2), and tries to control all phases of perceptual-motor function. In so doing it creates a busy mind, which quickly loses its ability to concentrate on the performance goal. In order to achieve good concentration we must find a way to "quiet the mind." Learning to trust the body is the first step toward achieving this goal.

Quieting the Mind

Quieting the mind means relaxing the mind, being able to concentrate totally on a given issue, person, place or thing without allowing thoughts or external distractions to interfere. Once this ideal state of mind is achieved, "awareness becomes acutely heightened while analysis, anxiety, self-conscious thought [and other forms of interference] are completely forgotten."[8]

To put it another way, quieting the mind allows us to learn through conscious awareness of our experience. This means being able to perceive, comprehend and realize fully and with clarity what we are actually doing. It allows the messages from our body-feedback mechanisms to "get through" to us with minimal distortion. This in turn allows us to evaluate our practice trials more objectively, so that succeeding trials can be more productive. In this context we can say that experience, which includes conscious awareness, is the best teacher. Similarly, the best kind of professional teacher is one who can help you increase your awareness of your own experiences. One way to quiet the mind and increase your awareness is through meditation, one of the most common techniques being that of learning to

---

[8]W. Timothy Gallwey, *Inner Tennis: Playing the Game* (New York: Random House, 1976), pp. 9, 10. Reprinted by permission.

concentrate on one's breathing. But as Gallwey points out, meditation is nothing more than pure concentration of the mind.[9] In this context, meditation, the ability to concentrate and quieting the mind are essentially synonymous.

Increasing Awareness

"[Awareness] is the energy of consciousness which makes it possible for us to experience events internal or external to our bodies."[10] Awareness allows us to truly hear, feel and see what we are doing.

According to Gallwey, "There is no learning, no growth, no action without awareness."[11] We learn through experience, which is our best teacher. Experience involves body feedback, and awareness is the means through which we are able to receive it. "Tuning in" to body feedback through awareness, therefore, makes all the difference between effective and ineffective learning.[12]

"The essence of the Inner Game learning process can [therefore] be summed up in two words: *increasing awareness*.[13] To better understand what this means let us again use the analogy of an artillery crew using trial-and-error adjustments in trying to hit a target. The crew leader can rely on his regular eyesight or he can use binoculars to evaluate the accuracy of the cannon shot in relation to the target. Through use of binoculars, he increases his awareness of what is really happening. Similarly, in perceptual-motor performance, "quieting the mind" allows us to use "sensory binoculars," which increase our awareness of body feedback.

Awareness Problems

While awareness is no doubt critical to our ability to learn, it is also an area where many of us experience special problems. Self 1 (our conscious brain) wants to judge performance and blame Self 2 for incompetence when it makes errors. This leads to various negative emotional states that cause us to lose concentration. Self 1 also likes to praise Self 2 (when deserved, of course), but this too causes us to lose concentration. Through "patting ourselves on the back" we think we can now perform well without trying at all. We become so relaxed that we begin making unnecessary errors. Then Self 1 takes over, chastising Self 2 for being such a fool, and our problems start all over again.

Self 1 (our conscious, analytical, left brain, which includes our emotions and ego) is thus our own worst enemy. Self 1 distrusts Self 2 and continually judges performance and tries to control it. In so doing it causes malfunction of Self 2's

[9]Ibid., p. 65.
[10]Ibid., pp. 20, 21.
[11]Ibid., p. 20.
[12]Ibid., p. 71.
[13]Ibid.

neuromuscular mechanism. Gallwey lists thirteen emotional states of mind that bring about this kind of malfunction.[14]

1. Fear
2. Lack of self-confidence
3. Self-condemnation
4. Poor concentration
5. Trying too hard
6. Lack of will to win
7. Perfectionism
8. Self-consciousness
9. Frustration
10. Anger
11. Boredom
12. Expectations
13. A busy mind

So, in order to avoid malfunction of the neuromuscular mechanism, we need to avoid these kinds of emotional states of mind through "quieting the mind" (Self 1). This in turn allows us to concentrate precisely on "what is" (awareness), and then we simply "let it happen."

Letting it Happen Through Nonjudgmental Awareness

"Letting it happen" means having Self 1 function like a distant observer who evaluates Self 2's performance in a calm, objective, detached way. It means simply to observe "what is" in a nonjudgmental way and to accept the learning process for what it really is, or at least what it should be: a routine process of trial-and-error practice. In so doing we are able to remain objective about our performance and avoid the negative emotional states cited earlier.

It is very important to understand that avoiding judgments does not mean ignoring performance errors. In order to improve performance we must be able to detect errors as well as correct them.[15] The secret in our being able to do this, however, lies in the way we approach this task. Emotionally based judgments affect our perception of reality by distorting it. Our perception is thus akin to a camera shot that is blurred and fuzzy. Boredom also affects our perception by distorting our awareness. It causes us to lose concentration and thus deadens our ability to respond actively to experience.[16] Therefore, we need to avoid all emotionally based responses to performance.

[14]Ibid., pp. 5, 6.

[15]W. Timothy Gallwey, *The Inner Game of Tennis* (New York: Random House, 1974), p. 36. Reprinted by permission.

[16]W. Timothy Gallwey, *Inner Tennis: Playing the Game* (New York: Random House, 1976), p. 47. Reprinted by permission

CONTROL OF MUSCULAR
TENSION THROUGH GOOD
POSTURE

As noted earlier, a prime symptom of most neuromuscular coordination problems is excessive muscular tension. This is defined as the tightening of too many muscles; that is, using more muscles than a given task requires. This kind of tension ruins technique, as we all know, plus all other aspects of musical performance.

The source of most performance errors can be traced to problems of mental dysfunction, which create excessive muscular tension. The most common *physical* source of performance problems, however, exists in poor posture, which also creates excessive muscular tension. As discussed in Chapter Two, posture is directly related to body balance, a reflex that is critical to athletes and dancers as well as musicians. In string playing, for example, good posture allows for balanced muscle action and thus has a direct influence on both bow and finger technique. In wind playing and singing it allows for good inhalation and ease in tone production. Reinhardt even goes so far as to say that good posture is "the very foundation to correct breathing."[17]

What is Good Posture?

When standing, good posture consists of the body being vertical, with the neck and head in line with the spine, and the eyes focused straight ahead. The lower back, just above the base of the spine, should be curved inward slightly. The feet should be positioned ten to twelve inches apart, with one foot slightly forward. To achieve good posture while seated, however, "you should sit as if you were standing, from the hips upward." This includes arching the lower back slightly inward, to allow for maximal inhalation.[18]

Keeping the neck and head vertical in line with the spine allows the vestibular mechanism to remain passive, thus allowing for balanced muscle function throughout the body. Keeping the lower back curved slightly inward prevents cramping of the abdominal area and thus allows for relaxed, unrestricted breathing. Keeping the feet separated, with one foot slightly forward, allows the upper body to move about freely without upsetting body balance.

Problems Caused by Poor Posture

The position of the head is the most critical aspect of good posture. If the head is lowered, the vestibular mechanism responds by sending messages to the appropriate reflex area of the lower brain to compensate by contracting various muscles and thus maintain body balance. The first muscles to contract are the neck muscles,

---

[17]Donald S. Reinhardt, *The Encyclopedia of the Pivot System* (New York: Charles Colin, 1964), p. 19. Reprinted by permission.

[18]Based on a personal conversation with Arnold Jacobs.

which cramp the throat, thereby interfering with good vocal and wind-instrument tone production.

But contraction of the neck muscles is only the first phase of what really happens when the head is lowered. Reflexive contraction of the neck muscles triggers additional reflexive contractions, mainly in the legs and the abdominal area. If the entire upper body is allowed to slump forward, this creates still more reflexive actions, initiated via messages to the lower brain from the vestibular mechanism. Ultimately what we have is a series of chain reactions. Abnormal balance in one part of the body is quickly compensated for in another part of the body's muscular system. The end result is excessive muscular tension, which precludes efficient motor performance.

Cramping of the throat muscles prevents deep, relaxed inhalation on the one hand while restricting open, free exhalation on the other. Cramping of the actual breathing muscles of the chest and the abdominal area creates similar problems. In order for the lungs to receive a maximal amount of air, the rib cage must be allowed the greatest possible freedom to expand upward and outward, and the diaphragm to contract downward. This can occur only if the upper body is fully erect and the muscles of the throat, chest and abdomen are relaxed. Good exhalation is likewise directly affected, excessive tension making good tone production virtually impossible.

In addition to breathing and tone production, excessive muscular tension also affects the tongue, fingers, embouchure and vocal cords as well. When we observe excessive tension in our students in any of these areas, our immediate response is to try to get them to relax. "Your throat is tense," "Your arms are tense," or "Your embouchure is pinched," we yell. "*Relax!*" Surely most of our students would be quite willing to respond to this directive if only they knew how. But most of them obviously don't know, and yelling at them doesn't help. It only creates anxiety and still more tension.

We can conclude, therefore, that the *physical* source of all muscular tension problems is that of body imbalance caused by poor posture. Consequently, regardless of what the problem symptoms are—cramped breathing muscles, tight throat, tense fingers or embouchure, check the student's posture first, before doing anything else. Poor posture is often *the* real physical source of tension, which manifests itself in other, more obvious parts of the body.

The bad effects of poor posture and resulting muscular tension are not limited to musical performance alone. The conductor whose head is continually tilted downward is also inviting unnecessary body tension, which is not needed. One of the more common symptoms of such a habit is soreness in the neck and shoulders, particularly after conducting for a lengthy period.

How To Achieve Good Posture

In order to help establish good posture and body balance from the start, I recommend that all performers (incuding wind players as well as singers, percussionists and string players) be required to stand during their lessons and in home practice sessions. The only exceptions to this rule are the obvious ones—bassoonists, cellists, pianists, harpists, and tuba players. Teachers of flute, violin, viola and voice have traditionally expected this of their students as a matter of routine. It is time that wind teachers in particular also make this an established procedure for the same basic reasons—to help insure muscle relaxation and thereby help to avoid excessive muscular tension.

There is yet another good reason for having students stand while playing: to help insure good playing position. Although repeated personal experience has convinced me of its value in this regard, it is not always a complete solution. Special attention should be given to flutists and saxophonists in particular, who begin by assuming excellent posture and end up ruining it when the instrument is brought into playing position. Be sure that flutists' hands are in proper contact with their instrument. Give special attention to the left hand, and make sure the elbow is down, not out. Be sure the saxophonist's neck strap is adjusted properly. The mouthpiece should enter the mouth at only a *slight* downward angle, almost horizontal with the floor. The right thumb should push the saxophone sufficiently forward to allow the player's head to remain erect. While these problems may persist to a degree even in a standing position, I have found them to be far worse with young students who do all of their playing sitting down. Standing up not only exposes an unnatural holding position for the student; it also makes the problem more obvious visually to the teacher.

Body Relaxation Through Movement

In the minds of many music teachers the essence of Suzuki's methodology lies in his use of the imitation method of teaching. Actually there is a great deal more to it than that, as a careful reading of his *Nurtured By Love* will reveal. One of the less obvious aspects of his teaching methodology has to do with preventing excessive muscular tension. This should not be surprising, since string teachers have long been conscious of this problem in the training of string players. However, Suzuki, along with other master pedagogues, such as Rolland, has developed a more elaborate strategy for dealing with this problem than we have seen in the past.

When I first saw and heard a group of Suzuki-trained students perform, I quickly noted the large amount of active movement used, mainly in the form of walking, and even running, *while* playing. My first reaction was that this was nothing more than a "stunt." I was reinforced in this view by other music teachers whose reaction was similar to mine. It wasn't until several years later, in a discussion of Suzuki with some specialists in physical education, that I changed my mind. Ironically, these physical educators were not interested so much in Suzuki's use of imitation as they were in his use of physical movement (walking and running) as a means of relaxing the body muscles, thereby preventing excessive muscular tension.

If string teachers find this approach successful, why don't wind and vocal teachers use it? I suspect the main reason is that they don't really understand its underlying purposes. I further suspect that there are others who hesitate to try something that seems so radical and unorthodox. But there is no logical reason for such an attitude. We usually don't think twice about the amount of physical movement involved when wind players march on a football field. Why, then, should we hesitate to ask beginning wind players to walk slowly around a room while playing, especially in view of the benefits gained through relaxing the body?

In addition to general body relaxation, walking while playing is equally valuable from still another standpoint. Let me explain. When we stand perfectly still, there is a tendency for us to use muscles above and beyond those we actually need to execute specific performance tasks. This results in excessive muscular tension, which in turn adversely affects the quality as well as the efficiency of our performance. Many of these ''extra muscles'' are the same ones we use for walking. If we walk while we play, this means we cannot rely on these muscles as much for playing. We are forced to rely mainly on those muscles we actually need to execute the specific performance tasks involved. This then promotes greater efficiency in the use of our bodies during performance.

In connection with this, we would do well to observe the efficiency of animal movements. They are always coordinated, because they use just enough muscular energy to accomplish their goal. They don't think about technique; they merely focus on the goal. They ''trust their bodies'' to perform at peak efficiency, without the need for outside guidance and/or interference.

It should now be obvious that posture, body balance and movement-training directly affect the quality of musical performance and learning. The following Figure (4-1) is used to further clarify and summarize this discussion.

FIGURE 4-1

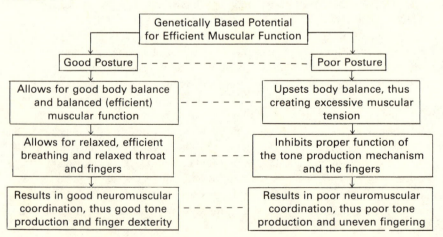

ATTENTION CONTROL
TRAINING

Attention control is nothing more than being able to voluntarily direct your attention; to concentrate in ways that are consistent with the demands placed on you by your home, family and job.[19]

Improving Self-Awareness Through Objective Self-Assessment

The first step toward developing attention control is to improve self-awareness through objective self-assessment. In other words, determine what it is that you are doing incorrectly and then decide what it is that you should be doing instead, through the use of mental imagery. In most cases this means learning how to relax; relieving ourselves of pressure, anxiety and stress so that our minds are free to concentrate fully on the performance task at hand. "[T]he key to controlling anxiety and concentration lies in controlling your attention."[20]

Focusing on Your Center of Gravity

The second step in attention control is to focus your attention on your center of gravity. Martial-arts instructors refer to this gravitational center as the "one point," a spot just behind and below your navel.[21] The purpose is to relax the body's muscles and control tension through achieving good body balance. Centering on the "one point," as discussed earlier, is also one of the meditation exercises Easterners use to achieve mind-body integration.

To achieve good body balance when standing, the legs should be about as far apart as the shoulders, with one foot slightly in front of the other and the knees bent slightly. When sitting, the back should be straight and the feet flat on the floor, with the weight of your upper body pushing down equally on each buttock. Then focus on your breathing. "Tune in" to the tension in your chest as you inhale; concentrate on the downward pull of gravity when you exhale. This process accomplishes two things: (1) it develops awareness of internal physical sensations and (2) it helps you learn to concentrate.[22]

The third and final step is to make a sound tape for rehearsal purposes that combines the use of mental imagery (step one) and centering (step two). (For specific details on how to prepare such a tape see pages 105 and 106 of *Attention Control Training* by Nideffer and Sharpe.)

[19]Dr. Robert E. Nideffer and Roger C. Sharpe, *Attention Control Training* (New York: Wyden Books, 1978), p. 23. Reprinted by permission.
[20]Ibid., p. 82.
[21]Ibid., p. 36.
[22]Ibid., pp. 84–89.

SUMMARY

Efficient perceptual-motor performance depends upon four prime elements: good mental conception, relaxed concentration, awareness of body feedback and good posture. Of these four, concentration is the most important, because it directly affects the other three. In fact, the ability to concentrate is probably the most important key to success in almost everything we do. Concentration is the act of focusing one's attention. Good concentration means being able to focus completely on a specific goal, to be so absorbed that we lose all awareness of other things going on around us.

Musical conception involves the use of the brain's musical memory which stores musical images acquired through listening. To insure memory storage of superior musical images, the performer needs to listen to a great deal of good music performed by superior musicians. To reinforce listening as a means toward acquiring good musical conception, the performer should also be required to sing before playing. This helps to develop the musical ear more thoroughly. It also helps the teacher to decide whether the source of the performer's problems involves poor musical conception or purely technical difficulties related to manipulating the instrument.

The key to our relearning how to use The Natural Learning Process is to relearn how to focus (concentrate) on the goal, not the process. To accomplish this Gallwey provides us with several conceptual techniques designed to facilitate muscle relaxation, good concentration, and increase our awareness of kinesthetic sensations. All of these in turn allow our neuromuscular mechanism to function at peak efficiency.

The most common *physical* cause of performance errors is the tightening of too many muscles, which in turn results in excessive muscular tension. Poor posture, which creates body imbalance, is a major source of this problem. In order to help achieve good posture and body balance, I recommend the following: (1) have all performers stand up rather than sit during lessons and in home practice, whenever possible, and (2) promote body relaxation through movement. The latter also helps us avoid using more muscles than we really need to execute specific performance tasks.

One other formalized technique for development of good concentration and posture is Attention Control Training. It involves the use of mental imagery and body balance as key factors in improving concentration and body relaxation.

In conclusion, good performance depends upon good mental conception, acquired through listening and singing, plus relaxed concentration, awareness of body feedback and avoiding excessive muscular tension through the use of good posture. A good teacher, then, is one who can assist students in mastering these fundamentals, via The Natural Learning Process, faster and better than they could otherwise do on their own.

chapter five

introduction
to teaching

Every good teacher knows that teaching, when done well, involves far more than mere imparting of information to students. In addition to knowledge of the subject being taught, there are various professional and personal qualifications that a good teacher should possess. The main purpose of this chapter is to identify these and explain how they relate to the teaching-learning process. The second purpose of this chapter is to discuss one of the oldest methods of teaching, and probably the most popular: synthesis-analysis-synthesis.

PRELIMINARY
CONSIDERATIONS

What is teaching? What is good teaching? What is a good teacher? Why do students need teachers? In this section these questions will be answered briefly.

Teaching Defined

To teach means to give lessons or instruction. Teaching is a profession in which teachers give lessons or instruction to students on *how to learn*. Since teaching involves specialized techniques of instruction, it is, first of all, a skill.

Teaching is also a craft, because it involves specialized knowledge drawn from several disciplines. At the highest level, teaching has been called an art as well as a science. I believe it can be all of these, but first and foremost it is a skill.

A skill is the ability to demonstrate knowledge and/or proficiency through performance. Skill in teaching is the ability to *apply* appropriate methods of instruction successfully within a practical learning situation. Merely being able to analyze and verbally explain learning theory and methods of teaching is obviously not enough. In fact, real understanding of some teaching methods comes only *after* they have been used (applied) several times.

Skill in teaching is acquired in the same basic way that all skills are acquired—first through observation and then through trial-and-error practice (direct experience). In order to be fully effective, the teacher also needs to have developed a teaching philosophy and be well versed in teaching-learning theory as well as in specific kinds of methodology. These facts are self-evident. But without teaching skill, none of the foregoing, alone or in combination, can ever result in good teaching.

What is *Good* Teaching?

Really good teaching is an art. It is an art because, like other art forms, it cannot be fully analyzed or effectively described in verbal terms. Most experienced learners know when they have been exposed to good teaching, however. They remember it as a unique experience, one not easily forgotten. The results of such an experience usually manifest themselves through increased learner interest and understanding of the subject being taught. This usually promotes increased study and practice outside the formal classroom environment as well.

Good teaching is also a science, although to a much lesser degree. If teaching could be easily reduced to a list of scientific principles alone, then training good teachers would be much easier and we could produce many more good ones than we do now. On the other hand, I do not subscribe to the idea that good teachers, like good conductors, are born, not made. No one ever became a good teacher or conductor by living on a deserted island without any external environmental influences. Environment undoubtedly plays a significant role in teachers' and conductors' development, just as it does in learning to play an instrument. Good teaching ability, like good performance ability, therefore, is something that still has to be developed mainly through observation, correct practice and positive experience. Great teaching, on the other hand, probably requires all of these plus inherited ability.

What is a Good Teacher?

A good teacher is many things: a well-educated, intelligent person and a master pedagogue with an outstanding ability to lead and motivate students. He or she is also a superior human being who influences students' lives in highly positive, personal and significant ways. Equally important, a good teacher is one who has a real sense of what cannot and should not be taught and what is best left alone. Several aspects of perceptual-motor learning fit into this category, as we already know.

BASIC QUALIFICATIONS
AND FUNCTIONS OF A GOOD
TEACHER

Specific qualifications and functions of a good teacher include the following: (1) has the ability to communicate well, personally as well as pedagogically, (2) serves as a positive personal role model, (3) functions as a superior musical-performance model, (4) is able to teach students how to teach themselves, and (5) serves as a highly effective motivator. On a more basic level, students also need teachers to teach them things that parents find difficult (in some cases almost impossible) to teach to their own children.

Why Students Need Teachers

Students need teachers to help guide them through the process of "growing up." They also need assistance from teachers to become increasingly independent as they mature. That is, students need to be taught in such a way that they can eventually teach (learn) themselves. This is the only way they can ever become mature individuals, capable of making intelligent decisions on their own. In these contexts, therefore, students need good teachers for much the same reasons that children need good parents. The major difference is that, while the parent-child relationship is inherently an emotional one, the teacher-student relationship is usually based on a more objective set of circumstances. Teachers, therefore, are often in a position to relate to students and their needs in ways that a good many parents find difficult or impossible.

We need to be reminded, however, that learning is not a phenomenon unique only to the school and the home. The church or synagogue has always been a major influence in the life of a child who participates in it.

For today's children, television has also become a major source of learning, in some instances more important than the parents or the school. Yet the need for parent and teacher guidance continues to exist. Students need to learn how to teach themselves. The school and the home are the primary agencies that fulfill this function for all children.

The Basic Function of Teachers
and Schools

As stated earlier, the primary reason why students need teachers is to have someone teach them how to teach themselves. If this does not happen, then there is no real need for professional teachers to exist. Unfortunately, we see some teachers in class lessons and rehearsals presenting detailed verbal lectures on musical content with little or no instruction on how to learn and apply such information. It is as if the students should automatically know how to do this, but usually they don't. This is true even of students of high intelligence. Particularly in learning musical-performance skills, students need to be provided with concrete strategies (study procedures) for home practice. Many of these strategies also need to be nonverbal rather than verbal. Our basic function as teachers is not simply to teach music. Rather it is to teach students "how to learn music." As teachers of musical performers, our job is to teach students "how to learn to perform music," and in specific, concrete ways.

Probably the most common error most teachers make is to talk too much; and the more they talk and try to explain something, the more confused the students become. This is especially true in regard to musical performance teaching. We spend entirely too much time explaining and not enough time having the student actually doing it. Instead we should demonstrate the performance skill to the student and then let her or him learn it, mainly via imitation and trial-and-error practice.

In regard to the schools themselves, I believe that the primary justification for their existence is to help students learn those things they cannot learn on their own, outside the school. Correlated with this is the teacher's responsibility to provide a good learning environment, which will allow students to absorb these things as rapidly and effectively as possible.

Unfortunately, these objectives are all too often forgotten in some schools. Instead of trying to broaden students' knowledge and appreciation of new, unfamiliar musical composers and styles, we see some teachers catering mainly to musical styles that are readily accessible outside the school, on radio and television. In performance ensembles we also find too many instances where the band, choir and orchestra appear to exist mainly for the personal edification of the director, the public-relations goals of the school system and/or the competitive and entertainment desires of the community. Such situations must be avoided if we are to fulfill our function properly as teachers and institutions of learning.

The Importance of Good Communication

One of the most important skills a good teacher possesses is that of good communication with the learner. Without good teacher-student communication, there can be no learning, and thus there is no "teaching."

Teacher-student communication exists on two levels. One has to do with communicating specific skills and concepts. The other has to do with communication on a strictly personal level; it involves rapport, personal interaction and open sharing between teacher and student. At the peak level it involves genuine love, understanding and compassion on the part of the teacher.

To teach, then, ultimately means to communicate. But communication does not necessarily need to be verbal in order to be effective. Suzuki, for example, does not speak the English language very well, but this did not prevent him from communicating very effectively with the young American violinists whom I observed him teach. Like a good conductor, he communicated mainly with his eyes, via facial expressions as well as through musical demonstration. Thus the students could tell very easily that he loved music and violin playing. But, more importantly, they also soon realized, thanks to his expressive eyes and warm smile, that he liked them and seemed to be sincerely interested in them as human beings. In other words, I sensed in Suzuki a genuine love, understanding and compassion for humanity as well as a love for music and musical performance. The late Pablo Casals, both as a teacher and conductor, reportedly also related to people in a similar caring, humanistic way.

But what does it really mean for a teacher to have love, understanding and compassion for humanity? First of all it means feeling genuine affection, tolerance and empathy for all people. More importantly it means *demonstrating* these feelings in our interactions with people. Teaching is a service profession. Service professions require a large measure of giving to others. Among the most important things we can give, as teachers to students, are love, understanding and sincere interest in their personal as well as their musical well-being. But before you can give these things to others, you first need to be loving, understanding and compassionate toward yourself. How can you possibly give these to others if you yourself don't possess them? You can't. You have to have them in reasonable abundance in order to be able to share them with others. The kind of giving I speak of here involves giving openly and freely, "with no strings attached." Anything less than that is what we commonly call a "trade-off." But the real beauty of it all is that the more you give, the more you receive in return. (Show a sincere interest in others, for example, and they will soon become interested in you.) This, to me, is one of the greatest rewards that dedicated teachers receive.

A good teacher, therefore, is much more than someone who is able to impart information skillfully. Like a good parent, a teacher should be a good person, with humanistic sensitivity and the ability to communicate this to students. Good teaching, therefore, should include observing and assisting students with their progress and development as unique human beings. Our ultimate goal should be one of helping them become superior individuals as well as good performers.

The Teacher as a Personal Role Model

Students obviously learn from what we tell them, but they probably learn as much, if not more, from what they see us do. Particularly if we have their complete confidence and respect, students will tend to imitate the personal examples we set in terms of speech, dress, mannerisms and even moral values. They imitate us through a kind of unconscious osmosis. This is especially true of young children; it is also true of college- and university-level students. Consequently it is very important that we be aware of having this kind of influence and be highly sensitive to its consequences. We have the potential to touch human lives in very significant ways, both positively and negatively. Let us make every effort to insure that the bulk of our influence is a positive one.

The Music Teacher as a Performance Model

As has been stated repeatedly in this text, the first and most important step in the musical-performance learning process is the acquisition of good musical conception. In order for the student's conception to be a *superior* one, however, the performance model provided by the teacher must also be superior. The key factor here lies in the adjective "superior." Let's discuss this adjective in terms of what it really means.

First of all, there is no way a teacher can serve as a superior musical performance model without being a superior musician and performer to begin with. This is self-evident; and yet, in a number of colleges and universities across the country, prospective music teachers continue to be viewed and treated as second-class musicians. While such situations are deplorable for the music-teaching profession as a whole, they are especially unfair to music teachers in training. In trying to explain the reasons why they exist, it is all too easy to place the blame primarily on applied-music instructors and others, for promoting elitism among nonmusic education majors. But a more productive approach, in my opinion, is to look inward for answers to this problem.

One major reason why music teachers do not always value superior performing ability is that their music-education professors do not always seem to value it. We seem to value musicianship, at least philosophically, but we do not always demonstrate an interest or proficiency in those things that clearly establish us as having a "musical trademark." Musical performance is one type of musical trademark; conducting is another. Teachers of choral and instrumental teachers need to possess both. Otherwise we have second-class musicians responsible for training more second-class musicians. College and university music administrators have a responsibility for recruiting and hiring music-education faculty members who possess both of these trademarks. Only then can we begin to alleviate what in many cases is the real source of the problem.

The Teacher as a Motivator

Of all the qualifications and functions required of a good teacher, the ability to motivate students is the most important of all. Without this ability, even a good musician-teacher cannot be successful. With this ability, however, it is still possible for a second-rate musician-teacher to achieve a modicum of success.

There are two basic reasons why motivational ability is especially critical for instrumental and choral teachers. One has to do with the recruiting and retention of students in the program; that is, without students, there is no program. The other reason has to do mainly with getting students to practice at home. A teacher who cannot motivate students in these two basic areas will never be genuinely successful.

The importance of teachers' ability to motivate students is nothing new. Good music teachers have been acutely aware of this fact for a long time. What we sometimes forget is the degree of and reason for its importance. To better explain this topic, I shall use an analogy. When you and I were young children, our initial desire to stand upright was mainly self-motivated. Somehow we knew that standing up would allow us to see and reach more easily those special objects that intrigued us. Our primary motivation for walking also came from within. Walking allowed us to move about faster and thus investigate more of our environment more quickly. But in addition to our own, internal motivation, we were motivated by our parents. They encouraged us, praised us for the slightest improvement and told us with their smiling eyes and warm hugs that they were proud of us. Who can deny the importance of all of this positive reinforcement and encouragement in helping us learn to stand up and walk?

Good teachers also frequently use positive reinforcement and otherwise make special efforts to encourage their students. But these external behaviors, when viewed in isolation, do not give us the full picture. In order for them to be truly effective, they must come from within. In other words, they must be motivated by the teacher's genuine love, understanding of and *compassion* for students, as was discussed earlier.

Related to teacher motivation is the idea, promoted by some educators, that teachers must somehow convince students that learning is easy and fun. I heartily approve of trying to use the most efficient methods available to reduce the amount of time and effort involved in learning. I also see nothing wrong with trying to make the learning process as interesting as possible, but I am strongly opposed to perpetrating the notion that learning is always easy and fun, because much of the time it is not. Learning complex skills generally requires considerable time, patience and hard work. Frequently the bulk of that time and effort will be spent in repetitive drill, which may be quite boring, and students should be made aware of this fact. At the same time such information need not (and should not) be communicated in overly negative, discouraging terms. The student simply needs to know that, while some tasks may take a good deal of time and practice, learning them is well worth the effort. Furthermore, I tell students that I am convinced they can do it and that they will be glad they did when they are finished.

We also need to be reminded that children aren't always as naive as we sometimes assume them to be. They know that learning is not always easy. Learning to ride a bicycle, for example, is quite difficult for some youngsters; but once they learn how, they are usually very proud of their achievement. The same holds true for many other tasks or skills they may try to learn. Let us therefore not be guilty of being dishonest with them.

THE THREE STAGES OF
DEVELOPMENTAL LEARNING

So that you can better understand the learning process on a developmental level, I have divided it into three separate stages. Experience has shown that understanding of these three stages can be very valuable as a basic guide to teaching theory, particularly as it relates to the synthesis-analysis-synthesis method, to be discussed in the next section. Although the main focus of this book is directed toward the perceptual-motor domain, I shall first discuss cognitive learning for purposes of comparison.

Cognitive Learning

Let's say that our goal is to teach students that dependability is a virtue, one they need to have. We begin by defining the term, explaining the importance of dependability and the negative consequences resulting from undependable behavior. We further explain how this affects us and those with whom we associate. To facilitate understanding, we encourage students to ask questions, which we try to answer as logically as possible. This initial process we call the *cognitive-understanding stage*.

Let's assume that our discussion was remarkably successful, and that now the students understand and say they are convinced. In fact, you begin to see overt evidence of their trying to be dependable. They usually arrive at their lessons on time, and their practice assignments are noticeably better prepared. Once these things happen, they have reached the second stage, which we call the *voluntary application stage*.

During this stage there probably will be times when students occasionally arrive late, and it may even be necessary for you, the teacher, to review some of your discussion from the first session. This is a normal part of the voluntary-application stage; it is a time of trial and error and inconsistency. But eventually you find that there is no further need for verbal discussion, since the students are now dependable in all respects. Through conscious, repeated effort, dependability has become a habit for them. They now seem to be consistently dependable without even thinking about it. At this point they have reached the third and final stage of learning, which can be called the involuntary-application or *established-habit stage*.

Perceptual-Motor Learning

Like cognitive learning, perceptual-motor learning can also be divided into three separate stages. Of these three stages, only the first one is significantly different from that in cognitive learning. Perceptual-motor performance involves abstract concepts and neuromuscular skills that cannot be analyzed effectively or described with words. Thus they are best communicated and taught as outlined here.

The conceptual-understanding stage.   By listening to other musicians perform and observing what they do during the act of performance, students acquire mental concepts of what good musical performance is. These concepts may be specific, such as awareness of good upper-register tone or smooth legato style in the lower register, as well as more general ones, such as producing a good tone.

The voluntary-action stage.   Students make a conscious effort, through the use of mental imagery, to reproduce general and specific concepts through trial and error. After each trial they evaluate their performance, and try to repeat a good performance and avoid repeating a poor one. Mentally, they try to remember (memorize and store) good performance experiences and forget (discard) poor ones. Through this means, they begin the development of desirable neural patterns (memory recordings), leading to the third and final stage of learning.

The involuntary-action stage.   When performers reach this stage, their actions are essentially automatic. Given the proper quantity and quality of development in the voluntary-action stage, they no longer need consciously to direct their attention to individual specifics of performance. They merely decide what they want to do musically, and the unconscious brain takes over from there. Their performance skills are now at the level of a conditioned reflex (involuntary, unconscious function acquired through voluntary, conscious, repetitive practice).

SYNTHESIS-ANALYSIS-
SYNTHESIS

Early in my college-teaching career someone told me that the proper way to present a class lecture is as follows: (1) tell the students what you are going to tell them, (2) then give them the information and, finally, (3) tell them what you told them. This concept represents one of the oldest, most popular methods of teaching known to us all: synthesis-analysis-synthesis.

Synthesis-analysis-synthesis (hereafter referred to as S-A-S) is a three-stage teaching method derived from Gestalt psychology. Simply stated it means "from the whole to the parts and back to the whole." During the synthesis stage the teacher introduces the topic, concept, skill, object or whatever is the focus of instruction, in its broad context or complete, integrated form. Next the teacher divides the topic of instruction into its individual parts, so that each can be studied separately (analysis). At the end, all the parts are once again reassembled into a unified whole (synthesis, or resynthesis, if you prefer).

S-A-S is frequently used by conductors during the first rehearsal of a new piece of music. First the piece is played all the way through, without stopping, so that the ensemble players can obtain a general concept of the whole work. Next the conductor rehearses individual sections that need special attention. Then, before leaving the piece, the conductor has the ensemble go back to the beginning and play the piece again in its entirety.

As a very basic, general approach to rehearsal technique, S-A-S is highly recommended. It also works well as a general approach to the teaching of class lessons. The key factor is to begin with synthesis, not analysis. When the teacher begins by introducing the various parts of a new topic or rehearsing individual sections of a new piece first, students inevitably become confused, because they have no idea how the various parts fit together. They cannot see the forest, because the only thing they have been exposed to is the individual trees. If the teacher synthesizes the individual parts immediately afterward, this does alleviate some of the confusion; however, the fully *integrated* whole is usually more than the mere sum of its individual parts. This is why synthesis should precede as well as follow analysis.

Teaching the Whole Versus the Parts

While the foregoing explanation seems logical enough, some will argue that introducing the whole is often too complex to be adequately understood by many students. Holding seems to support this belief when he states: "The two most prominent factors determining the apparent superiority of whole or parts methods appear to be the difficulty of the task and the way in which the part is related to the whole task."[1] The whole method usually works best when dealing with more simple tasks. If the task is too difficult and the student achieves little success in coping with it, divide it into separate parts. This can be done in two ways:

1.   Practice each part separately and then put them all together at once, or
2.   Use the progressive parts approach, where the first two parts are practiced separately, then put together; then practice the third part, adding it to the first two; then practice the fourth part, and so on.[2]

Some also believe that the inherent ability and intelligence of the learner is an important factor to be considered; that is, bright students do better with the whole method, while slower ones need to study the parts. This may be true, but even more important is the type of learning involved: are we talking about cognitive learning or perceptual-motor learning?

In many types of cognitive learning, the parts method does indeed seem to work best. But in dealing with perceptual-motor skills like wind-instrument and vocal-tone production, the whole method is often preferable. The reason for this is that tone production is a highly complex, integrated process, which cannot easily be divided up into separate parts without losing the kinesthetic feeling for the whole. In other words, all the parts are interdependent in terms of kinesthetic sensation, and when they are studied individually, the sum of the parts does not correspond to the whole. In this sense parts study and practice may end up being directed toward the wrong goals, which may need to be unlearned later.

In applying all of this to an instrumental-class teaching situation I recommend that the whole method be tried first. If it works for even two or three students in the class, you will have saved those two or three students and yourself a lot of instructional time. If after a reasonable trial you determine that the whole method simply isn't working for the remaining students, then try the individual-parts approach. If necessary, also try the progressive-parts approach recommended by Holding. In the

---

[1]D. A. Holding, *Principles of Training* (London: Pergamon Press, Ltd., 1965), p. 87. Reprinted by permission.
   [2]Ibid.

final analysis, we need to be reminded that no two people are exactly the same, genetically or environmentally. Thus no two people will learn in exactly the same ways. Each person needs to be dealt with on an individual basis to a greater or lesser degree.

Rehearsal and Class Teaching Priorities

While I favor the whole method in introducing basic performance skills, dealing with ensemble skills in a rehearsal or class teaching situation is another matter. The analysis stage of S-A-S is usually the main core of these situations. It is also the stage where some of the real challenges in teaching take place. But before the teacher can make intelligent decisions about what to teach (analyze), a set of priorities is needed, at least in the back of one's mind. Like a business manager of a corporation or school district who must make budgetary decisions based on an established system of priorities, the teacher needs to know whether to begin work immediately on dynamics or whether rhythmic errors should be dealt with first. Let me state from the outset that there is no absolute answer to such problems that will apply to every situation. Every piece of music, like every rehearsal and teaching situation, will be somewhat different, and in some cases a major reordering of priorities may be required. Nevertheless, I believe that establishment of some general guidelines can be highly beneficial, if not essential, especially for beginning teachers. This I have already done in an earlier text, but I include these rehearsal-class teaching priorities again here, as outlined in Table 5-1, for quick reference.[3]

TABLE 5-1   From the Whole, to the Parts, and Back to the Whole

SYNTHESIS	ANALYSIS	SYNTHESIS
	Rehearsal-Class Teaching Priorities 1. Rhythmic Accuracy 2. Correct Notes[1] 3. Tone Quality and Intonation[2] 4. Articulation[3] 5. Precision[4] 6. Interpretation 7. Dynamics 8. Balance and Blend	

[1]Refers to correct fingering, pitch placement and key changes.
[2]I list these two together because I view them as being basically inseparable. (See Chapter 3 of *Instrumental Music Pedagogy*.)
[3]The more appropriate term for string players is bowing; diction in the case of singers.
[4]Includes attacks and releases as well as good rhythmic interpretation. (See Chapter 5 of *Instrumental Music Pedagogy*.)

[3]Daniel L. Kohut, *Instrumental Music Pedagogy: Teaching Techniques for School Band and Orchestra Directors*, © 1973, p. 226. Adapted by permission of Prentice-Hall, Inc., Englewood Cliffs, N.J.

SUMMARY

Teaching is a profession in which teachers give lessons or instruction to students about how to learn. It is a skill and a craft. At the highest level it is also an art and a science.

A good teacher is many things. Specific qualifications and functions of a good teacher include the ability to communicate, being a positive personal role model and a superior musical-performance model, being able to teach students to teach themselves and being a highly effective motivator.

Understanding the three stages of developmental learning can be very valuable as a basic guide to teaching theory. These stages include—

1. the conceptual-learning stage, where the student acquires mental concepts of what good performance is;
2. the voluntary-action stage, where the student tries to reproduce mental concepts through trial-and-error practice; and
3. the involuntary-action stage, where performance reaches the level of an unconscious, conditioned reflex.

Synthesis-analysis-synthesis is a three-stage teaching concept that means "from the whole to the parts and back again to the whole." When introducing individual performance skills, the "whole approach" is recommended, with use of the "parts approach" later, as needed. In ensemble and class teaching situations, both are recommended. Special consideration in these instances should also be given to rehearsal-class teaching priorities during the analysis phase of instruction. Otherwise one's teaching will be lacking in sequential focus and sense of organization.

In conclusion, good teaching involves far more than merely imparting information to students. It requires possession of various personal as well as professional qualifications. Of all these, the ability to motivate students is the most important.

CHAPTER SIX

THE PSYChOLOGY
OF TEAChiNG

The initial focus of this chapter will be on defining the terms associated with the process of learning. Of these, the most important is motivation. Related to motivation is the subject of competition, which will also be discussed in detail. Identification of self-image and self-esteem problems will be covered next, followed by a discussion of related developmental techniques. The chapter ends with a summary.

INTRODUCTION

Unlike the physiology of learning, discussed in Chapter Two, the psychology of teaching and learning has been an established, integral part of training music teachers for some time now. Most musicians realize that a good mental attitude, at the very least, is critical to good performance. Most physical educators also share this view. In fact, coaches of competitive sports have been among those most vocal about the importance of psychology in winning games. Nideffer, a sports psychologist, points out that one of his former coach's favorite sayings was: "Winning is ten percent physical and ninety percent mental."[1] Most of us probably agree with

---

[1]Robert M. Nideffer, *The Inner Athlete: Mind Plus Muscle for Winning* (New York: Thomas Y. Crowell Publishers, 1976), p. 1. Reprinted by permission.

this assertion, but what is it that really happens in many athletic practice situations? Practically all of the time and effort is devoted to the physical aspects of performance. The bulk of mental training usually comes in the form of pregame and half-time "pep talks." Even then, the best the coach may be able to offer is exhortations such as "You have to be mentally ready to play; you have to have the desire and will to win." But is this kind of psychological lip service of any real value? Do the players really understand? Probably not. After all, how can the players understand if the coach doesn't really understand?

Like sports, musical performance also requires a high level of motoric skill and mental conditioning. The kind of precision execution demanded of a concert artist is surely equivalent to that of a professional golfer, for example, and probably that of a heart surgeon as well. And yet how much time do we musicians really devote to the psychological aspects of musical training? In many respects we, like some athletic coaches, probably give more lip service than intelligent effort to this critical area. Part of the problem is no doubt due to the fact that research in this area has been necessarily limited. Our knowledge concerning the operation of the brain remains finite. Another problem has to do with the strong emphasis in this country on the verbal-cognitive training of students. Given these circumstances, research in motor learning has not kept pace with research efforts in the cognitive domain.

DEFINITION OF TERMS

What is learning? Asking such a question may seem a bit ridiculous, but in order fully to understand the process we need to consider all of its components. These include memory, retention, practice, experience and motivation.

Learning, Memory and Retention

In simplest terms, learning is the act of gaining knowledge or skill. In perceptual-motor learning, memory is the means or process through which we are able to remember. Retention has to do with the ability to memorize, retain or remember. Actually, the three terms are so closely related that many learning theorists consider them to be basically synonymous and therefore inseparable. Learning obviously requires both good memory and retention ability. Without them, learning is impossible.

There are two basic types of learning and memory: short-term and long-term. An example of short-term memory is to look up a telephone number in a directory and remember it just long enough to dial it correctly. Soon afterward, the number is usually forgotten. But if the same number is looked up and *used* frequently, it is eventually memorized, as a result of repetition. This is one type of long-term memory. If there is a specific purpose for learning (memorizing), such as when children need to know their telephone numbers and street addresses in case they get lost, memorization of such information is accomplished more quickly and becomes even more permanent in the long-term sense.

For musicians as well as others, there are two other aspects of memory that directly affect perceptual-motor learning and our ability to improve performance: recall and recognition memory. Recall memory allows us to reproduce prior learning. Associated with recall memory is relearning, or the time it takes to regain the performance level previously achieved. In this regard it is known that effective warm-up can decrease the amount of time it takes to achieve this. Recognition memory, on the other hand, serves as the evaluation standard we use in judging the quality of our performance. Therefore, recognition memory, together with KR (knowledge of results), discussed in Chapter Two, serves as a primary means for error detection and correction.

With regard to perceptual-motor learning, I want to remind you that the kind of memory we are talking about is largely nonverbal, not verbal-cognitive. Of greatest importance to us are the physical sensations of kinesthesia, which are stored in the motor-control section of our brain, and the musical images that are stored and catalogued in our "musical ear." Music is a nonverbal form of communication. Musical performance is the act of expressing musical ideas through the medium of sound, not words.

Repetition, Practice and Experience

Repetition is the act of doing something over and over. Practice, on the other hand, is repetition that is done with a specific goal or purpose in mind. When its specific purpose is to learn a new skill, practice consists of trial-and-error experimentation used to develop correct long-term memory patterns based on sensory feedback. When it is intended to reestablish previously learned skills, practice really amounts to no more than intensive warm-up or relearning achieved largely through recall memory. In any case, the purpose of practice is to learn. In the context of this discussion, it is viewed as self-instruction.

We have all heard the old adage "practice makes perfect," but this isn't necessarily true. Some students simply don't know what or how to practice, so they practice incorrectly. Others, who may lack motivation and merely practice because they are required to do so, also practice incorrectly much of the time. Mindless repetition while watching the clock is usually harmful, because it reinforces performance errors. Such waste of human time and energy must somehow be avoided.

According to Cratty, "Learning is the rather permanent change in behavior brought about through practice . . . motor learning is a stable change in the level of a skill as a result of repeated trials."[2] Performance, on the other hand, does not normally involve repetition, nor is it directly related to learning. It represents the composite results of practice within a gestalt context (the big, complete "musical picture"). It is the act of expressing musical ideas, usually to an audience of listeners.

I make an issue here of the distinction between practice and performance

[2]Bryant J. Cratty, *Movement Behavior and Motor Learning,* 2nd ed. (Philadelphia: Lea and Febiger, 1967), p. 245. Reprinted by permission.

because we sometimes function as if the two terms were synonymous, and obviously they are not. Practice often involves analysis of individual parts of the whole, but even then the focus should be on the goal desired in practicing an individual part, not the means for achieving that goal. In performance, there is only one goal—making music. Players who use practice analysis during performance only create needless problems for themselves. They will invariably make numerous technical errors in addition to producing a performance that is musically sterile. Their minds will be so busy that their neuromuscular mechanisms cannot function properly. Therefore, we must be certain to maintain a clear distinction between practice and performance. Practice is the means to performance. Performance is the end product.

We have all heard the statement that experience is the best teacher, but what is experience? In our specific case, experience is the actual "living through" of the performance act in which we happen to be engaged. It is what we learn as a result of our conscious and unconscious awareness of what is taking place during practice and performance. It consists mainly of what we sense and feel rather than of what we can describe verbally or analyze intellectually. It is largely a nonverbal type of knowledge, which is processed mainly by the nonverbal, intuitive, right side of the brain. It forms the basis of recall and recognition memory. The latter serves as a built-in error-detection-and-correction mechanism for us.

While memory, retention, repetition, practice and experience are all highly important to learning, the single most important learning component is motivation. Every musician knows that in order to learn how to sing or play, you have to practice. But how do you get students to practice? The answer is through motivation.

MOTIVATION

Motivation is an individual's inner desire or urge that provides the incentive for purposeful activity. In our particular case we usually associate motivation with a student's interest in singing or playing an instrument coupled with a sincere willingness to practice on a regular basis. Without genuine motivation, there will be no practice. Without practice, no progress will occur, and thus no learning. Without learning, the teaching-learning process finds itself at a dead end.

Internal and External Motivation

Internal motivation is basically synonymous with the term "self-motivation," which means that students who already possess a large measure of it have a way of making their teachers and parents very happy. External motivation involves using external incentives that "encourage" students to practice and participate for reasons that are not self-initiated. These incentives exist in various forms and can be applied in various ways, ranging from positive inforcement to what some call "fear psychology."

Of the two motivational types, internal or self-motivation is of course the ideal. In fact I've known some persons who believe that motivation for practice and performance should come almost exclusively from the student, not from the teacher. However, I suspect that most experienced teachers would disagree with this rather strongly. I have found that one of the biggest challenges faced by first-year teachers, if not *the* biggest challenge, is student motivation. Teachers' ability to motivate students, as stated in Chapter Five, is the most important qualification for becoming a successful teacher.

To further make my point: A student may own the best instrument made, have perfect reeds, an IQ of 150, the best teacher in the world and still never learn how to sing or play unless a regular routine of practice is established. Suzuki says repetition is the key to the development of superior ability. This is another way of saying that correct practice is the key to becoming a fine performer.

Getting students to practice faithfully has always been a major concern of music teachers, but the question is: how do we get students to practice? The answer is: They must be motivated. This only leads us to the question of exactly *how* to motivate them.

Common Causes of Poor Student Motivation

If a student appears disinterested and refuses to practice, it is all too easy to place the blame directly on the student. Some teachers also make a habit of blaming an alleged poor home environment. Still others may blame the administration and school board because of their supposed lack of interest in and support for the music program. In a few situations where certain influential individuals or groups are indifferent toward school music programs, problems such as these may indeed be an underlying cause for poor student motivation, and they will be difficult to overcome. But let's treat the issue honestly and objectively. In every school one finds some of these problems, to a greater or lesser degree; no school system is totally immune to them. Therefore we would do well to search a bit further into the reasons why poor student motivation seems to persist in some schools and not so much in others.

I believe that in the great majority of cases the true source of the problem can be traced directly to the teacher, whose problems may include anything from poor teaching and organizational skills to basic personality problems in dealing with students. Furthermore, I believe that students usually sign up to play the teacher, not the instrument. By this I mean that the teacher's personality has a direct influence on students' interest and motivation and thus cannot be ignored.

Teacher Self-Motivation

Finding effective ways to motivate students is difficult enough, but there is no way to sustain motivation on the part of the students unless you yourself are highly motivated. If you find it difficult to attract and retain students in your program, you should reexamine your own motivations for teaching music and working with students. It is here that a large share of alleged "student motivational problems" begin and end.

To be a highly motivated teacher, the following requisites are essential:

1. You must have a genuine love for music and musical performance and demonstrate that love concretely, enthusiastically and continuously.
2. You must have a genuine love for, interest in and concern for people and demonstrate these qualities daily in your teaching. Teaching is a "people business," and to be effective, you must be honest, sincere and enthusiastic.
3. You must be a highly competent musician, which includes knowing the music literature and being sensitive to the expressive qualities of music. This is learned through having had intimate contact with good musicians and good-quality musical literature of all styles.
4. You must be competent as a conductor and musical pedagogue and demonstrate confidence in these abilities. If you lack confidence, how can you expect students to have confidence in you?
5. You must be willing to work long, hard hours and at the same time be willing to accept a salary that is considerably less than most other professionals earn with equivalent education and experience. As a dedicated musician and teacher, a large measure of your rewards will come in the form of "musical thrills" from student performances and, perhaps even more importantly, from the personal satisfaction you receive from having made a real contribution to the aesthetic and personal growth of other human beings.

If you feel that you do not meet one or more of the foregoing prerequisites, you may well be in the wrong profession. If you feel that you do fulfill the foregoing criteria, I hope you find the following discussion helpful in further motivating your students.

Recommended Techniques for External Motivation

The following is a list of motivational techniques that have worked well for me. I urge you to add other techniques you know to this list and then put it in a prominent place, where you can refer to it frequently.

1. Gain the respect of your students by demonstrating your knowledge of music and ability as a musician. One of the best ways to do this is to perform frequently on at least one instrument, not just for demonstration purposes, but also to inspire them with your own ability and enthusiasm for playing or singing. (If students respect you and admire what you do, they are much more apt to work for you.)
2. Praise the students when they deserve to be praised, and do it enthusiastically and sincerely. Don't nag and criticize all the time. (If they like you as well as respect you, this makes working for you easier and more enjoyable.)
3. Give the students specific performance goals to work toward; provide them with a sense of purpose. Avoid trying to teach too much at once. This only leads to confusion

and frustration in most cases, and even to despair in others. (See Chapter 7 of Kohut's *Instrumental Music Pedagogy*.)

4. Give your students a sense of achievement. Point out both their short-term and long-term progress in concrete ways. One way of doing this is to have them play something they studied several months ago that now is easy for them. Another approach is to play a tape recording of their performance made several weeks earlier and compare it with their current abilities.

5. The best motivator should be the music itself. Provide interesting and challenging music for them to play, for practice as well as for performance purposes. Without good music, interest deteriorates quickly. Avoid synthetic "training literature," which is challenging only from a technical standpoint.

6. Schedule enough public student performances so that students always have a concrete goal, a real reason to practice and improve. (This is especially critical!)

7. Probably most important is to stress small ensembles. Producing beautiful music where one can easily hear the results of one's efforts in the company of other musicians can be a vital musical learning experience as well as an enjoyable social encounter.

8. Invite guest conductors to rehearse your ensembles, and guest clinicians to give master classes to your students. If finances are a problem, arrange to do exchange clinic sessions with a neighboring director. Often this can be just as beneficial for your students as having musical celebrities come in.

9. Provide a good balance between the study and practice of fundamentals (scales, arpeggios, long tones, lip slurs) and real music. Scheduling enough public performances usually automatically solves potential problems in this area.

10. In teaching beginners I highly recommend keeping a record of students' practice time, although I realize that this is a controversial issue among some teachers. The most successful approach I have found involves the establishment of a three-way partnership, between the parents, the student and the teacher. The goal is to establish the habit of regular daily practice. Once it is firmly entrenched, the practice record can usually be dispensed with.

There is one more item I would like to add here, which is adapted from Colwell: developing a tradition of excellence within the program. Public-school students, just like adults, like to identify with high-quality organizations. In the case of a school music ensemble with an established history of excellence, there tends to be a built-in standard that students accept without undue "prodding."[3] In my experience this built-in standard has much more than casual significance. It can be, and often is, the underlying basis for top bands, choirs, orchestras and winning athletic teams in certain school systems. In psychological terms, it represents a collective type of positive self-image and high self-esteem. It is, in a sense, a programmed attitude, one where the potential for success is built in.

Colwell also lists several other motivational techniques that he refers to as intrinsic motivation (which pertains to long-range planning) and extrinsic motivation (which pertains to immediate, or short-term, goals). For further information, read Chapter 4 of Colwell's text (see the bibliography).

[3]Richard J. Colwell, *The Teaching of Instrumental Music*, © 1969, pp. 41, 42. Adapted by permission of Prentice-Hall, Inc., Englewood Cliffs, N.J.

Synthetic Techniques
of Motivation

Synthetic techniques of motivation include such things as medals, pins, certificates, jackets, sweaters and other extramusical awards. Also included in this category are extended concert tours and trips commonly justified as "educational experiences."

My use of the word "synthetic" no doubt indicates my generally negative attitude toward this motivational category. At the same time I recognize that there may be times when a limited use of these techniques may be desirable. Extramusical awards can sometimes be especially helpful in sustaining interest on the part of very young students. Out-of-town "educational trips" can also be valuable in terms of social growth as well as personally enjoyable, but I believe the label "educational" is misleading, because this is usually not their primary function.

To some readers this attitude may seem unduly narrow and conservative. Let me note, therefore, that I am not opposed to students having fun together. I am intimately aware of the value of student social interaction as a means toward achieving greater *esprit de corps* and musical cooperation in performance. What I object to is the use of expensive forms of external motivation largely as a substitute for good teaching and high-quality musical learning. If directors have to rely heavily on extended trips in order to retain their players and have them practice, this indicates that the programs are in trouble, educationally and musically. In such cases, there needs to be a reexamination of the basic goals and philosophy of each program, followed by changes that will put them back on a sound educational and musical footing. Usually this requires a reevaluation of the directors' musical and pedagogical qualifications as well.

The main point I wish to make here, therefore, is that synthetic motivational methods, if used, should *supplement* the methods recommended earlier, not replace them. Also, any costs incurred for the purchase of expensive awards or for financing "educational trips" should be borne by the parents and/or students involved. School funds and monies raised by music booster clubs should be used mainly for purchasing music, large instruments and other instructional equipment and materials for the music department.

COMPETITION

Many music teachers view competition as a primary means of external motivation. Others are strongly opposed to it. Therefore, competition in school music has always been a highly controversial and sensitive subject. Ultimately the final decision about competition is a matter of individual judgment and choice; but I also believe that we should exert every effort to make that decision a rational one, not an emotional one. The prime purpose of the following discussion, therefore, is to help you arrive at a rational decision on the subject. (I wish to give credit to my colleague Thomas Wisniewski, for many of the ideas contained herein.)

Arguments in Favor of Competition

In our culture, competition is almost a fact of life. It is the bedrock of private enterprise, which was and is largely responsible for our economic and technological progress. Professional musicians also secure their jobs through competitive auditions. Strong national interest in competitive sports further emphasizes how basic competition is to our culture. Competition is the means through which we have been able to achieve high efficiency and superior performance in many ways. Consequently, those who denigrate the value and merits of competition often find themselves in the minority.

I believe competition is valuable for these reasons, but that, like all good things, it can be overdone and misused. An area of special concern to me has to do with school music competition. All too often the desire to win, to beat the other school, becomes the central focus of the entire program. Rather than being an important goal, winning becomes the only goal. Winning is everything! When this kind of attitude prevails, it is time to seriously reevaluate the program's basic educational and musical goals.

Arguments Against Competition

The principal function of school music ensembles should be to help students acquire a deeper understanding and appreciation of good music and high-quality performance. In cases where this goal is achieved on a practical level, the goal of superior musical performance is usually also achieved, but as a related by-product. The question is how to reach this desirable goal. Should we use competition as a prime motivator—student against student, school against school?

My answer to this question is a resounding no! It is precisely this kind of competition that causes us to lose sight of our basic educational and musical goals. Instead of concentrating on teaching musical understanding and the appreciation of good music and high-quality performance, we become so emotionally involved with the idea of winning that it becomes our main focus. Even worse, I have seen too many youngsters experience the "agony of defeat" without sufficient prior preparation, and long before they were emotionally mature enough to cope with it. Consequently these problems have caused me seriously to question whether or not competition has any place at all in school music, even at the high-school level.

Why We Have School Music Competitions

One reason we have school music competitions is that some school administrators and parents want it; in fact, they actively promote it. These school administrators view a winning band, like a winning football team, as a highly desirable public-relations medium for the school system. It enhances school spirit. Parents and other adults also benefit, in the form of community pride.

Taken to extreme, winning music contests has been (and probably still is) a major criterion for retaining one's job in some school systems. Given such a situation, the music director, like the athletic coach, often feels compelled to institute high-pressure forms of competition among students in order to get them to produce at their maximum potential. But such approaches often create severe anxiety, stress and paranoia, which in turn cause extreme nervousness, irritability and lack of self-confidence. At this point, the students are being used to advance the personal desires and goals of adults, who should know better. Here, competition has succeeded in enslaving and degrading the minds and characters of everyone involved.

As with other examples of failure in a school music program, it is all too easy for music teachers to place the primary blame on administrators, parents or others. But let us acknowledge the fact that music teachers themselves are often the primary instigators and promoters of music competitions. A winning trophy boosts their ego and provides them with greater status within the school and community. Some also see it as a means toward getting a better job in a bigger and better school system, while others view it as a stepping stone to a college position. The ends seem to justify the means, but do they really? Does the music program exist to further the professional goals of the teachers, or does it exist for the musical and educational needs of the students?

In an extremely competitive situation, supposing the director decides at some point to redirect the goals of the program—away from competition and toward a more realistic program of *musical* education. Is this possible? Unfortunately, in the majority of cases, it is not. Having grown a ''monster,'' the only solution is to keep ''feeding'' it. Even if the original director moves elsewhere, the succeeding director will probably be expected to maintain the same type of program. If he or she doesn't, the director's tenure will probably be a short one. Change, if it takes place at all, is usually a slow, painful process. Obviously, the best answer is to be aware of the long-term consequences of establishing a competitive philosophy before becoming involved in it. This is one reason why the study of music-education philosophy, goals and objectives is so important in the training of music teachers.

Meeting the Goals and Objectives of Music Education

As professionals in music education we share a major ethical and moral responsibility to music education, students and to ourselves. That responsibility is to help students obtain a deeper understanding and appreciation of good music and high-quality performance. Whenever external pressures are imposed on us that directly impede or prevent us from realizing these goals, we must not automatically yield to them. We must be willing to express our views in an articulate, tactful and yet forceful manner, not only for the sake of music education and the students we teach, but equally as much for our own personal welfare. As the old saying goes, when you look in a mirror, you won't always like what you see but you darn well better respect what you see. If you don't like or respect what you see, then there is only one person who can really change that.

One of the best ways truly to understand and appreciate good-quality performances is to become a good performer yourself. But in order to have a high-quality performing ensemble, you need to have good-quality performers in it. There are some who believe that the most efficient method to achieve this is to promote competition among individual players. Others, including myself, disagree. In an effort to resolve this question let us discuss what is really needed to achieve good ensemble performance.

Requirements of Good Ensemble Performance

In an ensemble, students are expected to listen for such elements as intonation, tonal balance and blend. If players hear that they are out of tune, playing or singing too loudly or too softly or that their tone doesn't blend well, they are expected to compromise and adjust to the rest of their section and/or the full ensemble. The ability to compromise and adjust requires a positive attitude toward cooperation and team work. Without these attitudes on the part of every ensemble participant, good ensemble performance is impossible.

Ironically, then, the very things needed to develop good ensemble performance—cooperation and team work—are the antithesis of intense competition, at least as far as individual players are concerned. We promote competition between individuals for chairs within a section (commonly called the challenge system), and then ask them to compromise, cooperate, blend their tones and work as a team in order to create a sensitive, musically intelligent performance. I find it difficult to resolve the apparent incompatibility of these two extremes.

The Challenge System

Many music teachers favor the challenge system because they consider it to be a highly effective motivational technique for persuading students to practice. True, it does get them to practice, but at what cost? Is it really worth the excessive student anxiety it usually creates? What about the sociological cost, borne by some students?

Every good musician knows that no musical ensemble can function well unless all parts are sung or played well. In essence this means that second and third parts are just as important to the total ensemble sound as the first part. And yet when we use the challenge system as a motivational technique, this implies that the upper parts, especially the solo chair, are the only ones really worth striving for; third clarinet, second violin and fourth horn really can't be that important. But shouldn't we be trying to teach exactly opposite attitudes? No band, orchestra or choir can ever sound good unless *all* parts are sung or played well.

Noncompetitive Alternatives to Challenging

There are two alternatives that can achieve the same goals as the challenge system, but without the ill effects cited earlier. One of these is having *every* large-ensemble player or singer participate in a small ensemble. Small ensembles are excellent vehicles for getting students sincerely excited about performance, helping them acquire a genuine love for and sensitivity toward music itself and motivating them to practice. Perhaps most important, small ensembles promote positive attitudes of cooperation, team work and consideration of other players' problems. Compromise, as a means for achieving good ensemble intonation, for example, becomes a routine good habit within a good small ensemble.

The other alternative to challenging is the use of rotating seating within a section. This process can be initiated first within like-instrument ensembles, such as clarinet quartets. This allows everyone to experience directly the importance of all four parts and to understand the need for having each part played well. This is also perhaps the best way to help insure that all of the large-ensemble parts will be performed well.

Rotating seating is also recommended for large ensembles, in a modified context. Shifting players from the back of the first and second violin sections toward the front after each concert, for example, can help promote added practice. It can also be used to emphasize the fact that *where* one sits in the section is not (and should not be) a major concern, so long as everyone is contributing to the ensemble to the best of his or her ability.

When rotating seating is used, the director must use good judgment in how and when the players are rotated. Good balance between all parts is critical and must be maintained. Also, once the seating is established, it should not be changed until after the next concert. Indiscriminate shifting of players at frequent intervals only causes frustration and confusion for everyone.

How to Compete Successfully

While I am generally opposed to the use of intense competition in school music programs, I recognize that our society is basically a competitive one and that all of us must learn how to function within it. In order to reap some of the greater benefits of school music, such as participation in all-city and all-state ensembles, the ability to compete and do it successfully is also necessary. In fact, competition can be good for us when it allows us to develop our potential, to improve both our abilities and our skills. But, as in almost all other aspects of teaching, competition itself is not always the biggest problem; it is the way in which it is introduced and used by the teacher that brings about many of the negative results considered earlier. Therefore, I include the following list of suggestions designed to help students learn how to compete successfully in a positive learning context.

1. Practice adequately in order to be fully prepared. Good preparation is a prime confidence builder.

2. Compete often, assuming you are well prepared each time. Experience is not only a good teacher; in some respects it is the only teacher.

3. When you make a mistake, don't panic. If you feel you are doing even better than you expected, don't pat yourself on the back. In both situations your emotional responses can cause you to lose your ability to concentrate. That is when the really big errors begin.

4. When involved in serious competition, give it all you've got. The goal is to win. Don't worry about friendships with other competitors during the competition itself. Be a good winner or loser *after* the competition, not before or during.

5. If you lose, realize that this is not directly involved with your inherent value as a person. The competition simply tested a particular skill that you were willing to "put on the line."

6. Don't expect too much too soon. Throwing nonswimmers into deep water to sink or swim may work in a few rare cases, but often it results in drowning.

7. Avoid excessive pressure of the type that creates severe anxiety. It simply doesn't help; it only makes things worse, and, in some cases, unbearable. Worst of all, excessive pressure can lead to emotional wounds, which result in negative self-image and low self-esteem.

8. Don't try to beat the other performers; let them try to beat you. Concentrate on your own performance, not on theirs. Why? To avoid unnecessary anxiety, stress and tension.

9. Losing to specific competitors once doesn't mean you will always lose to them. On any given day you may very well be able to beat them.

10. Most important, try to approach the idea of competition as a means of attempting to improve your performance skills. Try to learn from your competitors. Accept the challenge they provide for you (see Chapter 9 of Gallwey's *The Inner Game of Tennis*).

ACHIEVING HIGH PERFORMANCE STANDARDS

A traditional bit of advice given by conducting teachers to conducting students is that a good conductor knows what he or she wants and knows how to get it. The same applies to a good voice teacher or a good biology teacher. The issue is to aim for and achieve specific standards of performance.

As a teacher you will get only what you ask for, seldom more and frequently less. If the teacher's standards are low, so will be student achievement, and vice versa. Even highly motivated and talented students need to be "prodded" occasionally, and it is the teacher's responsibility to do this whenever necessary. At the same time we must be careful not to establish standards that are unreasonable. This can be as bad as, or in some cases worse than, having standards that are too low.

What Are Reasonable Performance Standards?

Reasonable performance standards are ones that are consistent with a given student's level of ability and degree of motivation. No two students will ever be exactly the same in either of these two areas. Even when there are definite similarities in age, environmental influence and heredity, individual differences will exist. Each of us is unique. Each of our students will be unique in his or her own special way.

This affects teaching and learning in three principal ways. First of all, no two students will be able to learn or progress at exactly the same rate. Some will progress very rapidly and others very slowly, with the majority somewhere in between. As teachers, therefore, we must learn to establish realistic goals of performance achievement that are consistent with each student's potential. Secondly, we must keep in mind that student self-motivation is a critical factor in student progress and achievement. Some students seem to be highly self-motivated; others are not. Finally, we need to find effective ways to motivate students who lack adequate self-motivation. Several methods for accomplishing this goal have already been provided in the discussion of motivation, earlier in this chapter. Further elaboration on this topic as it pertains specifically to teachers and their role in the process is provided in the following discussion.

Being Intense Versus Being "Laid Back"

Teachers with high performance standards are sometimes criticized for being too intense. "Don't push so hard; try to relax more" is a typical suggestion. There can be no doubt that sometimes as teachers we are guilty of pushing too hard. When we do this, we usually create excessive pressure, which tends to decrease rather than increase the rate and efficiency of learning.

In discussing the ill effects of pressure, Maltz states that overmotivation (pressure) of any type causes a breakdown in the ability to think clearly. We try too hard, fail to meet our expectations and thus create a negative self-image.[4] Overly zealous teachers contribute to this negative self-image when they demand more than students can give. But perhaps the worst kind of pressure is that which we impose upon ourselves in the form of perfectionism. Perfectionists seldom if ever meet their expectations. They view mistakes as unforgivable sins. They are constantly berating themselves for being foolish and incompetent. Like competition, perfectionism can be extremely destructive. When students feel this kind of pressure, we should relax more and not push ourselves or our students quite so hard.

But there is also a limit as to how much one should relax. We can easily go to the opposite extreme, being so "laid back" (to use the vernacular) that nothing gets accomplished. Concepts like fast progress and high achievement are either left to chance or ignored entirely. When this happens, the idea of goals and standards virtually ceases to exist. So does one's motivation to really live life, in my opinion. Here I am talking about the quality of one's involvement or participation in the act of living and life itself.

[4]From the book, *Psycho-Cybernetics,* by Maxwell Maltz, pp. 207, 208. © 1960 by Prentice-Hall, Inc. Published by Prentice-Hall, Inc., Englewood Cliffs, N.J. 07632.

How can anyone receive genuine satisfaction from an extremely laid-back existence? Some people no doubt believe that they can, but many of us cannot. The old adage that "you get back what you put in" still holds true, in my opinion. To get maximal rewards, whether it be in regard to musical participation or from living your life, will require intense and genuine effort. Many students never have the chance to experience great rewards from achievement because they've never had a teacher who "pushed" them far enough. It is my belief that such students have been denied the opportunity to experience truly some of the more satisfying rewards of human existence.

If excessive intensity and being too laid back are both undesirable, what is the solution? In teaching and learning, as in most other aspects of human existence and functioning, I believe the best antidote exists in the concepts of variety and balance. By "balance" I do not necessarily mean always functioning in the middle of the two extremes. Rather, I mean creating variety through the *balanced use* of both extremes. This helps to insure a certain unpredictability, spontaneity and excitement, both in one's personality and in one's personal involvement. To be consistently moderate in one's behavior, on the other hand, is to be extreme in another undesirable way. Like listening to a monotone voice or trying to interact with someone who has no sense of humor, the mere consistency and predictability of the experience can be boring, and even frustrating.

To summarize, we can reduce this discussion to a question of attitude. If you want the most out of life, you have to live it to its fullest. Life should not be measured quantitatively (number of years lived); it should be measured in terms of quality. If being laid back means making a minimum of effort and not being involved, I find that uninspiring, unsatisfying and generally unrewarding. If being laid back means being alert, aware and sensitive to what is really happening around you, I am fully supportive of it. A good teacher, then, is one who is both intense and relaxed. This means he or she is sensitive to variety and balance. These concepts, combined with experience, seem to be key factors that determine success in obtaining a reasonable performance achievement from each student.

Dealing with Special Problem Cases

In Chapter Five I said that of all the qualifications and functions required of a good teacher, the ability to motivate students was the most important. Directly related to this is the degree of confidence and respect students have for their teacher. A teacher who is highly admired and respected by one's students will likely be one whose students meet high performance standards without the need for frequent prodding. But even the best-liked, most highly respected teachers will usually have a few students who seem to lack adequate motivation (are not working) and thus make minimal progress. What can one do to change this? This important question is one I have yet to solve to my complete satisfaction. In addition, teaching experience will quickly prove that the same approach cannot be used with everyone. Some students respond to a heavy-handed, punitive approach, possibly because this is how they were taught (learned) to respond within their home environment. Others, especially those with problems of self-image and self-esteem, will need to be dealt with in much more subtle and sensitive ways.

Being able to decide which approach to use with which student, therefore, is where the real challenge lies. In some cases the only alternative may be one of trial-and-error experimentation. In such a situation I would begin with firm but sensitive "persuasion," progressing toward an increasingly more intense level of insistence. Being firm but fair is still a good policy, but being overly firm can in some cases produce very negative attitudes, which are often difficult to change later. It is better to be cautious at first and give the students time to know you as a musician and person rather than to be too demanding too soon.

SUMMARY

Learning is the act of gaining knowledge or skill. In perceptual-motor learning, memory is the means or process through which we are able to remember. Retention has to do with the ability to memorize, retain or remember. Repetition is the act of doing something over and over. Practice is repetition that is done with a specific goal or purpose in mind. Experience is the actual "living through" of the performance act we happen to be engaged in. Motivation is the desire or urge within an individual that provides the incentive for purposeful activity. Of all the components related to learning, motivation is the most important. It is *the* key to all learning!

There are two basic types of motivation: (1) internal motivation, which is essentially synonymous with the term "self-motivation," and (2) external motivation, which involves the use of external incentives, usually devised by parents and teachers, to persuade students to participate and practice. Successful teachers are ones who are able to capitalize on internal motivation while knowing how to apply external motivation techniques in a functional way. But there is no way a teacher can sustain continued motivation on the part of students unless the teacher is also highly motivated. Among the most important prerequisites in this area are genuine love of, interest in, concern and enthusiasm for music, musical performance and the students themselves. A music teacher who meets these criteria is one to whom most students will be devoted. They will have great confidence in and respect for such a teacher.

A primary method of external motivation used by some teachers involves competition. Since competition is so deeply rooted in our culture, I believe we need to teach students to use it in constructive ways. At the same time I feel very strongly that we must be careful not to misuse the competitive spirit in ways that can cause serious psychological damage to students. Winning contests is not, and should not be, the principal goal of school music ensembles. Helping students obtain a deeper understanding and appreciation of good music and quality performance is, and should be, the principal goal.

How can students really learn to appreciate high-quality performances unless they participate in top-quality ensembles? First of all, learning to appreciate a good performance is not totally dependent on playing in a top-notch ensemble. It can be accomplished best through the use of small ensembles and rotating seating. Through these means students are able to learn the concepts of cooperation, compromise, responsibility and team work, all of which are critical to all types of good ensemble performance.

While I am generally opposed to the use of intense competition in school music programs, I recognize that our society is basically a competitive one and that all of us must learn how to function within it. When involved in competition, try to view it as a means of improving your skills, and try to learn from your competitors. Accept the challenge they provide for you.

A good music teacher is one who knows what he or she wants in terms of students' performance standards but whose expectations are also reasonable. Reasonable performance standards are ones that are consistent with a given student's level of ability and degree of motivation.

Teachers with very high performance standards sometimes create excessive pressure, which tends to decrease rather than increase the rate and efficiency of student learning. But perhaps the worst kind of pressure is that which we impose upon ourselves, in the form of perfectionism. Since perfectionism, like competition, can be destructive, we need to learn to relax and not push ourselves and our students too hard.

At the same time there is a limit to how much one should relax. We can easily go to the opposite extreme—being so laid back that nothing is accomplished. The solution lies in proper proportions of balance and variety; variety in being intense and laid back, but also making a balanced use of both extremes.

No matter how highly admired and respected a given teacher may be, there will usually be a few students who lack adequate motivation and thus make minimal progress. There is no single, simple answer to solving this problem, but it is recommended that one begin with firm but sensitive "persuasion" and progress toward an increasingly intense level of insistence. Avoid being too demanding too soon.

Knowledge of the psychology of teaching, therefore, is vital to becoming a successful teacher. It has a direct impact on motivation, which is the key to all learning. Without motivation, there can be no genuine learning. Without learning, the teaching-learning process finds itself at a dead end.

CHAPTER SEVEN

INTRODUCTION
TO PERFORMANCE PEDAGOGY

In order to better understand where we should be going pedagogically, it is helpful to be aware of where we have been. In addition, we need at least a basic introduction to the aesthetic aspects of music and musical performance, the focus of our pedagogy. Both of these areas will be covered in the first portion of this chapter, followed by a review and evaluation of three selected teaching methods.

PROBLEMATIC ASPECTS
OF MUSIC METHODOLOGY

In the introduction of this text I said that one of the biggest problems we face is the large number and diversity of methods we have for the teaching of musical-performance skills (428 methods in the case of vocal breathing alone, according to Hutton's 1951 survey).[1] The purpose of this section is to examine some of the reasons we find ourselves in this predicament.

The Nature-Nurture Question

Are superior intelligence and ability inherited or are they developed after birth? Is musical talent mainly a result of heredity or is it acquired primarily through

---

[1]Charles L. Hutton, Jr., *A Survey of Research Pertaining to the Singing Voice* (unpublished Master's Thesis, Department of Speech, University of Pittsburgh, 1951), p. 19.

training in a superior environment? The real truth, of course, is that no one really knows the answers to these questions, since we still have no way of absolutely proving or disproving them. But since we obviously inherit observable physical characteristics and potentials from both of our parents, it seems logical that we inherit mental characteristics and potentials as well. After all, intelligent parents usually produce intelligent children. But this only brings us back to the original question: what really produced the superior child—inheritance alone, or the home environment provided by the intelligent parents?

Because there is no simple answer to this question, most authors generally avoid taking a strong stand on the issue. One notable exception is Eccles, whose position is explained in the following:

> There is much misunderstanding and downright error in popular beliefs today that environment is dominant in the creation of intelligence. It can be stated quite categorically that brains are built by the complex processes resulting from genetic endowment and all the secondary instructions deriving therefrom in fetal life . . . Geniuses are born, not made! . . . The environment is important simply for discovering and using what we have inherited. This is the essence of the age-old nature-nurture problem![2]

Regarding musical talent, Suzuki specifically states, "Talent is no accident of birth."[3] I find this difficult to accept. Had Suzuki said that superior *ability* is not inherited, I would find it much easier to agree with him. Superior ability is obviously something that has to be developed through environmental adaptation (learning through experience). On the other hand, some people seem able to learn (adapt to certain aspects of their environment) with greater speed and sensitivity than others. Even Suzuki agrees with this.[4] Aren't these special qualities, then, the essence of talent?

In response to this question, let me ask still another: what real difference does it make to us as teachers whether or not talent is inherited? From a purely practical standpoint, there is absolutely nothing we can do about our heredity or that of our students. That issue was settled at the time of conception, so why worry about it now? We have no control over it. Environment, on the other hand, is something that is definitely under our direct control. Therefore, it is the area toward which we should direct our teaching energies. If we fail to do this, we fail in our function as teachers. To put it more succinctly, if teachers fail to exercise proper control over the learning environment of students, there is no compelling reason for professional teachers to exist!

I suspect that even Suzuki would agree with most of this. Regardless of what he means by the opening statements in his book, if one reads further, Suzuki makes it reasonably clear that his basic philosophy is that of an environmentalist. As a teacher who strongly believes that environment plays an important role in the

---

[2]John C. Eccles, *The Understanding of the Brain* (New York: McGraw-Hill Book Co., 1973), p. 222. Reprinted by permission.

[3]*Nurtured by Love* © 1969 by Shinichi Suzuki. Reprinted by permission of Exposition Press, Smithtown, N.Y.

[4]Ibid., p. 24.

development of human potential or talent, I of course agree in principle with most of what Suzuki has written. At the same time I also agree with Eccles that geniuses are born, not made. To accept completely the environmentalist philosophy, to the total exclusion of heredity as a factor in human potential and development, doesn't make sense. Both factors appear to be intimately involved in the realization of superior skills. My own study of human physiology and close observation of fine musicians and dancers as well as superior athletes supports this view. Inheritance definitely plays a significant role in an individual's performance potential. Otherwise, how do we explain a Dick Butkus or an Olga Korbut? How do we explain a Mozart or a Paganini? Can we really say that such superior abilities are the direct result of environmental learning and training alone?

On the other hand, there seems little doubt that a positive environment is necessary in order for superior potential to be developed. I am also convinced that poor and/or misguided training can adversely affect the development of such potential. In some cases I suspect that use of incorrect and/or inappropriate teaching methods can virtually eliminate the potential of highly talented individuals. If all this is true, then the methods of training we use should not be selected casually. As teachers we are obligated to select mainly those methods that are tested and proven or else show maximal promise for success. Doing less than this, it seems to me, represents a neglect of professional responsibility.

Weaknesses in Music-Teacher Training

As teachers of musical performers we have yet to establish a sound philosophical-scientific foundation on which to base our theory and practice of teaching. In the teaching of beginners, for example, we have no standardized principles to guide us in the teaching of new skills. Nor do we have any well-defined procedures or strategies for accurate diagnosis and solution of problems experienced by intermediate and advanced performers. Lacking such principles and procedures, most of us simply teach the way we were taught. We use a wide variety of disparate methods handed down by various former teachers, without necessarily understanding why we use them or questioning their reliability. Beyond that many young teachers learn to teach mainly via trial and error. While trial and error can be desirable and in some cases necessary, continual experimentation, even on the part of a first-year teacher, is difficult to justify. Our colleges and universities ought to do better than this in the preparation of vocal and instrumental teachers.

In order to be certified, all of us were required to study educational history and philosophy, psychology, and methods of teaching. Why, then, do we not apply more of these theories and methods to the live music lesson and rehearsal setting? Part of the problem stems from the fact that knowledge in the perceptual-motor domain has been, until rather recently, severely limited and often misguided. Lacking any real understanding or appreciation of our bodies' extreme physiological complexity, we have erroneously focused on trying to control muscle action and other physiological functions through conscious means. In so doing we have created more problems than we have solved.

Another perhaps more important answer to the problem lies in how we were taught to teach. Traditionally the primary emphasis in most teacher education curricula has been on teaching theory during the first three years, with a brief period of practice (student teaching) at the very end. But such an approach violates two established pedagogical principles: (1) experience should precede (or at least accompany) theory, and (2) we learn to do by doing. While there have been some recent changes in teacher education at several institutions, in the form of increased teaching and observational experiences prior to the senior year, we have yet to solve the problem in any substantive or comprehensive way. We need to strive for a much better balance between theory and practice (experience) in our training of new teachers as well as work toward improved coordination and sequencing between the two. Until we achieve these goals, the perennial gap between theory and practice will continue to exist.

Another important factor is that the practice of teaching (learning *how* to teach) does not end upon completion of senior-year student teaching and receipt of one's teaching credentials. As my dentist once candidly pointed out to me, the "practice of dentistry"—like the practice of medicine, teaching, law and other professions—is, during the first few years, literally a time for practice. During this period we continue to rely on trial and error to some degree, accompanied, ideally, by all due caution and concern for the patient, student or client. To try to argue that this is not true is to deny the reality of how all human beings, including highly skilled professionals, learn to improve and perfect their skills.

In summary, then, a major share of our current problems in music methodology stems from two primary sources: (1) lack of an adequate philosophical-scientific foundation on which to base our teaching methodology, and (2) the continuing gap between teaching theory and practice. This, combined with the tendency of our educational institutions to emphasize training of the verbal, left brain to the neglect of the nonverbal, right brain (as explained in Chapter Three), has created some major problems for us. But music teachers are not alone in this dilemma. Teachers in other fields face similar internal problems. To understand the difficulty in a broader perspective, let us next examine one of the most important influences within our society during this century: science and its methodology.

The Influence of Science and Its Methodology

There can be no doubt that science and the technology it has produced have had a profound effect upon all of us living in civilized cultures. The evidence is all around us. It has affected the way we live, work and play. It has also affected the way we view the world, and even our view of life itself.

A specific outgrowth of all this is that we have come to view most things in overly complex terms. Nothing seems easy, simple or natural any more. Within even the smallest particle of dust or a single drop of rain, there lies the potential for a detailed research study and a lengthy verbal or written dissertation. This, unfortunately, has caused some people to assume that real knowledge and understanding, regardless of the subject under consideration, is possible only through detailed scientific study and analysis. In the case of breathing, for example, we think we have to study the anatomic and physiological aspects of the breathing mechanism in order fully to understand, and thus control, the process.

But what is good for the hard scientist is not automatically appropriate for all other disciplines. Nor are the methods of hard science especially helpful in dealing with matters of human function and behavior. Instead we often find exactly the opposite to be true. In regard to singing specifically, Reid points out that we have yet to find a singer trained via scientific methods who has achieved any notable success.[5] To understand the reasons for this we first need to be reminded that the singer is first and foremost "a complex human being, not a scientific equation."[6] As complex human beings our behavior is not always consistent, nor is it entirely predictable. For this reason it is difficult, if not impossible, to establish specifics of methodology (beyond a few very general principles) that will work with one person, much less a large group. But even more important is the fact that singing and the teaching of it, like all other types of musical performance and related pedagogy, is a creative process, one that depends upon musical conception as its stimulus for action.[7] Musical conception comes out of mental imagery, not scientific analysis. Scientific analysis has nothing to do with the creative stimulus; its function is limited to dissection of the response.

Historically, Reid also points out, "the available evidence indicates that the teaching practices employed up to the middle of the nineteenth century were superior to those which came later."[8] We know this because "present day singers simply haven't the technique to overcome the difficulty contained in the dramatic works written prior to the time of Verdi."[9] One of the basic reasons for this is that voice teachers in that time knew nothing about vocal anatomy and physiology. But soon after Garcia invented the laryngoscope, around the middle of the nineteenth century, teachers attempted to have students exert direct control over vocal function, and, as Reid states, "the result has been chaos."[10]

SPECIAL PROBLEMS
RELATED TO WIND AND
VOCAL PERFORMANCE

An integral part of assisting students in the improvement of their performance is the proper diagnosis of performance problems and a knowledge of how to correct them. In this section I will discuss two special items related to this process, particularly as it pertains to wind instruments and the human voice.

[5]Cornelius L. Reid, *The Free Voice: A Guide to Natural Singing* (New York: Joseph Patelson Music House, Ltd., 1965), p. 5.

[6]Ibid., p. 6.

[7]Ibid.

[8]Ibid., p. 3.

[9]Ibid., p. 5.

[10]Ibid., p. 3.

Diagnosing Internal Physiological Function

The usual approach to solving performance problems is first to identify the problem, then observe the symptoms, diagnose the source and finally prescribe corrective procedures to solve the problem. This is relatively easy in the case of pianists, string players and percussionists, where most problem symptoms are external and therefore clearly visible. In the case of wind players and especially vocalists, the problem symptoms are largely internal and are thus hidden from the eye except through use of special X-ray techniques. In this sense voice and wind teachers are like doctors of internal medicine, who must rely on their knowledge and understanding of how the human body functions, in order to make an intelligent, accurate diagnosis of the source of the problem.

But most musician-teachers have little if any knowledge of and training in human anatomy and physiology, which makes the task of diagnosing internal problems a particularly precarious one, fraught with the potential for frequently making inaccurate diagnoses. It becomes all too easy to focus on a tight embouchure as the source of a tone production problem, for example, when in fact the real source may exist in the breathing apparatus or some other part of the body. If, in this instance, the teacher focuses on working with the embouchure, one is merely treating the symptom rather than the true source of the problem. It is something like an M.D.'s prescribing aspirin for a headache caused by a brain tumor. Such diagnoses and solutions should, of course, be avoided.

Problems in the Use of Literal Verbal Instructions

Since most symptoms and sources of problems in wind and vocal performance are primarily internal, verbal analysis and description of what is and should be happening is difficult. In fact, literal verbal instruction in such cases seldom helps; usually it only creates more problems. Cratty states that if any literal verbal instructions are given, they should be directed toward the gestalt (general principle concept).[11] In regard to early musical performance, however, I suggest that any real need for literal verbal instruction will be rare; and even then the only verbal instructions I view as having any immediate practical value are words like *listen, watch* and *concentrate.* Musical performance is also a nonverbal form of artistic expression, not a verbal one, as will be discussed in more detail later.

The main problem with verbal instruction lies in what can best be described as overteaching. Not only do we give the student detailed descriptions of what *should* be done; we also tell him or her what should *not* be done. When we add all of these instructions together, we find that the student has too many things to think about. Since human beings basically function with one-track minds when learning new skills, trying to remember numerous instructions is essentially impossible.[12]

[11]Bryant J. Cratty, *Movement Behavior and Motor Learning,* 2nd ed. (Philadelphia: Lea and Febiger, 1967), p. 59. Reprinted by permission.

[12]J. A. Adams, "Motor Skills," *Annual Review of Psychology,* Vol. 15, pp. 181–202, 1964.

Master pedagogues like Pestalozzi and Suzuki were obviously aware of this, since both recommend teaching one thing at a time, and teaching it thoroughly, before moving on to the next step. Gallwey takes us a step further, by saying that "sometimes verbal instruction to a conscientious student seems to *decrease* the probability of the desired correction occurring."[13] If this is true, the need to avoid excessive verbal instruction needs no further justification.

A PHILOSOPHICAL BASIS
FOR PEDAGOGY

In order to know what to teach, we need a reasonably clear understanding of our subject. In the next paragraphs I will provide that information by asking two basic questions: what is music, and what is musical performance? These questions will be followed by a discussion of how the brain processes information related to both music and musical performance.

What is Music?

According to Langer, "Music is the tonal analogue of the emotive life."[14] It consists of aesthetically organized sound and silence existing in time and space.

Of special importance to us is the fact that music—like painting, dance and sculpture—is a nonverbal form of artistic expression. It is an aural art that is symbolic in nature, not literal. Its modes of expression are sound and silence, not words. Being the "tonal analogue of the motive life," words cannot be used to describe effectively or explain music any more than they can effectively describe feelings like love and grief. Yet, all too frequently, music teachers try to teach music primarily through verbal means. This is a serious mistake and should be avoided, as was explained earlier.

Contrary to popular opinion, music is also not a "language" in the strictest sense. It cannot function as a language because language is a form of communication through which rather specific meanings and concepts can be conveyed. Music cannot and does not do this; it is a form of artistic *expression*, not communication. To prove this to yourself, ask any group of people what they feel or think as a result of listening to a given piece of music. No doubt you will find that their responses will all be different. No two people will hear or imagine exactly the same things. The same holds true for program music and absolute music. Who can tell the story of a programmatic piece on first hearing unless someone has told you the story *before* the piece was played?

---

[13]W. Timothy Gallwey, *The Inner Game of Tennis* (New York: Random House, 1974), p. 18. Reprinted by permission.

[14]Suzanne Katherina Langer, *Feeling and Form: A Theory of Art* (New York: Schirmer, 1953), p. 27.

What is Musical Performance?

Musical performance is the *act* of producing aesthetically organized sound and silence within time and space. It involves reproduction of musical ideas or concepts (mental images) that are conceived within the musical mind of the performer. As was explained in Chapter Four, the creation of musical images within the brain is called musical conception.

The source of musical conception, of course, exists within the musical mind of the performer, but musicians often use the term ''musical ear'' rather than ''musical mind'' when discussing such conception. The musical ear is that aspect of brain function that deals with musical memory. It is analogous to the artistic eye of the painter or the analytical eye of the scientist who spends hours viewing specimens under a microscope. Like a fine musician who hears things laymen do not, both the painter and scientist see things that you and I miss entirely.

Which Brain Should We Train?

As was discussed in Chapter Two, the two sides or hemispheres of the brain operate in two, separate modes of consciousness. The left side (left brain) operates in what is essentially a verbal, analytic mode. The right side (right brain) operates in what is predominantly a nonverbal, intuitive mode. The right brain is also responsible for mental imagery and spatial orientation within the environment. Therefore, since musical performance is a nonverbal form of artistic expression, which relies on the use of mental imagery as its basic stimulus for action, it is clear that the primary focus of our training should be on the right brain. This means programming it with superior musical images rather than purely verbal concepts associated with the left brain.

But since most of our training in school is directed toward development of the left brain, there has been a strong tendency among teachers to rely mainly on verbal and cognitive-oriented teaching methods in all subjects, including sports, dance and musical performance. This has resulted in what was described in Part One as paralysis through analysis.

REVIEW AND EVALUATION
OF THREE SELECTED
TEACHING METHODS

I have labeled the first two teaching methods to be discussed, as follows: the physiological-analysis–conscious-control method and the recipe-cookbook approach. Both represent what I consider to be arbitrary and misguided teaching, as I will explain in detail. The third type to be discussed is the Imitation Method. In this instance the primary focus will be on how to apply it within a practical teaching situation.

The Physiological-
Analysis–Conscious-Control
Method

Support the tone with the diaphragm; lift the chest and keep it high; relax, you are too tense; open your throat; use more air pressure in the upper register. All of these generalized statements are examples of what I call the physiological-analysis–conscious-control method of teaching. Used in isolation outside the context of viable principles of learning, they represent focusing on the process rather than on the performance goal.

The main thing wrong with the physiological-analysis–conscious-control method is that it is based upon several erroneous assumptions: (1) that correct physiological function can be reduced to the proper operation of a single muscle or body organ, (2) that we can easily exercise conscious control over complex involuntary functions like breathing, the speech-vocal mechanism and muscular action generally, (3) that conscious control is best achieved by concentrating directly on the individual muscle, organ or mechanism itself and, worst of all, (4) that the *key* to good physiological function is to have a verbal-intellectual understanding of it. All of these assumptions are false, as was pointed out in earlier chapters. Perceptual-motor function in musical performance is basically involuntary, not voluntary. It is controlled by the unconscious brain, not the conscious brain. Like music itself, perceptual-motor function exists in the realm of the nonverbal, not verbal.

To review some specific reasons why all this is true, we need to remind ourselves that the human body is by far the most complex organism in the universe. Its mechanical, electrical and chemical operation is so intricate that physiologists readily admit that we are just beginning to understand some of its more basic operations. It is also designed to operate in a perfectly balanced, integrated fashion, like the most precise piece of machinery imaginable. Even though physiologists have classified body function into separate categories like breathing, blood circulation and digestion, we cannot isolate individual functions from what is going on in the rest of the body. In the case of breathing, for example, the entire body is involved to a greater or lesser degree, not just the so-called breathing apparatus. As a specific example, body balance and posture have a direct influence on breathing efficiency, as was explained in Chapter Four.

Since the brain is the control center for all bodily functions, even seemingly simple movements like standing up or sitting down are controlled by the brain, not by the individual muscles involved. A complete physiological analysis of such movements would show that they are not as simple as they seem. They involve proper balance of muscular tension between the more than two hundred pairs of muscles. If we consider more intricate movements, such as performing a chromatic scale on a clarinet, then a detailed physiological analysis would become totally overwhelming not only in complexity but in the time it would take to do such an analysis.

Finally, we need to remind ourselves that no two people's bodies are exactly the same or function in exactly the same ways. Human bodies do share general similarities and function similarly up to a point, but they are not exactly the same physiologically. (One cogent example of our physiological differences exists in the fact that no two people have ever been known to possess the same fingerprints.) Even in the same family there will be major physiological differences, which include multiple births. Differences in inheritance and environmental background preclude this possibility.

Even if it were possible to analyze psychophysiological function for one human being, trying to apply it to another human being wouldn't work. Researchers have tried to do this by analyzing skills of expert performers through the use of slow-motion photography. Analyzing the process (individual components of a specific skill) and having others try to imitate those components did not work. Focusing on the goal (performance result) thus remains the best, most practical solution. We have to do it our own unique way!

What happens when we ask a student to analyze physiological function during practice or performance? We create excessive muscular tension. In asking Gallwey's Self 1 to involve itself in Self 2's job (unconscious body function), we end up "trying too hard," which creates still more tension. For example, try to imagine yourself attempting to produce a tone on a flute for the first time. Your teacher begins with a lecture on correct inhalation, verbally describes the embouchure, talks about using the tongue to release the air and explains that the airstream must be "split" properly across the outer edge of the embouchure hole in order to produce a sound. You listen carefully, take a deep breath and blow, but nothing happens. You try again, but still no sound. The teacher decides the problem lies in your embouchure, so correct embouchure formation is reviewed for you, this time in considerably greater detail. You try again with no results. Maybe you are covering too much of the embouchure hole with your lower lip, your teacher says . . . only one-quarter to one-third should be covered and so on.

How many times have you observed this kind of approach to teaching? Did you teach this way when you first started? Do you still teach this way? If you do, I hope that the rationale provided in this text is sufficiently convincing to help you stop. Learning to sing or play an instrument does not require intellectual knowledge and understanding or conscious control of physiological function. It requires good musical conception, relaxed concentration, awareness of body feedback, practice and experience. It requires focusing on the goal, not the process.

If the teacher is well versed in human anatomy and physiology, there is often an intense desire to communicate these to one's students. However, this should be avoided. Manuel Garcia, the famous nineteenth-century voice teacher who invented the laryngoscope, probably knew a great deal about vocal and respiratory physiology, but he reportedly never discussed any of it with his students. Instead he merely used this information as part of diagnostic procedures for identifying the source of students' performance problems. This is also the way we as teachers should use it.

In closing, let us realize that if we tried to teach children how to walk and talk using traditional analytical methods of teaching, it is quite possible that they might never learn how. If they did learn primarily through this means, then it is likely that they would walk like robots and speak like computers. I believe that this same concept applies equally to some of the basic music-performance skills we musicians try to teach. Even though our intentions may be very sincere, our pedagogical focus is often misguided—it is far too analytical in most cases. Consequently our students learn to execute skills in a stilted, robotlike fashion but find great difficulty in achieving the elegance, refinement and smooth coordination associated with genuinely artistic performance. We need to change that through the use of more effective methods of teaching.

The Recipe-Cookbook Approach

Some teachers use the following systematized procedure for teaching tone production to beginning brass-instrument students. First the students buzz their lips without the mouthpiece, then with the mouthpiece alone, and finally add the entire instrument, but only after they can successfully execute the first two steps. This is an example of what I call a recipe-cookbook approach to teaching. If you use all of the right ingredients and add them in proper sequence, then certain predictable and consistent results should emerge each time the recipe is used.

At first this type of methodology seems quite practical because of its logical structure and simplicity. It is also easily communicated by the teacher and understood intellectually by most students. But its main flaw lies in the assumption that all people are built the same in terms of neuromuscular function and that they also learn in exactly the same ways. This assumption, of course, is false: we are not built the same, and we do not learn in exactly the same ways. In the case of brass tone production, for instance, experience has shown that while buzzing the lips alone is unduly difficult for some youngsters, these same youngsters can sometimes achieve better results when allowed to buzz directly on the mouthpiece. Still other students achieve remarkably good results by blowing through the entire instrument the first time. So why insist that every student go through all three steps when it is totally unnecessary for some and retards progress for others? Since every person is unique physiologically and psychologically, this requires that the teacher deal with each student somewhat differently, even in class situations. To reinforce this belief I quote from Galamian:

> Many things are being taught by the various present-day methods that I would not care to endorse. . . . The first of these is the contemporary insistence upon compliance with rigid rules for everyone. . . . In violin playing, as in any art, that which can be formulated is not a set of unyielding rules but rather a group of general principles that are broad enough to cover all cases, yet flexible enough to be applied to any particular case.[15]

I fully agree with Galamian that what we need is a set of general principles, not rigid rules and cookbook formulas. General principles provide us with a basic

---

[15]Ivan Galamian, *Principles of Violin Playing and Teaching,* © 1962, p. 1. Reprinted by permission of Prentice-Hall, Inc., Englewood Cliffs, N.J.

foundation for teaching, but without locking us into a rigid structure that fails to take individual differences into account.

The recipe-cookbook type of teaching, therefore, is much like "painting by the numbers" as compared to creating a genuine work of visual art. Both of the former are sterile because they lack variety and creative imagination. In teaching and learning, as in painting, individuality must be considered if we are to achieve artistic levels of achievement. A specific style that meets this criterion is the Imitation Method.

The Imitation Method

The essence of the imitation method lies in the following: (1) being able to develop good musical conception via listening repeatedly to a superior musical-performance model, and (2) learning to reproduce musical conception via trial-and-error experimentation. The following is a lesson plan designed for the first several lessons of a beginning instrumental class. For best results I recommend that one or both parents of each child also attend separate classes for similar instruction, so that they can understand the learning procedures and thus assist their child during home practice sessions.

1. The teacher plays the starting note as a long tone of a specific length, and the students are asked to imitate it exactly via singing it first, then playing it later. This means they should start and stop *together*. To do this they must listen very carefully to each other.

    At first, the teacher should indicate the start of the tone by giving a small downbeat with the bell of the instrument. Avoid counting off or giving a downbeat with the right hand. Both of these methods are time-consuming and cumbersome. Remember that the goal is to get the students to listen to one another as well as to themselves and to watch you carefully for your downbeat. In addition to developing the ear, such experience is also invaluable for aiding precision in ensemble playing, which each student will no doubt be involved with at a later date. Playing or singing exactly together in a band or choir involves far more than merely watching the conductor's beat and responding to the ictus. Ensemble performers must also learn to listen to one another in order to perform exactly together.

2. Next, the teacher plays some short, simple rhythmic patterns on a single pitch, with the students singing and then playing each pattern back to the teacher. (See Example 7-1 for specific ideas.)

3. As soon as the class learns two pitches, melodic as well as rhythmic imitation is possible. Example 7-2 includes ideas that can be used with a beginning clarinet or cornet class whose pitch vocabulary includes notes E, D and C (see Example 7-2). As additional adjacent pitches are introduced, they should be integrated accordingly into similar imitation exercises.

4. As soon as reasonably possible, the tempo, dynamics, articulation, musical style and expression should be varied. The ultimate goal is to make every tone or group of tones musical. Without musicality, it is impossible to express musical ideas, which is the essence of genuine musical performance.

EXAMPLE 7-1

EXAMPLE 7-2

Items 2, 3 and 4 are adapted from Chapter Two of Kohut's *Instrumental Music Pedagogy*, published by Prentice-Hall, Inc. For a list of recommended songs for use in imitation teaching, see pages 37 and 38 of that text.

Now let's discuss some of the rationale behind this approach to teaching. The main focus of imitative teaching is ear training. By ear training I mean teaching the student to know what to listen for, including tone quality, attacks and releases, articulation and musical expression as well as pitch, rhythm and duration. I stress the importance of singing for the reasons cited in Chapter Four. I also recommend that there be minimal verbal communication except for positive reinforcement, when deserved, and encouragement in dealing with challenging aspects of performance. The principal type of communication between teacher and students should be a nonverbal musical dialogue via the media of tone and silence.

Next let us consider what should not be done. There should be no verbal instructions about how to sing, no extended verbal explanation about the diaphragm, use of vocal cords, size of throat opening or any other complex physiological function. There is also no need to mention note names, since these are irrelevant at this time. Note names assume their greatest importance once music reading is introduced. The same is true relative to rhythmic note values. Don't mention them now. What is necessary is to teach correct fingerings as new pitches are introduced.

What should the teacher do if the students cannot reproduce a given motif correctly on their instruments? First, slow down the tempo. If the problem is a specific note or interval within the motif, then isolate the note or interval and practice it alone several times before putting it back into context. Demonstrate the wrong way and the right way. Let them try it several times both ways. Also try to develop the virtues of time and patience in helping them overcome performance challenges. Give the Natural Learning Process a fair chance to work. When it is evident that special assistance is needed, however, do not hesitate to diagnose the problem and prescribe appropriate exercises for its correction. (For more specific, detailed information, read Chapter Two of Kohut's *Instrumental Music Pedagogy*.)

But what if performers cannot reproduce the musical model they hear mentally and wish to convey to their listeners, even after years of practice? Does this mean the imitation method is invalid? David Taylor says no; the problem lies elsewhere, usually as a result of extraneous involuntary actions or reflexes that are difficult to control.[16] More often, however, I believe that the problem is due to

[16]David C. Taylor, *The Psychology of Singing* (New York: The Macmillan Co., 1908), p. 248.

random repetition without any specific musical goals in mind. This inevitably leads to establishment of bad habits (poor programming of the unconscious brain) which necessitates remedial work at some later date. Therefore, as teachers we need to do all we can to prevent such a situation from developing in the first place. More specifically, we need to be sure our students know how to practice correctly.

How does a student reproduce the teacher's musical model when practicing at home, where the teacher is not present? One simply forms a mental image of the teacher's performance or that of some other fine performer whom one greatly admires, and tries to imitate it. In either case, the student needs to think and concentrate before playing, listen critically and evaluate the results immediately afterward. These procedures form the core of the development of good musicianship.

Trying to duplicate the performance of an artist-player obviously requires considerable trial-and-error experimentation. Naturally, students' first attempts usually will not be very successful. As in learning to speak or walk, they will falter at first. Only after considerable repetition do they begin to achieve any noticeable degree of success. The same applies to the development of musical-performance skills. We practice long and hard until we are finally able to do what we originally set out to do. The critical factor is that we have an aural conception of what is ideal and what is not. In final analysis, then, the most fundamental pedagogical purpose the teacher serves is to provide a superior model for students to imitate, while at the same time being careful not to expect too much progress too soon. The rest lies mainly with the students in terms of quantity and quality of practice time. There is no substitute for correct practice, and lots of it! (The subject of practice will be discussed in detail in the next chapter.)

SUMMARY
AND CONCLUSIONS

Are superior intelligence, ability and so-called talent inherited or are they developed after birth, through training within a superior environment? We have no definite answer to this question, but it seems logical that both heredity and environment are significantly involved. As far as teachers are concerned, however, environmental influence is their only area of practical concern, since it is the only one over which they have any direct control. Teachers should therefore exert every effort to insure that the environment they create is a superior one, which allows for the maximum development of ability.

Most teachers tend to teach the way they were taught, not the way they were taught to teach. Part of the problem stems from the fact that we still lack an adequate philosophical-scientific foundation on which to base our teaching-learning theory. Another part of the problem lies in the gap that continues to exist between teaching theory and practice. The result of all this has been a mass proliferation of personalized and questionable theories on how to teach. Some of these theories are directly conflicting in their basic orientation; others are totally misguided in terms of both logic and scientific facts. Most experienced teachers are well aware of this problem, and most have managed to succeed in spite of it all. But those with whom I am most concerned are our young teachers in training, who must somehow try to make sense out of all the confusion. Which methods should they accept? Which ones should they reject, and on what basis?

The logical answer is that those involved in higher education who are charged with the responsibility for training and certifying teachers should be expected to alleviate this problem. As a teacher of teachers myself, I agree fully and I accept that responsibility. I am keenly aware of problems such as these. It is a major reason why I decided to study and research these areas.

In order to know *what* to teach, we need to understand clearly our subject—in this case, music and musical performance. Music is aesthetically organized sound and silence existing in time and space. Musical performance is the act of producing aesthetically organized sound and silence within time and space. Since musical performance is also a nonverbal form of artistic expression, the primary focus of our training should be directed toward the nonverbal, right brain. This means programming it with superior musical images rather than purely verbal concepts, associated with the left brain.

Unfortunately there has been a strong tendency among teachers to rely mainly on verbal and cognitive-oriented methods in all types of training, including musical performance. A specific method in question is one I have labeled the physiological-analysis–conscious-control method. Here the focus is on an analysis of physiological function combined with conscious attempts to control it. But such an approach violates everything we know about perceptual-motor function and learning. The unconscious phase of this function cannot be controlled consciously and thus should be left alone.

Another method is what I call the recipe-cookbook approach, which consists of a structured sequence of learning steps designed to approach instruction systematically. But the main problem with this method is that it fails to take individual differences in functioning and learning into account. As such its value is limited, and it can also be a waste of time in many cases.

What we really need is a set of general principles of teaching, not rigid rules and formulas. We also need functional procedures for diagnosing and solving problems. These provide us with a basic philosophical foundation for teaching, but without locking us into a rigid methodological structure.

The only specific method I subscribe to is the Imitation Method, mainly because it is based on The Natural Learning Process. Its primary focus is on the performance goal, not the process. It relies mainly on nonverbal communication, not verbal. In these respects it is consistent with the principles of perceptual-motor learning identified in Chapter Four and the definitions of music and musical performance cited earlier.

chapter eight

developmental
and remedial
teaching

From a methodological standpoint there are two basic types of teaching: developmental and remedial. The purpose of this chapter is to provide the teacher with principles and techniques of instruction appropriate to both types.

GENERAL TEACHING
PRINCIPLES

As stated earlier, one of the prime pedagogical functions of a teacher is to serve as a superior performance model. Another function is to know how to assist the student properly in the improvement of his or her performance. Fulfilling these functions involves developmental as well as remedial teaching techniques.

Developmental and Remedial
Teaching Defined

In simplest terms, developmental teaching involves the teaching of new skills, while remedial teaching is associated with getting rid of bad performance habits. More specifically, developmental teaching involves instructional methods designed to properly introduce and improve new skills so that they become established as desirable performance habits. Remedial teaching, on the other hand, is designed to eliminate undesirable performance habits by replacing them with new, desirable ones. It means relearning and retraining; thus its purpose is to rectify the ill effects of poor developmental teaching and learning.

Therefore it seems obvious that if correct developmental methods are used, there should be no real need for remedial teaching later. Essentially this is true, but we need to realize that some negative factors, such as excessive muscular tension, have a way of "creeping in" without being noticed easily. Mental problems such as poor concentration ability and negative self-image can also remain hidden for some time before they are clearly diagnosed. Finally we must remember that most of our students have lived (and learned) on this earth for several years before we as teachers first meet them. Since education begins on the day of birth, this means that at least some of our instruction will necessarily have to be directed toward the remedial area. No student will be totally without mental and physical problems that affect performance. We must therefore be prepared to deal effectively with both the remedial and developmental aspects of teaching and learning.

Developmental Principles

As a general introduction to developmental teaching, here are some related principles:

1. Program the brain with superior musical images. Provide a performance model through which the student can acquire a good conception of what superior musical performance sounds like.
2. Allow students to learn to do by doing. Let them experience performance via imitation and trial-and-error practice before trying to discuss its cognitive aspects. The principle involved here is that experience should precede theory.
3. Teach the student how to concentrate on musical conception and how to focus on the musical goal. Without good concentration, superior performance is, of course, impossible.
4. New cognitive concepts are best introduced by proceeding from the known to the unknown. This principle is especially applicable to the teaching of musical notation. (See Chapter Two of Kohut's *Instrumental Music Pedagogy,* published by Prentice-Hall, Inc., for details.)
5. Complex new skills are best taught by going from the whole to the parts and back again; that is, by synthesis-analysis-synthesis.
6. Teach students how to practice correctly. Teach them what to listen for and how to "tune in" to kinesthetic sensations.
7. Finally, learning depends upon the desire to learn (motivation). Teaching, in turn, is the art of making students want to learn (the teacher must be a good motivator).

Principles 2, 4, 5 and 7 are adapted from Holz and Jacobi.[1] Even though these authors refer to them as principles of class instruction, I suggest that they are

[1]Emil A. Holz and Roger E. Jacobi, *Teaching Band Instruments To Beginners,* © 1966, pp. 47–50. Adapted by permission of Prentice-Hall, Inc., Englewood Cliffs, N.J.

relevant to all types of instruction. In fact, all of the principles cited here are intended to be broad enough to be applied to almost any situation, yet flexible enough to meet individual student needs.

Learning Transfer

Related to Principle 4—proceeding from the known to the unknown—is the concept of learning transfer. Learning transfer is the effect that the practice and performance of one task has upon the learning and performance of another (usually related) task. It comes from a development of insight based upon experience. Insight comes from a generalization or set of principles concerning a given task that can be reapplied to a new task. Learning transfer is therefore valuable when it decreases the amount of time required to learn a new, yet related, skill.

An interesting comment on this topic is one made by Fitts and Posner: "After the first few years of life, learning an entirely new skill is rare. For the most part, new skills are built out of already existing ones. The learning of skills is therefore largely a transfer of prior habits to new situations."[2] If this is true, the importance of learning transfer needs no further justification. It is obviously a major key to human learning and performance.

The function of the teacher in regard to learning transfer is to assist the student in developing insights in the form of generalizations or sets of principles that transfer from a learned task to a new one; that is, relating the known to the unknown. This is important not only for its own sake but also because it is the key to students' eventually being able to teach themselves. Teaching oneself requires an understanding of basic principles or generalizations that can be applied to several situations. Examples of such generalizations useful in perceptual-motor learning are learning via imitation and being sensitive to kinesthetic feedback.

Remedial Principles

How do you change a bad habit? The answer is, you can't. All habit patterns exist in the form of conditioned reflexes, which are controlled by the unconscious brain. Once they have become deeply engrained through hours of practice and performance, they cannot be changed (altered or modified) merely through a conscious effort of will. Trying to do so is essentially an exercise in futility. The best we can do in most cases is to learn a new habit to replace the old one. Then, through lack of use, the old habit eventually can be discarded.

For a better understanding of this, let us imagine that a habit, once firmly established, exists in the form of a rut or groove in the brain. Each time we are presented with a given stimulus, we are locked in to the related rut we have established for ourselves. Like traveling the same muddy dirt road in a car, our wheels want to follow the rut in the road. The only way to avoid the old rut is to

---

[2]Paul M. Fitts and Michael I. Posner, *Human Performance* (Belmont, Cal.: Brooks-Cole Publishing Co., 1967), p. 19. Reprinted by permission.

make a new rut. If we stop using the old rut and allow the rain and wind to do their work, it will no longer be so prominent. In time it will essentially disappear.

On a more specific level, remedial teaching and learning can be expressed in the form of two basic principles. Both of these incorporate the basic concepts explained thus far.

Principle no. 1.   The first principle involves going from one playing extreme to the other. In the case of a student with major tonguing problems, for example, stop using the tongue entirely for several weeks. Then reintroduce its use as if for the first time. In the case of a saxophonist who bites the reed, push the mouthpiece onto the neck as far as it will go and force the student to drop the jaw in an extreme fashion in order to get down to the correct pitch. In the case of a brass player with a pinched tone due to clenched teeth, place a thick piece of cork between the back teeth to force the mouth open far more than normal. The source of such exaggerations should eventually be removed, of course, but with the result that the student will now be able to perform correctly without it.

Principle no. 2.   This principle involves changing the playing environment. For example, a partial change in the playing environment can be achieved by temporarily changing to a different mouthpiece, a different-strength reed or an instrument with a different-size bore. Another possibility would be to change all three items at the same time. The most extreme use of this principle would be, for example, to have a trumpet player change to euphonium for a period of time, especially if repeated attempts at trying to get the student to ''open up'' the tone have been unsuccessful.

In connection with this, research has shown that radical change in the performance environment is often preferred because it virtually eliminates psychophysiological interference between the old method and the new one. In the case of the typewriter, for example, we know that the present keyboard design is second-rate. Attempts to incorporate a few changes in the design have not worked, because they interfere with skills already learned. Thus the answer is to redesign the keyboard so radically that entirely new skills are required to use it. Interference will be absent if old and new skills are totally unrelated.

Problems with student motivation.   Since remedial learning usually requires starting all over, this inevitably results in a degree of frustration for the student. Worst of all, it usually means that overall performance will temporarily become worse instead of better. In some cases, this lasts for an extended period of time. Anyone who has ever undergone a radical change in embouchure, for example, will understand this dilemma quite well. But the critical first step is to explain this to the student from the outset. One needs to be fully aware of what to expect, that it will take time, patience and concentrated effort on the part of all concerned.

Equally important is the need for the student to be convinced that the change is really necessary. This requires that the teacher be able to demonstrate the practical, desirable results that one can eventually expect from this change. In this context let us use the example of children learning how to walk. Children don't have to break the habit of crawling in order to learn how to walk. They simply concentrate on walking because they are motivated to do so. They know from observing others that it is a faster, more efficient way of moving from place to place.

Directly related to this, of course, is student respect for and confidence in the teacher, as was discussed in Chapter Five. While students' attitudes toward the teacher are very important in all types of learning, they are *critical* with regard to remedial learning. Before you deal with your next major remedial teaching problem I recommend that you reread Chapter Five. It could mean the difference between success and failure in dealing with major problems in remedial teaching and learning.

THE FOUR LEVELS
OF DEVELOPMENTAL
TEACHING

Developmental teaching, as it pertains to perceptual-motor learning, can be conveniently divided into four general levels: (1) pretraining, (2) preventive training, (3) introduction of new skills, and (4) performance improvement. Each of these will be discussed below.

Pretraining

According to Suzuki, education begins at the time of birth. With regard to musical education he recommends that children be exposed first to good recorded music from early infancy onward and to live performances as soon as possible. He further states that good environmental conditions produce superior abilities. "What does not exist in the environment is not developed."[3]

What Suzuki is referring to is called pretraining, which involves development of good musical conception through listening and also through singing, as explained in Chapter Four. As such, pretraining is directly related to the first learning stage (conceptual understanding), also discussed in Chapter Four.

All of the foregoing seems obvious, yet I suspect that many of us fail to give it the consideration it deserves. We are all products of our environment. If a child's environment contains very little music, that child's musical growth will be stunted. As stated earlier, what does not exist in the environment is not developed.

If young students should be taught to sing as well as listen, should they use letter names, numbers or solfege syllables? Should wind players use appropriate articulation syllables like "toh," "doh" or even a neutral syllable like "lah"? These questions are answered in Chapter Two of Kohut's *Instrumental Music Pedagogy* published by Prentice-Hall, Inc., and thus will not be discussed here. But the

---

[3]*Nurtured by Love* © 1969 by Shinichi Suzuki, p. 23. Reprinted by permission of Exposition Press, Smithtown, N.Y.

main point I wish to make is that the mechanics of *how* you do it are of secondary importance. Of prime importance is that you in fact have your students do it regularly since good musical conception is the first and foremost aspect of good musical performance.

Preventive Training

Preventive training involves methods designed to help the neuromuscular mechanism function at peak efficiency. One method is to have students stand during practice, to help promote good posture and body balance. Another method is to have them move about while practicing. In both cases the main goal is to help avoid excessive muscular tension, as was explained in Chapter Four. But an even greater cause of muscular tension is the existence of various mental states, such as anxiety, which interfere with good relaxed concentration, as was also explained in Chapter Four. Unless problems such as these are identified and alleviated early, remedial teaching will inevitably be necessary later.

Introduction of New Skills

This third level involves methods used to help the student in the first attempts to execute new skills. As such it is related to the second stage of learning—voluntary action—discussed in Chapter Four.

There are three different times when a teacher can assist the student during practice trials: before, during and after the trial. Each of these will be discussed separately below.

Before the trial.   Pretrial instruction can be administered in three ways: (1) performance demonstration by the teacher, (2) symbolic verbal cues and (3) literal verbal instruction. Of these three, performance demonstration should receive primary emphasis. Symbolic verbal cues should be used when deemed appropriate, and literal verbal instructions used very rarely, as was explained in Chapter Seven.

During the trial.   During the practice trial, the teacher can assist in one of three ways: (1) through manual guidance, (2) by giving single-word or other brief verbal suggestions or (3) by playing along with the student. Manual guidance of the type used often by string teachers can be very helpful, particularly if the student seems unable to solve the problem alone after several practice trials. But excessive manual guidance for too long a period, like any other crutch, can be harmful, as it deprives the student of kinesthetic learning. Development of kinesthetic sensation is of course necessary to serve as a basis for guiding the student's own movement. Therefore, manual guidance is best done in front of a full-length mirror, so that students can observe what they are doing as well as see what the instructor wants them to do. This kind of visual KR will allow students to better evaluate their own performance later, during successive practice trials in front of a mirror, and also to correct their own errors. At the same time they will be developing appropriate kinesthetic feeling without the delay caused by the kind of instructor guidance described earlier.

Brief verbal cues from the instructor while the student is playing, such as "support the tone" or "softer," can also be helpful on occasion, but experience has shown that too much of this can be confusing and frustrating to the student. Assuming the student is trying very hard to concentrate, excessive verbal cues can interfere with and possibly even disrupt concentration entirely. If the student frequently needs active feedback while playing, this might be better accomplished by having the instructor actually play along with the student. In this way, the student has a direct means of comparing his performance to that of the model and can also use action KR in its most appropriate context. Through this means again, we provide the means for allowing the students to teach themselves. The teacher also serves as an aid to learning rather than simply as an external judge of performance.

After the trial.   Once the trial is completed, the most important feedback (evaluation) students receive is their own. The instructor, therefore, should encourage students to evaluate themselves in specific terms at this time. Was the attack a clean one? Was the tone properly centered? Any feedback given by the instructor should come afterward and serve to supplement the student's self-evaluation.

If as a teacher you are not accustomed to stressing student self-evaluation in your teaching, then I realize that changing your approach will not be easy. But if you agree that developing the ability to evaluate oneself is important, especially if you want the student to get the maximum out of home practice sessions, a change in your approach is essential. Otherwise all you really accomplish is teach the student to be continually dependent on your feedback as the principal means toward improvement. Ultimately this means that a significant amount of time spent in home practice will be wasted because you, the teacher, aren't there to help.

Performance Improvement

The essence of performance improvement lies in knowing how to practice, which is our next topic. It also involves use of reliable error-detection and -correction procedures, which will be discussed later in the chapter. But an essential prerequisite to both of these elements is the development of good musical conception. As stated many times previously, good musical conception is the first and foremost requisite to good musical performance.

Also highly important is that the student approach trial-and-error practice with the realization that performance errors are natural and inevitable, especially during the first two stages of learning. It doesn't help to berate oneself for making mistakes; this only makes things worse by precipitating negative emotional stress, which induces excessive muscular tension. Given enough time, patience and intelligent practice, performance accuracy and consistency will eventually improve. A good teacher can help students greatly by showing students how to practice intelligently. In fact, the major focus of beginning lessons should be on teaching students how to practice.

TEACHING STUDENTS HOW
TO PRACTICE

To become a fine performer, the traditional answer for musicians has been a rather simple one: you seek out the best teacher you can find and then you practice, practice, practice. But *what* should one practice?

Several years ago I attended a clinic session given by the famous bass trombonist, George Roberts, who is especially noted for his lyrical renditions of slow popular ballads. Someone in the audience asked him what he felt were the primary secrets of his performance success. He responded as follows: (1) practicing long tones . . . lots of them, (2) practicing lip slurs and (3) learning to play songs, in the lyrical style of the human voice. This seems simple enough; and combined with the fact that every person possesses the innate ability to learn on one's own via body-feedback mechanisms, this would seem to answer the question adequately. But the big question that remains is *how* to practice. Hours and hours of mindless repetition obviously will not produce high-quality results, but a good teacher can prevent this and make one's practice efforts far more productive.

Broad Objectives of a Good
Practice Session

Galamian lists three broad objectives for a good practice session: (1) building time, (2) interpreting time and (3) performing time.[4] To these I wish to add one other, which should precede these—warm-up time.

Warm-up time.   Warm-up is a time for activating and preparing the brain (specifically the musical ear) and the muscles for the intense concentration and efficient coordination that will be needed later, in the more formal parts of the practice session. Warm-up time is also designed to establish continuity with the goals of the previous practice sessions and to reestablish previously learned skills (relearning).

The specifics of the proper way to warm up vary depending on the instrument concerned and the performer's level of advancement. Because of this I will not attempt a comprehensive discussion of this topic here. My comments will be limited to principles of a general nature.

The first principle of good warm-up is to begin slowly and softly. This seems to be the most logical and natural way. One of our best clues in this regard is to observe the behavior of animals awakening from a deep sleep. They yawn, stretch their muscles and move about very slowly and quietly at first. More strenuous activities usually come later.

Principle number two is to warm up on long tones and give close attention to the three phases of tone production: starting, sustaining and ending each tone. If

---

[4]Ivan Galamian, *Principles of Violin Playing and Teaching*, © 1962, pp. 94, 95. Reprinted by permission of Prentice-Hall, Inc., Englewood Cliffs, N.J.

errors are detected in the attack, for example, this phase should be isolated and worked on until it is at least somewhat improved. The same applies equally to sustaining and ending the tone, of course.

After that each instrumentalist and singer will use diverse warm-up exercises, which may include anything from scales, arpeggios and lip slurs to individual routines designed for a specific instrument or individual performer at a given stage of advancement. Whatever technique is used, the goal remains essentially the same for everyone—to prepare the brain and muscles for the next stage of the practice session, which is building time.

Building time. Building time is designed for the development of performance technique. It may include work on new scales, etudes or other technical exercises. It can also include "working out" technical problems in music being prepared for performance. In brief, it is a time when the performer works on technical skills involved with the second stage of learning, described in Chapter Four.

Good performance technique is developed mainly through repetitive, *slow* drill. I emphasize the word "slow" because this is where many students fail. They need to be reminded that before one can be expected to run, one first needs to learn how to roll over, crawl, then stand up and walk steadily. The same applies to performance technique. We must avoid expecting too much from our students too soon. Asking students to run before they can walk or even crawl inevitably means that they will fall. They may even be seriously hurt. This obviously interrupts and may even greatly retard future progress.

Slow practice is also valuable in that it allows the student to listen and evaluate a performance more easily and more accurately. Hearing music in slow motion is akin to watching a slow-motion film. Suddenly we are able to hear problems that we could not hear at all when played up-to-tempo.

Another reason for slow practice is that it allows the student to concentrate on and become more aware of kinesthetic sensations in the body. Remembering how it feels when something is performed correctly is an integral part of perceptual-motor learning. It is also a key factor in achieving consistency in future performance.

Another facet of efficient technical drill has to do with learning how to identify specific performance problems (notes, intervals or motifs), isolate them from the larger context of the phrase in question (analysis) and create appropriate drills for solving them on an individual basis. After adequate drill, the problem area should be put back into context (synthesis) and the phrase played in its entirety before one goes on to something else.

This seems so obvious that one may wonder why it should even be mentioned. Yet we often find intermediate students and occasionally even advanced performers who need to be reminded of this basic practice approach. In the case of beginners one often finds them practicing an entire measure over and over, for instance, because they have difficulty playing one note in the middle. At worst some will even go back to the very beginning and drill the entire exercise. It is as if they feel a strong need to punish themselves for making a minor error. Obviously, this is a waste of time and energy and should be avoided.

Interpreting time.   Interpreting time is when the performer works on performance literature that has been mastered technically but needs attention from an expressive standpoint. The real basis for success in this area lies mainly in the quality of the performer's musical conception. While listening to a good recording, if one is available, can be very helpful, what the performer usually needs most is live demonstrations performed during the lesson itself by the teacher. This is when a high level of musicianship in the teacher is especially critical.

Once good musical conception is clearly established, practice procedures for improvement of interpretation are essentially the same as those for technical facility. One begins by isolating individual notes, intervals and motifs. Then you work on entire phrases and sections, expanding this to include entire movements and eventually the whole composition.

In summary, then, the goal up to this point is to master all of the technical and interpretive challenges of a given piece so that they no longer require conscious analysis. When this level has been achieved, the performer is ready for the fourth and final phase of the practice session, performing time.

Performing time.   Performing time means playing the entire piece without stopping, preferably with an accompanist if the piece requires one. The goal is to concentrate on the act of musical performance itself and to function at the third and final stage of learning. This type of practice is essential and must not be neglected. No more analysis, no more stopping and going over "trouble spots" at will. One must learn how to keep going despite any technical problems that may occur. The focus of one's concentration should be on the musical gestalt, the total performance goal.

Even though lengthy practice periods will often include all four of the practice objectives discussed here, this does not mean that every one of them must be included in each practice period. A shortage of practice time on a given day may make this impractical. Other than warm-up time, which always comes first, there is no rule that says the other three should follow exactly in the order given here. At certain times it may be more appropriate to go directly into interpreting time and end the practice session with intensive work on scales and arpeggios. My purpose in discussing these four practice objectives is simply to try to focus on the various types of practice one needs to do.

Mental Practice

Normally we think of practice as being primarily a physical act. We go into a practice room and produce audible musical sounds in the course of warming up, followed by various types of drill and repetition of the music being studied. But this is only one way to approach the task of practice. Another, equally valuable way is to practice mentally. We therefore have two kinds of practice: physical practice (hereafter referred to as PP) and mental practice (hereafter referred to as MP).

MP defined.   MP is the symbolic or imaginary rehearsal of performance activities without observable movement or sound. In music it is the mental repetition of a given task without the instrument. In brief, it means to practice silently.

There are actually two types of MP. The first involves using our imagination (conscious brain) to formulate positive mental images of ourselves accurately doing specific musical tasks. This type of MP directly relates to Maltz's theory of mental imagery, discussed in Chapter Four, and is perhaps best labeled imagery practice. The other type of MP involves training the unconscious brain to efficiently process and organize information (goals specified by the conscious brain) and transform it into specific nerve signals to the muscles. In this context MP is directed toward development of neuromuscular coordination.

How do we know that nerve signals actually travel from the unconscious brain to the muscles during MP? We know this because of electromyographic (EMG) studies that have measured electrical activity in specific muscles involved during MP. (An electromyograph is a device that measures electrical activity in muscles.) E. Jacobson was the first to prove this, in 1932. He also demonstrated that such muscular activity also occurs during imagery practice.[5]

The value of MP.   But before going any further, let us ask whether MP is of any real value. Based upon our own experiences alone, I think most of us would agree that it is. But I also suspect that most of us do not really understand *why* it is beneficial or how to use it most effectively. This is why I have included this topic in our discussion.

First of all, MP is not unique to musical performance. Golfers, bowlers, sports and physical-education people of all types have long recognized its value, and many have strongly advocated use of it in their teaching. To illustrate the degree of their interest in MP, more than fifty research studies, articles and books have appeared in recent years on this topic alone. I will not attempt to survey each of these here; rather, I will simply summarize important points that I feel have immediate relevance to musical performance. What we really need, however, is intensive MP research directed specifically toward musical performance. It is my strong suspicion that this area may hold many important keys to more efficient learning in our field.

According to Maltz, "Your nervous system cannot tell the difference between an actual experience and one that is vividly imagined."[6] (This statement is supported by the electromyographic research cited earlier.) It is therefore possible to

[5]Edmund Jacobson, "Electrophysiology of Mental Activities," *American Journal of Psychology,* Vol. 44, p. 677, 1932.

[6]From the book, *Psycho-Cybernetics* by Maxwell Maltz. © 1960 by Prentice-Hall, Inc. Published by Prentice-Hall, Inc., Englewood Cliffs, N.J. 07632.

work on neuromuscular coordination away from the instrument. We can also do MP when there is no suitable place to do PP (physical practice). Fritz Kreisler reportedly had little choice but to use MP as his primary practice approach while on tour. PP was not a practical option while riding on a train or in a hotel room late at night.

How valuable is MP? The findings of various research studies in physical education are mixed. Some report that it is more valuable than PP, others say it is of equal value and still others say it is less valuable. The only certain conclusions we can draw are qualified generalizations:

1. The more familiar the task, the greater the relative gain that can be expected from MP. (This assumes, however, that task familiarity has been acquired mainly through PP.) With regard to the development of neuromuscular coordination it appears, therefore, that MP first becomes valuable somewhere around the second stage of learning.
2. For effective MP the teacher should instruct students to try to imagine how it would feel and sound if they were actually playing the instrument. Obviously this means that a significant amount of prior PP is necessary.

The problem of motivation.   The only problem encountered in the use of MP is decreased levels of motivation on the part of some students. When we use PP, we get immediate concrete feedback (knowledge of results) on how we are doing. This serves as a reinforcer, which makes us want to practice more and harder. Since we receive no concrete feedback during MP, motivation tends to wane rather quickly. Therefore, in order for MP to be valuable to us, it needs to be judiciously alternated with PP. In this way the two types of practice can supplement and complement each other.

It has been my experience that the best time to use MP is probably before playing a piece of new music for the first time. Begin by mentally performing the melody, figuring out how it should sound rhythmically, melodically and expressively. Also identify any alternate fingerings, bowings, breath marks or other technical problems that can be ascertained easily. The process used is in a sense similar to that of a conductor studying a score before the first rehearsal. The benefits to be gained from this process are also similar. In this connection first impressions tend to be lasting ones. A first mistake will tend to persist in future practice trials. Through proper use of MP before the first playing of the piece, we would hope to avoid making those first mistakes, or at least minimize their number.

Practice Procedures for Instrumental Beginners

One of the best ways to teach beginners how to practice is to design the first several lessons on the model of what a good home practice session should be. The following is a list of specific procedures to be used with beginning instrumental classes:

1. Begin by playing long tones. Have the class sing them first and then play them. Continually stress the importance of listening to the pitch, the beginning, middle and ending of each tone, both in singing and playing.

2. Remind the students *in each lesson* that in the absence of the teacher at home practice sessions, they must always have a proper mental image of the tone they wish to reproduce *before* actually doing it. This is an essential first step in any and all practice and musical performance.

3. Teach the students what to listen for via correct and incorrect demonstrations of tone production. Then ask them to evaluate their own performance verbally for you. In other words, make student self-evaluation an active process right from the start. Eventually students need to be able to evaluate and really teach themselves in home practice sessions.

4. In addition to evaluating themselves aurally, students need to know how to evaluate themselves visually. Ask the students to evaluate their own embouchure, posture, instrument-holding position and/or other relevant visual factors while standing in front of a mirror. Again, teacher evaluation should be included as needed, but only as a supplement to student self-evaluation.

5. In the two foregoing points I have specified use of student self-evaluation as opposed to peer evaluation. The reason for this is that I want students to develop the habit of evaluating themselves honestly and without inhibition. Peer evaluation introduced too soon can be inhibiting and even embarrassing to some youngsters. Silent mental evaluation by other class members, on the other hand, should be encouraged from the very beginning. As in any class situation, students can learn a great deal from listening, observing and evaluating one another's strengths and weaknesses. Eventually the teacher may want to add some verbal peer evaluation as part of the regular class routine. When and how much this is to be done will depend upon the teacher's judgment of its appropriateness.

6. Once the class begins playing short rhythmic and melodic motifs, the emphasis on singing before playing should continue. So should the emphasis on self-evaluation. If a given student's musical conception is a good one, as evidenced by the singing performance but he or she still has difficulty reproducing that conception on the instrument, show the student how to isolate the problem note or interval in the manner described earlier. Above all, don't assume that the student will know instinctively how to do this.

7. Continually stress the importance of slow practice by actually doing some of it in every lesson. Also stress the value of mental practice, and show students how it works. Remind them that mental practice can also be a very valuable substitute for physical practice during times of illness or when the instrument is being repaired. Again, teach the techniques of mental practice by doing some of them in each lesson.

8. As an aid to insuring slow practice at home, have your students buy a metronome, and show them how to use it. Also encourage them to tape-record themselves at home and use this as an additional means for self-evaluation.

Although the foregoing procedures are intended mainly for beginners, the basic concepts involved apply equally to intermediate and advanced students. This is especially true with regard to musical conception and to evaluation of performance errors. In this context there is no such thing as beginning, intermediate and advanced practice procedures. The fundamentals of practice apply to all performers regardless of their level of advancement.

Other Considerations

What is the best time of the day for practice? For many people morning is better than afternoon or evening, because they are more alert and thus able to concentrate better. But this generalization does not apply to everyone, of course.

Some persons do their best work in the evening. Whatever time is selected, however, the important thing to keep in mind is consistency, not only in terms of daily practice but in establishing a definite time for practice so that it becomes a routine or habitual matter. If physical practice with the instrument is not possible, for whatever reason, mental practice should be used instead.

Quality of practice is, of course, far more important than quantity. Beyond reasonable and general guidelines, rigid adherence to a specific time schedule of minutes or hours should be avoided. Practice when one is physically fatigued is detrimental because it can cause embouchure problems and excessive muscular tension, both of which are counterproductive to good performance technique. Excessive mental fatigue can also lead to numerous errors, which is equally detrimental. Ultimately each student must learn to determine how long he or she is able to practice and still achieve optimum results. Clock watching should definitely be avoided.

BASIC ERROR-DETECTION
AND -CORRECTION
PROCEDURES

An integral part of teaching and learning is the ability to accurately detect and correct performance errors. The following discussion concerns three areas related to this process: evaluation, diagnosis and problem-solving.

Performance Evaluation

In most teaching and rehearsal situations there never seems to be enough time to accomplish all that we might have hoped for. Consequently the potential for making hasty evaluations and diagnoses of performance problems is ever-present, and we must carefully guard against it, particularly if we are inexperienced as teachers. To guard against this, try to develop the habit of listening carefully to a student's performance for a reasonable period of time before making any specific evaluations or diagnoses. Avoid making snap judgments, especially if you and the students are new to one another. Premature evaluation and diagnosis can easily result in the creation of additional problems that will have to be undone later.

Note that I said LISTEN to student performance in the above paragraph. Listen for phrasing and musical expression first and then for tone quality, intonation and articulation or diction. Avoid visual observation at first. Above all avoid focusing on a "pet area" like embouchure formation or breathing, and do not start trying to change it immediately.

After you have listened long enough to make a valid evaluation of the student's performance, begin by identifying and praising one or two of the student's principal strengths. As stated in Chapter Six, positive reinforcement is a key factor in motivating most of us toward higher levels of achievement.

FIGURE 8-1   Performance Evaluation Procedure

Listen for an extended period to musical phrasing and expression; then listen to tone quality, intonation, articulation or diction.

↓

Identify one or two principal performance strengths and praise the student for them.

↓

Identify the *principal* performance problem within a musical context.

↓

Demonstrate the correct way and the incorrect way. Have the student try to imitate the correct way.

Next, identify what you believe to be the student's principal performance problem, within a *musical* context. Save technical analysis until later. Briefly describe the problem to the student and demonstrate both the correct and incorrect ways of solving it. Then have him or her try to imitate the correct way. This is often sufficient to solve the problem.

Note that I said you should focus on the student's *principal* problem first. Every student will possess several performance problems, all of which need to be identified and solved eventually—but not all at once! A complete critical analysis of all aspects of one's performance can be very intimidating and discouraging, especially for a new student. Work patiently on one thing at a time. Don't try to accomplish too much too soon. (For additional discussion of this topic, see Chapter Six of Kohut's *Instrumental Music Pedagogy,* published by Prentice-Hall, Inc.)

For a summary of accurate performance evaluation procedure, see Figure 8-1.

Problem Diagnosis and Solution

Assuming you have gone through the procedures outlined in Figure 8-1 but without noticeable success in solving the principal performance problem, the next step is to begin diagnosing the technical source of the problem. Generally this means applying logical deduction and the process of elimination as methods for diagnosis and solution of the performance problem.

Let us first be reminded that the ultimate objective of good musical performance is to express musical ideas artistically. Basic to this is the quality and appropriateness of the performer's musical conception. Thus the first step in diagnosis of performance problems is to determine if the student's conception is clear and accurate. Many performance errors are simply the result of a fuzzy mental picture of the performance goal or one that is ill-conceived. To alleviate such problems, have the student sing the motif or passage in question, as recommended in Chapter Four. This should be done for two basic reasons: (1) to make the student focus more clearly on the musical idea he or she is attempting to express and (2) to allow you the teacher to determine if the problem is a conceptual or technical one.

Assuming the performer's musical conception seems satisfactory, the next step is to focus on the key elements of musical performance—tone quality, intonation and articulation or diction. If deficiencies are found in any of these areas, the initial step in trying to solve them should be through teacher demonstration and student imitation. Again we are dealing mainly with nonverbal, artistic concepts, not verbal, analytical ones. Only after we are reasonably sure that proper artistic concepts have been adequately instilled should we proceed any further.

I wish to emphasize the need for focusing on musical conception (including phrasing and expression) as well as tone quality, intonation, articulation or diction as items of foremost importance, as opposed to technical areas such as breathing, embouchure and fingering, which are of secondary importance. The latter area is the *means* toward achieving the former. We must not allow the means to become ends in themselves.

To apply the foregoing concept, let us use the technical area of breathing as a specific example. Breathing is the means through which we achieve several musical ends, the main ones being tone quality and expression. But before correct breathing can be of any real value to the performer, one first needs a good concept of the tone and expression one is trying to produce. Otherwise one operates in a musical vacuum, by not knowing whether one's breathing is helping one to achieve desirable musical results or not.

Mastery of technical fundamentals is undeniably important to good musical performance. This I do not question; but when technical fundamentals are allowed to become ends in themselves, as can easily happen, the expressive qualities of musical performance inevitably suffer. Likewise, pedagogy should serve as a means toward achieving musical ends. It should never be used as an end in itself. Unfortunately, as teachers we are sometimes guilty of transforming what is basically a simple, natural act into an overly complex one, through excessive verbal description and analysis. In so doing we end up impeding student progress rather than accelerating it.

The proper procedure in diagnosing and solving performance problems, therefore, is to focus first on conception of musical phrasing and expression and the elements of artistic performance—tone quality, intonation and articulation or diction. Unfortunately these are the specific areas that are often skipped entirely by some teachers. Such teachers also neglect to look for the prime sources of muscular-tension problems—mental-emotional problems or poor posture—and focus immediately on obvious symptoms, such as lack of breath support or a tight, pinched embouchure. We need to be reminded that the latter are the *means* toward realizing musical goals. They are part of the performance process, not the goal. They should not be allowed to become ends in themselves (primary goals), as they are apt to if this is where the teacher's diagnosis and solution begins and ends.

Assuming that the student's problem *is not* a purely conceptual one, however, the next step is to look for visual symptoms of excessive muscular tension, which indicate problems of poor neuromuscular coordination. First look for evidence of poor posture as the major source of the problem. If the posture-tension problem is mentally based, the solution will not necessarily be a simple one. It will require knowledge and techniques such as those described in the next discussion.

DEALING WITH MAJOR
REMEDIAL PROBLEMS

As stated in Chapter Four, the most common cause of performance errors is excessive muscular tension—caused by poor posture and even more by negative emotional states such as anxiety and boredom. In fact, it seems that one of the biggest problems of today's society is general tension and stress. Most of us realize we are tense and need to learn how to relax, but the question is how.

Relieving General Tension
and Stress

One major step toward relieving general tension and stress is to establish a good routine of physical exercise. This not only helps us feel better physically and emotionally; it also improves our posture and our personal self-esteem. What could be more basic to our physical health and thus more important to our mental health? Yet few of us really take it seriously enough. We rationalize, procrastinate and otherwise neglect exercising as much and as often as we should. Some of us don't exercise at all. I strongly believe that exercise is the first and most basic step toward solving problems of stress and tension and urge you to do more than merely agree with me. I ask you to put this idea into action.

Other Techniques for Relieving
Body Tension

If the body seems generally tense, have the student stand up straight and focus on the "one point". Then ask him or her to move the upper body from side to side, then forward and back. If the feet are too close together, the knees locked or the legs otherwise improperly positioned, relaxed upper body movement will be impossible, of course.

A technique for relaxing the upper body is suggested by Colwell: "Have the student flop over from the hips, letting the top of the body fall in a limp, rag-doll fashion. Rotating the head around in as large an arc as possible will help relax the shoulders and the neck."[7]

If there appears to be tension in the arms, hold the student's hands at chest height, horizontal to the floor. Then let go of the student's hands and let them drop down and swing back and forth until they reach a position of rest at the student's sides. The goal is to have the student relax the arm muscles while you are holding

[7]Richard J. Colwell, *The Teaching of Instrumental Music* © 1969, p. 104. Adapted by permission of Prentice-Hall, Inc., Englewood Cliffs, N.J.

them and let them fall like dead weight when you let go of them. In this way the student learns kinesthetically how the arms should feel when properly relaxed.

Another relaxation exercise is to hold the student's hands and have the elbows swing in and out. According to Rolland and Mutchler, this helps relieve tension in the shoulders.[8]

All of these exercises, incidentally, are equally valuable in the teaching of conducting. As in vocal and instrumental performance, the primary physical source of conducting errors is excessive muscular tension.

Despite the most sincere efforts of teacher and student alike, there will be times when excessive muscular tension is difficult to avoid. One of these is just prior to a solo or contest performance, when the performer is apt to be quite nervous. According to Fillebrown, "The breath of nervousness is quick, irregular and shallow, therefore, take a few, slow, deliberate, deep and rhythmic inhalations of pure air through the nostrils" to overcome this condition.[9] Another occasion is when the air is inhaled too soon and held back prior to the initial attack. Not only does it create tension in the shoulders, neck and abdomen, but it also upsets the natural timing of the attack, thus creating tension in the tongue and embouchure. To rectify this situation, concentrate on making the inhalation-exhalation process a continuous, uninterrupted movement, the way it is in normal breathing. In ensemble performance, begin inhaling when the conductor starts the preparatory beat. Exhale on the downbeat.

In the final analysis, the ideal muscular condition can best be described as "controlled tension," in the form of good muscle tone. Suzuki, for example, has his violin students do deep knee-bends, walk around the room while they play, and engage in other similar physical activities in order to achieve the goal of controlled tension while at the same time striving to relieve undesirable tension in other parts of the body. Wind and vocal teachers would do well to consider adapting this concept to their own particular needs, especially in the area of breathing pedagogy.

Other specific techniques for alleviating stress and tension exist in the Inner Game and Attention Control techniques, discussed earlier. Maltz also reminds us that in order to solve tension and nervousness problems we need to approach them from a mental perspective rather than a physical one. Since the brain controls all of our behavior, he recommends the use of mental imagery to solve all tension problems, regardless of their source. (For specific techniques, see Chapter 4, pages 59–63 of Maltz's *Psycho-Cybernetics*.)

The Effect of Anxiety
on Neuromuscular Coordination

According to Nideffer, ". . . the major factor affecting both the mental and physical functioning of athletes, and thus their ability to integrate these functions, is

---

[8]Paul Rolland and Marla Mutschler, *The Teaching of Action in String Playing* (Urbana, Ill.: Illinois String Research Associates, 1974), p. 181.

[9]Thomas Fillebrown, *Resonance in Singing and Speaking,* 3rd ed. (Boston: Oliver Ditson Co., 1911), p. 27.

anxiety.''[10] I believe the same applies equally to performing musicians. Hours' of training and conscientious practice directed toward technical and musical skills alone will not automatically insure performance success. Anxiety can literally ruin what otherwise could have been a superior performance.

What is anxiety? It is a mental attitude associated with the emotion of fear. Anxiety involves fear of making mistakes or errors, fear of performing poorly. In the case of performers who know they are poorly prepared for performance because they have practiced insufficiently, the presence of anxiety is normal and perhaps justified. In most cases, however, anxiety is a self-imposed, unnecessary detriment. There is no logical reason for its existence, but we need to be reminded that human behavior is not always logical. Our emotions often interfere with our intellect and vice versa.

What are the effects of anxiety on performance? Anxiety interferes with mental concentration. It also causes nervousness, which leads to excessive muscular tension. Given the existence of these two mental and physical obstacles, good perceptual-motor function becomes impossible.

What are the causes of anxiety? The main cause is negative self-image, often coupled with low self-esteem. The lack of confidence ensuing from these factors prevents us from viewing our performance potential in a positive way. But there is one other cause of anxiety that is equally harmful—perfectionism. The perfectionist is one who cannot accept the possibility of human error on one's own part. Such a person has to be perfect or feels he or she has failed. When carried to such extremes, this attitude spells automatic failure. There is nothing wrong with striving toward perfection—within reason. The problem lies with self-deprecation by the individual who fails to reach unrealistic expectations.

How can we rid ourselves of anxiety? If we can't do so completely, are there ways at least to bring it under control? One solution exists in learning techniques of meditation. Another lies in the use of various relaxation exercises. (See page 160 and following of Nideffer's *The Inner Athlete* and page 61 and following of Maltz's *Psycho-Cybernetics.*) Still another, perhaps preferred, solution is to work on improving our self-image, which is often the primary cause of anxiety problems. But first I wish to summarize the basic problem diagnosis and solution procedures discussed up to this point (see Figure 8-2 on page 136).

Identifying Self-Image and Self-Esteem Problems

In Chapter Three, I explained how self-image sets the boundaries of our potential. Persons possessing a negative self-image perform below their potential, while those with a positive self-image perform much better, in some cases better than might be expected. Great athletic coaches often accomplish the latter team-wise in the form of upset victories. Fine musical conductors accomplish the same

---

[10]Robert M. Nideffer, *The Inner Athlete: Mind Plus Muscle for Winning* (New York: Thomas Y. Crowell Publishers, 1976), p. 7. Reprinted by permission.

FIGURE 8-2   **Basic Problem Diagnosis and Solution (Using Logical Deduction and the Process of Elimination)**

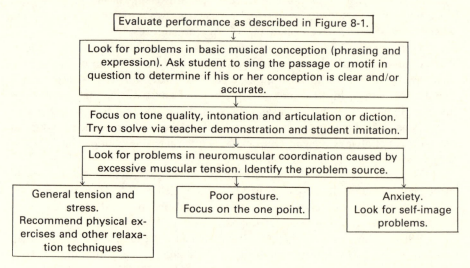

when they have their ensembles "rise to the occasion" during the performance of a very challenging piece of music.

In trying to understand such phenomena let us begin by considering the so-called typical school-music-ensemble or athletic team. Let's face it; the great majority of these students have but average ability. Only perhaps one or two out of a hundred will possess what is often called star potential. And yet the performance quality of musical ensembles and athletic teams in some schools always seems to be above average. Even in a lean year, the band or football team in a given school always seems to achieve far more than anyone had a right to expect.

How does a music director or athletic coach get average students to perform above and beyond what seems reasonably possible? Increased practice time and superior methods of teaching are two of the most obvious answers. But equally important is the ability of the director or coach to convince the players that they can in fact perform better. Practice alone will not automatically produce positive results. You have to believe in yourself. In short, the director or coach must focus on improving the players' collective self-image of their potential for success.

To improve player self-image you first have to eliminate negative self-image. To do this you need to be able to identify some of the symptoms. Then you diagnose the causes and effects.

The symptoms, causes, and effects of negative self-image.   The usual symptoms of negative self-image are fear, anger, shyness, anxiety, and other forms of emotional stress. The basic cause stems from negative evaluations of past performance. The process begins with significant others (parents, teachers, friends) telling us we are failures. In time we become convinced of this and begin telling ourselves the same thing.

What are the effects of negative self-image? It stifles our potential for success through adversely affecting the quality of our mental imagery. In musical performance specifically, our self-image directly affects the quality of our musical conception. Without good musical conception, good musical performance is impossible.

To approach the subject from a positive frame of reference . . . good musical performance requires good musical conception. Good musical conception depends upon our ability to formulate positive mental images of our performance potential. If the image we hold of our performance potential is unnecessarily limited, our performance results will likewise be limited. Self-image and performance results are inextricably related.

Let us now apply the above on a specific level. Let's say a child expresses the desire to begin violin study. He or she expresses this desire to the parents who look at the child with disbelief and say, "You, playing the violin? The violin is the most difficult instrument to learn how to play, you know, and there is no musical talent in our family. Besides, the violin requires lots of practice and you never have stuck with anything for long. You started Little League baseball and quit. You enrolled in swimming lessons and quit after the first week. What makes you think you can stick with the violin and learn to play it? You've got to be kidding!''

Despite the extremely negative nature of this statement, it is not too far removed from reality in a significant number of home environments. Even when the child's interest is so strong that he or she somehow convinces the parents to let him or her start violin study, the war is far from being won. The child desperately needs encouragement and positive reinforcement in order to get past the early stages. The early attempts in performance will not be perfect; numerous and repeated errors will be made. What is important is that the child realize that making errors is normal—a necessary part of everyone's learning development—not evidence of failure. The parents must be sensitive to this and support rather than denigrate the student's honest efforts.

Over an extended period of time, the effects of negative self-image can be devastating. We become locked into a cycle in which failure breeds still more failure, eventually leading to self-condemnation and possibly even self-hate. When things sink to this level, the problem has gone beyond mere negative self-image. It is now a problem of low self-esteem.

The symptoms, causes and effects of low self-esteem.   Primary symptoms of low self-esteem include feelings of futility and hopelessness. The person with very low self-esteem has lost all confidence in his or her worth as a person. The main cause of low self-esteem is a long history of repeated failures. Receiving consistently poor grades in school is a specific example. Continual negative evaluation and destructive criticism from parents, teachers and friends can also bring about low self-esteem. Conversely, we have all heard the old adage that success breeds success. Positive reinforcement, at least in the form of sincere encouragement, can do much to turn a history of past failures into future successes.

The effects of repeated failure and negative evaluation on a person's behavior manifest themselves in the loss of self-confidence and self-respect, the key ingredients of self-esteem. Whatever potential for success the person may have had previously is now effectively stifled. One is no longer able to function as a normal human being. He is psychologically dead.

Self-Image and Self-Esteem Development Techniques

Self-esteem is our personal evaluation of who we are, as a result of past experiences. To change the established negative pattern of the past, we have to establish a pattern of positive experiences in the present and the future. To do this we first have to work on improving our self-image. In other words we have to develop a positive attitude about our potential for success. One of the best means toward acquiring a positive attitude is through the help of a good teacher in whom we have confidence and trust.

What can we do as teachers to help students with problems in these areas? Problems of low self-esteem should be referred to the school psychologist, if there is one available. In any case, expert professional counseling by someone other than the teacher is definitely recommended. But most students experience problems with negative self-image, not low esteem. They are so-called average students whose performance achievement is below their potential, and it is below that potential for no apparent logical reason. What can we do to help them? The answer is to begin by changing their mental attitude about themselves and the performance task in question. The following is a generalized example of an approach that has worked with measurable success for me.

Changing a student's mental attitude.   First I ask the following questions. How do you view yourself as a musical performer? How do you view yourself as a person? Give me some good reasons (not excuses) for why you believe these things about yourself. Convince me that it is impossible for you to be a better player. Convince me that you cannot change and improve as a person and as a player. (Assuming I have been successful in pointing out the irrationality of the students' attitudes about themselves, I then move on to the next stage.)

Everyone born into this world is a unique person, I explain. You are a unique person. You are unique because of your heredity and your unique life experiences. There is no one else in the world quite like you. There is no one else in the world quite like me. I too am unique. I'm not like you or anyone else and never can be. So let's stop comparing ourselves to other people. We can't be like them; they can't be like us.

Who are we? You and I are both unique people with amazing potential. Most human beings possess truly amazing potential, but few people are aware of this as it relates to them personally. Most people don't have the slightest idea of how much potential they have; thus they never realize it. True, our potential is predetermined to some extent by our heredity, but this is not the real source of the problem with most of us. We simply don't believe in ourselves; we have little confidence in our abilities.

But we can change all of that. You can change it; I can change it. Both of us have significant control over who we are and what we can become. We can become pretty much what we want to be so long as we are personally convinced that it is possible and are willing to exert the necessary extra effort to achieve our goals. In other words, we must not only have a dream, but we must also possess the willingness to work hard to make that dream come true. Without a dream or goal to begin with, there is no chance for improvement. Without effort, there can be no possibility of improvement.

Self-image, then, begins mainly with one's personal attitude. Develop a positive attitude about the possibility of improving your self-image, and you open up the potential for major improvements in personality and performance achievement. We are what we think we are. We can become what we wish to become, but only if we believe our goals are within the realm of reality. In my experience, reality is usually what we choose to make it.

Gallwey provides us with two specific suggestions for improving self-image. One is through role playing. The other is to get past one's negative self-image by concentrating on a given task so intensely that you "lose yourself" in the process.[11]

Role playing.   A major key for changing self-image is to acquire new experiences through direct action. One way to do this is to pretend that you are someone else, someone whom you greatly admire or even some mythical individual drawn from your fantasies. Then try to think, act and perform as you think that person would.

I once observed Arnold Jacobs applying this concept as follows: Jacobs asked a high-school trumpet player to play "America." The player's pitches and rhythm were accurate enough, but musically the performance was without style or feeling. Without giving the student any evaluatory feedback, Jacobs then asked the student to name his favorite trumpet player. The student responded with the name of Adolph Herseth. "Now pretend *you* are Adolph Herseth, and play 'America' the way you think he would play it," said Jacobs. The second playing was amazingly better than the first one. Then Jacobs asked the student to name another one of his trumpet idols. The name given was Doc Severinsen. The student was asked to play it like Severinsen, and again the degree of improvement, especially in terms of style, was remarkable.

What does this tell us? It tells us that mental imagery based upon a superior self-concept (in the form of role playing in this instance) can greatly improve the quality of performance. The student's awareness of Jacobs's reputation as a teacher and the accompanying respect he had for him was no doubt also a contributing factor. At the same time, however, the student's image of his own performance was

---

[11]W. Timothy Gallwey, *Inner Tennis: Playing the Game* (New York: Random House, 1976), pp. 114, 120. Reprinted by permission.

decidedly inferior to the image he had of both Herseth and Severinsen. The major element that improved his performance during the second and third trials, therefore, was the vast improvement of his conception—musical self-image.

Getting past the image barrier.   In discussing self-image, Gallwey uses the term "image barrier." The image barrier has to do with all of those aspects of negative self-image that prevent us from performing our best. They also keep us from making steady progress in learning to perform. They include such things as impatience, self-doubt, anxiety and other symptoms of low self-esteem cited earlier.

To break through the image barrier, Gallwey suggests: "One of the easiest ways . . . is to focus your attention so completely on something that you 'forget' to be afraid as you are about to exceed your expected limit."[12] I interpret this to mean that we should try to lose our conscious selves through the power of concentration, so that our unconscious brain is able to take total charge of our performance. Through this means we are able to transcend the performance limitations imposed by our conscious brain and thus achieve the full potential we are capable of at that particular time. Some of this losing oneself through concentration no doubt happened to the trumpet player in the role-playing example cited earlier. This apparently also happens with persons skilled in techniques of meditation.

Positive reinforcement.   One of our functions as teachers is to evaluate student performance. Most of us are very good at this when it comes to pointing out performance errors. But we must not forget that good evaluation should include feedback on performance successes as well. In fact, I believe that most evaluatory sessions should begin by listing the positive aspects of performance. This makes it easier for the student to accept the inevitable "constructive criticism" due to follow. In other words, fill the cup before you take some of the contents away.

This is very important when dealing with a student who has a poor self-image. Rather than hearing more criticism, such a student needs to be built up, needing patience, understanding and moral support. One specific technique for providing this is to take a piece of writing paper and construct two vertical columns, one column for listing the student's strengths as a performer, the other for the student's weaknesses. Invariably, students with a poor self-image will come up with a long list of weaknesses and with very few strengths. The teacher's role, then, is to help the student identify additional strengths and possibly delete some of the weaknesses, which don't really exist except in the mind of the student.

Assuming we have a student who is able and willing to accept constructive criticism, we need to recognize that there are right and wrong ways to administer it. First of all, making mistakes (errors) is not an unforgivable sin. It is a normal, acceptable and necessary part of the learning process. Students need to realize, therefore, that fear of failure is foolish. Sometimes the only way to succeed is to fail

---

[12]Ibid., p. 119.

first. Secondly, our criticism should be positive, not a negative, tearing-down process. We should treat people not as they are but as we wish them to become. A good teacher must have faith in one's students and in one's ability to help them. Otherwise both teacher and student are defeated before they even begin.

The ability to approach the teaching-learning process positively, therefore, is critical to eventual success. The ability to deliver criticism in such a way that it can be received by the student without undue anguish is an attribute all teachers should consciously and continuously strive to cultivate. Both of these concepts are integral to great teaching.

TECHNIQUES FOR THE CORRECTION OF SPECIFIC PERFORMANCE ERRORS

Probably the most valuable thing a teacher can do to assist students in both error detection and error correction is to *increase* their awareness of what is and/or should be happening during performance. Good teachers do this through the use of three primary techniques: (1) verbal imagery, (2) kinesthetic reinforcement and (3) augmented feedback.

Verbal Imagery

As discussed in Chapter Seven, excessive use of verbal instructions should be avoided. If any verbal instruction is to be used, I recommend the use of verbal imagery. By verbal imagery I mean symbolic verbal cues that involve the use of similes, metaphors and other psychologically based descriptions to communicate nonverbal and abstract concepts and ideas.

One specific example of verbal imagery is to think of the sound of church bells before performing a series of *sforzandos*. In trying to have singers produce a darker tone, voice teachers may ask them to think of deep, rich red velvet. Another example is to ask wind players trying to produce a soft legato attack to think of the tongue operating like a soft, artist's brush. Still another example is to ask young brass players to think of blowing bubbles when forming the embouchure.

It has been my experience that voice teachers tend to use verbal imagery much more in their teaching than do instrumental teachers. I have also heard some instrumental instructors criticize voice teachers for this, in the belief that verbal imagery is a synthetic and ineffective way to teach performance skills. I do not agree. Other than teaching via direct imitation itself, some concepts are best communicated through symbolic rather than literal explanations.

There is a good reason why voice teachers tend to rely rather heavily on the use of verbal imagery. Unlike wind, string and percussion instruments, the vocal mechanism cannot be taken apart and put back together again. More importantly, the voice box and its contents are extremely complex, and beyond simple conscious control. Voice teachers are therefore left with little choice than to use indirect methods such as verbal imagery to teach many primary vocal techniques. Direct analytical, pseudo-scientific approaches seldom work. Often they only serve to create additional performance problems associated with muscular tension.

Wind players have problems similar to those of vocalists in these areas. Most of their tone-production mechanism also exists inside the performer's body. Much of this internal mechanism also operates involuntarily. I suggest therefore that wind teachers take a cue from voice teachers and try to make greater use of verbal imagery in their teaching since there are many aspects of wind technique and interpretation that also defy verbal description and analysis. (See Harrison, S. "Problems of Piano Playing" *Ergonomics,* Volume 1, pages 273–276, for further discussion of this topic.)

Kinesthetic Reinforcement

As stated in Part I, kinesthesia is an integral part of The Natural Learning Process. We don't have to acquire it; we already possess it. What we need to do is increase our awareness of it and thus use it more effectively in learning and performance.

I explained in Chapter Four that we increase kinesthetic awareness through quieting the mind, which is made possible once we are convinced that it is both valid and proper to trust the body. Having mastered these two concepts, we are then able to achieve a high level of concentration, which allows us to tune in to kinesthetic feedback.

Kinesthetic sensations are especially important during the first two stages of learning. A specific technique for developing an increased awareness of them at these times is the use of slow-motion practice. Slow practice allows us to concentrate better on what is going on inside our bodies and thus increases our awareness of what is.

A good teacher can increase our awareness of kinesthetic sensation through two principal means: (1) helping us achieve a state of relaxed concentration and (2) reinforcing kinesthetic sensations experienced during accurate performance. A typical, teacher's comment in regard to the second means is, "That's it; that is how it should feel. Now try to remember how it felt and play the passage again in the same way."

The use of kinesthetic reinforcement is not new to music teaching, of course. Many teachers use it frequently, in an almost instinctive sort of way, without even knowing what to call it. But it is important to understand that it does little good for a teacher to try describing a specific kinesthetic feeling to a student or anyone else who has never experienced that feeling before. In a sense, specific kinesthetic sensations are things, like love and extreme grief, that a person can identify and comprehend only *after* having experienced them. In kinesthetic learning, as in all other types of learning, experience should precede theory.

Augmented Feedback

Augmented feedback, sometimes also called added feedback, is sensory information received by the performer that amplifies the normal types of body feedback discussed in Part I of this book. The most common type of augmented feedback is the verbal feedback provided by a teacher, but this has its limitations, as was explained earlier. Other types of augmented feedback exist mainly in the form of various audiovisual aids.

Evaluating our own performance is sometimes similar to evaluating our own personality. It is difficult to be genuinely objective about it. Sometimes we see and hear only what we choose to see and hear. At other times we are simply unable to perceive what is really happening. Our teacher points out a negative aspect of our performance, such as poor intonation or articulation, and we simply don't hear it the way the teacher does. This, in particular, is where the special value of augmented feedback exists. Use of a stroboscope to ''illuminate'' the reality of poor intonation on a given pitch can resolve the matter in question very quickly. (For specific information on how to use the stroboscope in solving tone quality and intonation problems, see pages 114–119 of Kohut's *Instrumental Music Pedagogy*.)

Probably the most common audiovisual aids used by music teachers are the mirror and the metronome. The ways in which a mirror can be used are so obvious that I will not take time to discuss them here. Regarding use of the metronome, I refer you to pages 188–190 of Kohut's *Instrumental Music Pedagogy*. I will discuss three other audiovisual aids here: prerecorded disc recordings, video- and sound-tape machines.

Disc recordings can be used in two principal ways: (1) as a means for communicating general musical concepts to a large ensemble and (2) as a means for studying a given solo piece during the process of learning it. As far as the second way is concerned, the goal is to memorize the piece aurally. Once students learn to play the piece reasonably well, they should tape record themselves for self-evaluation purposes. Having acquired a concept or standard of performance through repeated listening to the prerecorded model, students are now able to make intelligent comparisons between the model and their own performances. The goal of self-teaching is thus realistically achieved. In this context the tape recorder may well be the musician's most valuable teaching aid. It is indeed unfortunate that we don't use it more often.

When taping one's performance for later evaluation, I hasten to emphasize the importance of using it mainly for self-evaluation. Ask students to evaluate their own performances first. Any evaluations made by the teacher should come afterward, in a supplementary context, such as pointing out additional errors the student may have missed. In some cases the teacher may need to focus mainly on the positive features of the performance if students are overly critical of themselves. Nothing is really all bad, and some students need to be reminded frequently of this important fact.

While use of video-tape recordings can also be beneficial, particularly to singers and string players, the emphasis on student self-evaluation remains equally important. In my experience in teaching conducting through the extensive use of video recordings, most students seem to improve faster when they (rather than the teacher) do most of the evaluation, at least initially. Even during later stages of development, this approach continues to be important. In this context we need to be reminded that someday conducting students will have little choice but to improve through self-evaluation. We won't always be there to help them.

There is one other type of augmented feedback that deserves special mention here. This is biofeedback, referred to by some as "electronic yoga." Biofeedback involves the use of electronic equipment to measure muscle tension. The more tension there is, the more electrical activity. This electrical activity is sent through an amplifier and used to operate a loudspeaker. As the muscle tension increases, the pitch goes higher, and vice versa.

There are two aspects of biofeedback that appear to have some relevance to musical-performance training. One of these is being able to discriminate between Alpha and Beta brain waves and being able to "call up" the Alpha state on demand. (The Alpha state is quite similar to the meditative state of mind, feeling a oneness with nature.) The other relevant aspect is, of course, in monitoring and controlling muscular tension.

SPECIAL PROBLEMS IN
TEACHING INSTRUMENTAL
BEGINNERS

Deciding what to teach and in what sequence to teach it can be overwhelming for the instrumental teacher faced with a first class of beginners. There is so much to cover: breathing, embouchure, tone quality, tonguing, intonation, fingering, hand position, posture, dynamics, phrasing, musical style, rhythm and even musical notation. The list seems endless, but the key is to cover one thing at a time, in logical sequence, and teach it thoroughly before moving on to the next. Since we function with one-track minds when learning new skills, we need to be especially careful not to expect too much too soon from the beginner. It takes time (at least eighteen years, according to law), for youngsters to mature into adults. Musical maturation also takes a good many years, and we need to keep this in mind, especially when working with the very young.

Preliminary Objectives

Obviously the first things an instrumental beginner needs to be taught is how to assemble the instrument, then disassemble it and put it properly back into its case. Basic care and maintenance should also be discussed at this time, with an information sheet sent home to the parents that outlines both of these.

The next step involves forming the embouchure through use of various syllables and producing a sound on the mouthpiece alone. (Specific syllables will be
provided in Chapter Eleven.) Next, the mouthpiece should be inserted into the
instrument, accompanied by instructions on how to hold the instrument. All of this
should be done while the student is standing, and should be taught mainly via
demonstration and imitation. The less verbal description and explanation, the
better.

Tone Production

The first performance objective is to produce a reasonably centered tone, one
that is characteristic of the maximum resonance potential of the instrument being
played. This too is best achieved through imitation.

Tone production is a highly complex, integrated process, as will be explained
in Part III. For this reason it should be introduced to a beginner in as simple and
direct a way as is possible. Initially the focus should be on the total process, not on
its individual parts. Later, if individual parts fail to function properly or bad habits
begin to appear, the individual parts should be dealt with in isolation. Also, younger
players in particular do not need to know the intricate details of how their body
functions during performance. In fact such knowledge can be very harmful, as
discussed earlier. But the teacher needs to know and understand this information as
an aid to an accurate diagnosis of performance problems.

Tone production is best taught through the nonverbal process of imitation. If
the student is unable to achieve acceptable results after several trials, and the source
of the problem is specifically diagnosed to be an incorrect use of the breathing
mechanism, for example, then a brief but simple explanation of proper breathing
technique may be in order. But again be careful not to give up too soon on the
student or give up prematurely on the imitative method as a viable learning approach; trial-and-error experimentation in home practice between the first and second lessons may, in the long run, prove to be the easiest and best way to learn.
Especially resist the temptation to use excessive verbal description and analysis.
Whenever verbal instructions are given, try to make them as brief, direct and simple
as possible. There is ample evidence that cognitive learning is relatively easily
forgotten. On the other hand, motor skills, which are learned by doing, are generally retained much longer. In fact, skills such as swimming or riding a bicycle, once
learned, are never forgotten. We are not entirely sure why this is true, but some
believe that it may be the result of the amount of overlearning that is required in
order for these skills to be executed properly in the first place.

Three additional tone-production techniques are outlined next.

1. Have beginners play at the loudest dynamic level that they can control. Avoid early use
    of *p* or *pp* dynamic levels. Learn to *move air through* the instrument. Don't blow *at* the
    mouthpiece!
2. Consider use of Middleton's BRIM (Breath Impulse) Technique. Ironically, this sys-
    tem was originally designed for teaching rhythmic reading, not breath support, but it

appears to be equally useful in promoting good tone production. Since this technique has already been reviewed in the author's earlier text, *Instrumental Music Pedagogy,* pp. 28, 29, it will not be discussed in detail here. James A. Middleton's unpublished doctoral dissertation, "A Study of the Effectiveness of the Breath Impulse Technique in the Instruction of Wind Instrument Performers," University of Oklahoma, 1967, is also available through University Microfilms, Ann Arbor, Michigan.

3. Finally, be especially watchful for beginners who relax their embouchure and breathing muscles after each note and reset both for each subsequent note. This faulty habit is sometimes called "huffing and puffing for each note." This problem is especially prevalent among beginning flutists but often shows up with horn and tuba players as well. In the case of the flute, the problem is brought about by the fact that the embouchure provides the only real source of resistance to the air. If the embouchure is weak or poorly developed, the air escapes almost immediately, causing a frequent need for new air. With horn and tuba players, this habit is usually brought on by the offbeat-downbeat parts in their music. To solve this problem, have students sing the melody or exercise, then ask them to play it the way they sang it. This should make the error evident to them. If it does not, then the teacher must demonstrate the wrong way, followed by the right way. Ask the students which version they prefer. Follow this by telling them to think of singing through their instruments.

Ear Training

The first and foremost musical objective in working with a class of instrumental beginners is to train the ear toward developing a good musical conception. If prior experiences in general music classes have been positive and beneficial, this will, of course, make the instrumental teacher's job that much easier. But regardless of prior experience, continued emphasis on ear training through the imitative method is necessary.

Every experienced teacher knows that posing a question like "Do you understand?" to a class of youngsters is essentially a waste of time pedagogically. It is easiest for the student to say yes. Those who should be saying no are often too embarrassed to speak up, fearing it will demonstrate their ignorance in front of their peers. Therefore, if the teacher really wants to know if the students understand, they should be asked to demonstrate that understanding in a concrete way.

This is especially true in teaching good musical conception to instrumentalists. Before they can play a given note, motif or phrase correctly, they need to form a clear mental picture of it in their "musical ear." The best way to determine if they know how to do this is to have them sing it first and play it afterward. This literally forces them to think before they play.

The Method Book: Its Purpose and Limitations

Through the years instrumental teachers have devoted considerable verbal effort to the pros and cons of like-instrument methods versus full-band methods, and one full-band method versus another method. The implication here seems to be that the real answer to teaching success lies mainly in finding the "right" method book. But this is confusing the issue. The main purpose of most method books is to serve as a means toward learning to read musical notation, which is, or at least should be, separate from developing good musical conception and performance skills. The teacher still has to do the real teaching of music and performance techniques. No method book can accomplish these tasks even though some of the more recently published play-along methods with programmed cassette tapes and/or disc recordings can function very well as supplementary aids. Therefore, I recommend these programmed materials highly, but for supplementary purposes.

Since the main function of most method books is to provide a logical, sequential approach to the teaching of musical notation, any drill material designed to improve individual performance skills within a class usually results in numerous compromises between instruments, particularly in the case of full-band methods. Ear-training and instrumental-performance techniques are best learned through other means. Therefore, before using any method book, begin by teaching ear training and individual performance skills via imitation alone. Teach one thing at a time, and teach it thoroughly. Provide your students with a good visual and aural model to imitate. Encourage them to create, to learn familiar melodies on their own, to experiment, to compose, and to improvise. Supplement this with method-book instruction later, but only after students have had sufficient experience in ear training via imitation. Never lose sight of the fact that high-quality musical conception is necessary for high-quality practice and performance results.

In closing this discussion, I wish to make it absolutely clear that I have nothing against the majority of published method books presently available, especially full-band methods. In fact, full-band methods are preferable in most cases to other types, since they allow easier scheduling and grouping of wind instrument classes. My point is simply that students learn mainly from the teacher, not the method book. The teacher, not the method book, spells the real difference between efficient and inefficient learning.

Teaching the Gifted Student

As teachers we realize that most of our students are not geniuses, but often we have students of above-average ability who exhibit special musical skills or talents. How should we deal with these students?

First of all, we need to be alert in identifying such abilities in students and providing a stimulating environment for their natural, maximum development. Secondly, we need to be extremely cautious in selecting methods of training for these students, so that we don't retard their progress. Often the best approach is simply one of providing the appropriate environmental stimulus (learning situation), then staying out of the students' way and letting them develop naturally on their own. In some instances it may be advisable to alter the environmental stimulus temporarily to see if there is any increase in motivation and/or skill development. Most importantly, the teacher would best avoid encumbering the student with traditional structured methods of learning. Such methods can interfere with natural ability and thereby inhibit special skill development. When this happens, teaching in fact becomes a "subversive activity," as described in a book by Postman and Weingartner entitled *Teaching as a Subversive Activity,* published by Delacorte Press.

Maintaining Student Interest[13]

Do this by—

1. occasionally changing the daily routine.
2. occasionally changing seating arrangements.
3. planning in a manner that will avoid becoming bogged down on a given point; students may need weeks to master a particular type of technique. Do not expect to complete the job in one class period. A judicious (usually brief) amount of time every day for several days or several weeks (in proportion to the difficulty in question) will usually produce improvement without boredom or rebellion.
4. developing the ability to judge the point at which immediate further study of a problem is useless. Turn to something else for relief, and try again at a later time.
5. seizing upon every opportunity to point up the progress that has been made by the class; for instance, doing an occasional review reading of an earlier exercise or piece that proved difficult in the first performances.
6. scheduling the use of material with much consideration for continuity. By this means the students are made to be aware of steady forward progress. Indiscriminate skipping around in the book results in carelessness, a feeling of futility, and frustration.
7. selecting challenging goals and materials that are justified by past preparation and performance and do not present difficulties of such magnitude as to be completely discouraging.
8. praising a good performance but remembering that there is always room for improvement. Be prompt, direct, and specific in stating where and how such improvement may be made. Human performance seldom reaches perfection. When your class, band, or orchestra reaches the point at which you can suggest no further improvement, you are in a serious predicament!
9. knowing your students as individuals and establishing with each one a personal contact that is your line of communication, spoken or unspoken, as the occasion demands.
10. remembering that your attitude and manner will often be reflected by your students. The confidence and enthusiasm that will be evident as a result of the common-sense effort you spent in preparing to teach your class or your large group will do much to evoke a similar response from your students. A mutual realization of joint effort in the direction of a common goal is an invaluable aid. A tardy teacher finds oneself with tardy students; a sleepy teacher with sleepy students, and so on.
11. being patient! It is often true that a technical problem, which is difficult now, becomes no problem at all six months hence, largely because of students' maturation.
12. striving to avoid a monotonous or mumbling manner of speaking. Speak distinctly, modulate your voice and inject a change of pace in your general speaking manner.

SUMMARY

From a methodological standpoint there are two types of teaching: developmental and remedial. In simplest terms developmental teaching involves teaching new skills, while remedial teaching is associated with getting rid of bad performance

---

[13]This entire section is taken from an unpublished educational handbook written by Dr. S. M. Trickey, School of Music, North Texas State University. Used with the author's permission.

habits. Getting rid of a bad habit involves replacing it with a new one. Remedial teaching and learning, therefore, is a time for reteaching and relearning.

There are four levels of developmental teaching, which are classified as follows: (1) pretraining, (2) preventive training, (3) introduction of new skills, and (4) performance improvement. While all four levels are important, performance improvement is perhaps most important to us in this chapter because it relates directly to teaching students how to practice.

There are two types of practice: physical practice and mental practice. Physical practice involves learning to do by actually doing, while mental practice is the symbolic or imaginary rehearsal of performance activities without observable movement or sound. While we all accept the validity of physical practice, mental practice as a bona fide learning technique has not been as widely discussed. There seems to be little question regarding its value, however, and its use is especially recommended before actually playing a new piece of music.

The first step in the diagnosis and solution of performance problems is to evaluate performance carefully and accurately by listening to (not watching) the student from a musical (not technical) standpoint. Then try to solve the principal performance problem, initially through the use of the teacher-demonstration–student-imitation method. If this fails to achieve satisfactory results, then have the student sing the passage in question to determine if the musical conception is clear. If the problem appears to be one of poor neuromuscular coordination due to excessive muscular tension, look first for poor posture, then for general tension and stress and finally for anxiety problems. A major source of anxiety is negative self-image and accompanying low self-esteem. Self-esteem problems should be handled only by a psychological specialist, but a good teacher can do much to improve difficulties in the self-image area.

Techniques for the correction of specific performance errors include the use of verbal imagery, kinesthetic reinforcement and augmented feedback. In all cases the goal is to assist students in increasing their awareness of what is and/or should be happening during performance. The most common audiovisual aids used in providing augmented feedback are the mirror, metronome, stroboscope and video- and sound tape-recording machines.

In the teaching of instrumental beginners, probably the most challenging aspect is deciding what to teach and when. As recommended in the first part of this book, the primary emphasis at first should be on ear training, which is taught via imitation. Beyond that, the next greatest challenge is to maintain student interest.

Despite the length of this chapter, it is hoped that this summary has served to crystallize the basic evaluative, diagnostic and problem-solving procedures of teaching into a set of easily defined principles. For further summarization I recommend a review of Figures 8-1 and 8-2.

CHAPTER NINE

ANATOMY AND physiology of THE TONE-production MECHANISM

Soon after I first began writing this chapter I considered moving much of the material to the appendix or leaving it out altogether. Who needs another tedious discussion on the physiology of breathing and other functions associated with tone production? We already have enough confusion in this area. Perhaps the less said the better. Yet I eventually decided that this is the very reason this subject needs to be discussed here in some detail. We need to eliminate some of the confusion by exposing some of the myths and other erroneous concepts currently surrounding the subject. These need to be replaced with reliable information that can be used by teachers to more accurately diagnose tone-production problems. Herein lies, therefore, the main purpose of this chapter.

The tone-production mechanism consists of the following basic components: the breathing apparatus, the glottis and the oral cavity. For singers, however, we must add the voice box and the lips, which are used for the forming of consonants. In the case of wind players we add the embouchure, and for reed players the reed itself. In this chapter the primary focus will be on the anatomy and physiology of the breathing apparatus, followed by a brief discussion of the oral cavity. Detailed discussion of the oral cavity, embouchure and reed function will be included in Chapter Eleven.

THE BREATHING
APPARATUS: BASIC
INFORMATION

The breathing apparatus consists of three anatomical sections: (1) the upper respiratory tract, (2) the chest (thoracic) cavity and (3) the abdominal section. The upper respiratory tract consists of the nose, mouth, throat (pharynx), the glottis (opening between the vocal cords) and the windpipe (trachea). In breathing, the primary function of these components is to serve as passageways for air going in and out of the lungs. So long as these passageways remain relaxed and open, efficient breathing is possible. When the throat or glottis is reduced in size owing to excessive muscular tension, inhalation and exhalation are both adversely affected. To insure maximum throat and glottis opening during inhalation, think of whispering the vowel sound ''oh.'' During exhalation, think of whispering ''hoh.'' Further discussion of vowel sounds as they affect tone quality directly will be included in Chapter Eleven.

The chest cavity includes the rib cage, the rib (intercostal) muscles and the lungs. The rib cage contains a total of twenty-four ribs, twelve on each side of the sternum, or breastbone. All are attached to the vertebra in the spine. In front, the first six ribs from the top are attached to the breastbone, the next four ribs are attached to the rib immediately above in each case and thus are indirectly attached to the breastbone structure. The eleventh and twelfth ribs are not attached to any source in the front and are therefore called floating ribs (see Figure 9-1).

The rib cage cannot initiate any action or movement on its own. It is totally passive and reactive. The principal agents that cause it to move are the rib muscles

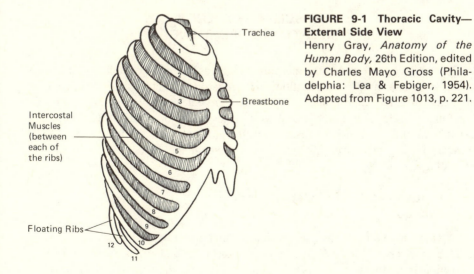

FIGURE 9-1 Thoracic Cavity— External Side View
Henry Gray, *Anatomy of the Human Body,* 26th Edition, edited by Charles Mayo Gross (Philadelphia: Lea & Febiger, 1954). Adapted from Figure 1013, p. 221.

(intercostals), which occupy space between each of the twelve pairs of ribs. These muscles and their function will be discussed separately later.

Everyone knows what the lungs are, what function they serve and the fact that every normal person has two of them. Not so well known or understood is the fact that their mode of operation is basically a passive one, since they can neither expand nor contract on their own. Active movement of the lungs is dependent almost entirely upon the action of various muscles, which increases and decreases the size of the chest. These muscular actions provide the lungs with additional space to fill up with air during inhalation and to be compressed and expel air during exhalation.

In the abdominal section, the organs pertinent to breathing are the muscles used to initiate inhalation and exhalation. Physiologists tell us that there are at least twenty-five muscles used for these functions, the primary ones being the diaphragm and those of the abdominal wall. The rib (intercostal) muscles, mentioned earlier, are also significantly involved. A review of writings by musicians concerning specific muscles used in breathing, however, reveals several contradictions. One author states that the whole science of breath control depends upon proper use and control of the intercostal muscles. Another author maintains that the intercostals should remain passive, since they are too poorly distributed to use with force and should, therefore, leave the job of supporting the air to the larger, stronger muscles of the abdominal wall. (No scientific support is provided for either of these assertions.) Still another author expresses the belief that two sets of muscles should be used—the intercostals and the diaphragm. All of these statements cannot possibly be true. The first two happen to be incorrect physiologically, and the other is at best misleading. Since correct muscular function is the single most important aspect of breathing, it is critical that it be clarified.

MUSCLE PHYSIOLOGY
RELATED TO BREATHING

In Chapter Two I referred to the muscular system as being responsible for the output phase of human mind-body function. With regard to breathing, the same concept applies. Once the appropriate nerve signals are released by the brain, it is the breathing muscles that do the actual work necessary to bring about inhalation and exhalation, not the lungs themselves. But before we can discuss the breathing muscles intelligently, we first need to understand the fundamentals of muscle physiology.

Fundamentals of Skeletal Muscle Function

There are only two basic things that skeletal muscles can do: they can contract and they can relax. During contraction they exert force and produce motion. During relaxation their function is basically a passive one. They cannot exert force or pressure when in a relaxed state. In order to keep this discussion brief, an outline of what skeletal muscles can and cannot do is provided here.

1. Individual skeletal muscles do not function alone; they operate in groups of muscles that oppose one another. To initiate a movement, one group (agonist) is activated through contraction, while the other group (antagonist) is inhibited through relaxation. To stop a movement, the function of these two muscle groups is simply reversed.

2. The action of each muscle group is a highly integrated process. The higher the quality of muscle-group integration, the smoother and more coordinated the resulting movement. Poor muscle-group integration manifests itself in jerky, awkward, robot-like movements.

3. Skeletal muscles also contract and relax instantaneously. While certain muscles, such as those in the walls of the intestines, can contract and relax slowly, skeletal muscles cannot do this. Their action is immediate, in response to nerve signals from the brain.

4. When skeletal muscles contract, they contract fully and totally. The same is true with regard to relaxation. They cannot be partially contracted or partially relaxed, any more than a regular light switch can be set to a partially on or partially off position. Skeletal muscles do not operate like dimmer switches such as you might have in your dining room. Skeletal muscles operate on an all-or-nothing principle: fully contracted (switch on) or fully relaxed (switch off). There is no in between.

If this is true, then how do we explain the difference in muscle strength needed, for example, to lift a ten-pound weight versus that needed to lift a one-pound weight? Increased strength or force is achieved mainly through using a larger *number* of skeletal muscles. The more muscles contracting at any one time, the more strength we have at our disposal. The fewer muscles used, the less potential strength we have. Each individual muscle can be strengthened further, of course, through appropriate physical exercise. But the fascinating aspect of this process is that it all happens unconsciously, and thus automatically. Appropriate muscles in the proper quantity contract and relax without any conscious direction from us. All we do is decide on a movement goal, such as picking up a pencil, for example, and the unconscious brain (Self 2) does the rest. It decides which muscles and how many are needed to accomplish a given goal and sends appropriate nerve signals to each of them. Our conscious brain (Self 1) is not normally involved in this specific process, nor should it be.

The Lungs

As stated earlier, the function of the lungs is basically a passive one, since they can neither expand nor contract on their own. They depend almost entirely upon the action of various muscles that increase and decrease the size of the chest. When the size of the chest cavity is increased during inhalation, this creates a partial vacuum inside the lungs in relation to external atmospheric pressure. To equalize this pressure, air automatically comes into the lungs, assuming the oral passageway is clear. During exhalation, air inside the lungs is expelled, mainly as a result of muscle relaxation, which automatically decreases the size of the chest cavity. The air can also be expelled more rapidly through contraction of various expiratory muscles, as is necessary in musical performance, but again the lungs themselves are not directly involved. Their function is essentially a passive, reactive one, not an active one. They can neither expand nor contract on their own.

In trying to explain lung function, however, music teachers sometimes tell students that the air from the lungs is expelled in much the same way as it is from a balloon or automobile inner tube. At first the air is expelled rapidly and in large quantity, followed by a gradual decrease in volume and speed, until all of the air is gone. Then the lungs have to be "blown up" again in preparation for the next phrase. While this analogy has no doubt been helpful to some students, it is not really accurate physiologically. The elasticity of the lungs, as compared to a balloon or inner tube, is minimal. Lung expansion and contraction is mainly a reactive response to external atmospheric air pressure and muscle action, as explained earlier. Filling a balloon or inner tube with air requires use of compressed air above and beyond normal atmospheric pressure. Both are able to expand and contract because of the elasticity of the rubber of which they are made. The lungs cannot and do not do this, because their elasticity is minimal.

If you feel compelled to use an analogy to explain lung function, I recommend comparing the lungs to hand bellows, of the type used for starting a fire in a fireplace. When the interior size of the bellows is increased, this creates a partial vacuum, which causes external air to be drawn inward in order to achieve a balance with the external atmospheric pressure. A decrease in the internal size of the bellows forces the air out, this decrease in size caused not by elasticity of the bellows but by the action of the person using them. Therefore, the lungs might be best described as human bellows.

The Diaphragm

Support the tone with your diaphragm! How many times did we hear our teachers say this to us when we were students? How many of us use exactly this terminology today? But it is wrong! The diaphragm *cannot* actively support the tone during performance. Read any physiology text and you will find that the diaphragm is basically passive and nonfunctional during exhalation. It performs its active role during inhalation instead. X-ray research done in the 1960s by musicians, which I will discuss later, also verifies this.

The information that follows is available in almost any physiology textbook. I include it here in outline form for your convenience. The diaphragm—

1. is a muscular, membranous partition that separates the chest cavity from the abdominal cavity (see Figure 9-2).
2. is actually made up of several individual muscles, which work together in a highly integrated fashion.
3. is a skeletal muscle, since it is attached to the inside of the lower ribs, the backbone and the breastbone at a slant from front to back, the highest portion being near the

FIGURE 9-2

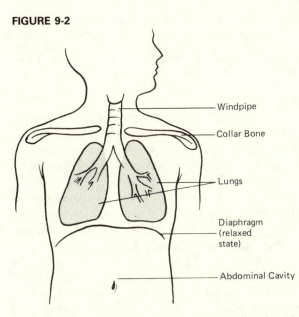

Windpipe

Collar Bone

Lungs

Diaphragm
(relaxed
state)

Abdominal Cavity

breastbone. Consequently, it extends well up into the chest cavity inside the rib cage. It is not located near the front waistline, as some music teachers suggest.

4. is a thin membranous structure much like a drumhead, as personal inspection of several cadavers has shown. It is not a large, thick structure, as some teachers imply in their teaching. At the same time it is true that some diaphragms are noticeably thicker than others. Although I am not certain, I suspect this means that the diaphragm can be made thicker and presumably stronger through proper exercise.

5. contracts and relaxes quickly. It cannot contract or relax slowly, as some musicians seem to believe.

6. *cannot* be kept firm, partially contracted or partially relaxed during exhalation, as some musicians seem to think. As it is a skeletal muscle, it operates on an all-or-nothing principle. It is either fully contracted or fully relaxed; there is no in between.

7. is basically an involuntary muscle. According to Zemlin:

..... there appears to be little if any voluntary control over diaphragmatic action. Wade . . . and Campbell and Jellife . . . examined diaphragmatic movements in physiotherapists and singing teachers who believed they had voluntary control of their diaphragms. Although these subjects were able to control rib movements during breathing, there was no evidence of voluntary control over the regular muscles of inhalation, particularly the diaphragm.[1]

8. is the primary muscle of inhalation, not exhalation. Like all other skeletal muscles, it produces motion through contraction and can only contract (exert force) in one direction—downward. It is incapable of exerting *direct* force upward, against the base of

[1]Willard R. Zemlin, *Speech and Hearing Science: Anatomy and Physiology,* © 1968, p. 88. Reprinted by permission of Prentice-Hall, Inc., Englewood Cliffs, N.J.

the lungs. Therefore, to bring about inhalation, the diaphragm contracts downward. To allow for exhalation, it has to relax upward. (Jacobs likens its operation to that of a piston moving up and down within the chest cavity.) In fact, the only way that air can be released from the lungs is for the diaphragm to relax first. To continue exhalation, the diaphragm must remain relaxed. Otherwise airflow is interrupted each time it contracts.

In summary, the diaphragm has no active function during exhalation. Instead, the only thing it can do is help bring air into the lungs and keep it there. Based on these facts, therefore, the whole idea of actually supporting the tone with the diaphragm is a major misconception on the part of musicians and without physiological basis.

Isn't it frustrating to be told something all your life, only to discover that you have been given the wrong information? And this misinformation is not limited to verbal instruction in the teaching studio. It also appears in numerous books and periodicals written by music teachers. (See Taylor, Robert Boynton, *A Study of the Concepts of Breathing as Presented in Literature Dealing with Tone Production for Orchestral Brass-Wind Instruments,* Unpublished Columbia University Ed. D. thesis, 1968.) But to clarify matters quickly, allow me to review some research by musicians done in the early 1960s at North Texas State University. The purpose of this research was to analyze diaphragmatic action of several trumpet players during the act of performance, through the use of a fluoroscope. (The fluoroscope is a machine used for examining internal structures, such as the diaphragm, through indirect use of X-rays.) According to Douglas Smith:

> All the diaphragm can do is bring air into the lungs and keep it there. Concerning the theory of keeping the diaphragm firm during exhalation, several people took turns, all trying to keep the diaphragm tensed while pictures were taken with a fluoroscope. Not one person could keep it firm . . . the diaphragm relaxed and moved upward in every case. So why mention the diaphragm at all? Basically it is an involuntary muscle over which we have minimal control.[2]

I agree! Don't mention the diaphragm in your instruction. But if the diaphragm cannot be used to support the tone, then how do we achieve good breath support? We do this through the use of numerous other muscles, primarily the abdominal and external intercostal (rib) muscles.

The Abdominal Muscles

The abdominal muscles used in breathing are those of the abdominal wall, shown in figures 9-3 and 9-4. They serve as opposing muscles (antagonist and agonist) to the diaphragm, which means that when the diaphragm is contracted they are relaxed, and vice versa. During inhalation, for example, the abdominal muscles

---

[2]Douglas Smith, "The Diaphragm: Teacher's Pedagogical Pet," *The Instrumentalist* (March 1966), 87, 88. Reprinted by permission.

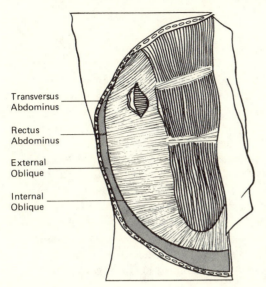

Transversus
Abdominus

Rectus
Abdominus

External
Oblique

Internal
Oblique

FIGURE 9-3 Abdominal Muscles—Vertical View
Adapted from Carl C. Francis and Alexander H. Martin, *Introduction to Human Anatomy,* 7th ed. (St. Louis: The C. V. Mosby Co., 1975), p. 114. Reprinted by permission.

are relaxed, allowing the abdominal wall to move outward, thereby providing additional space for the diaphragm's downward contraction. During exhalation, for singers and wind players, for example, the abdominal muscles contract inward. This creates pressure against the internal abdominal organs, which must move backward, downward and also upward. The upward movement results in pressure against the underside of the relaxed diaphragm, which causes it to press upward against the base of the lungs. The diaphragm thus exerts pressure indirectly during exhalation in response to abdominal muscle contraction.

So there we have it. It is the contraction of the *abdominal* muscles that provides us with breath pressure for musical tone. The diaphragm is only *indirectly* involved. Even so, the problem is mainly one of physiological semantics rather than substantive pedagogical error. Telling a student to support the tone with the abdominal muscles rather than the diaphragm will not in itself significantly aid the student in achieving better breath support. The real answer to good breath support lies elsewhere.

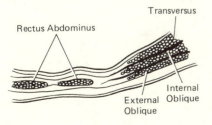

Transversus

Rectus Abdominus

Internal Oblique

External Oblique

FIGURE 9-4 Abdominal Muscles—Horizontal View
Adapted from Catherine Parker Anthony, *Textbook of Anatomy and Physiology,* 7th ed. (St. Louis: The C. V. Mosby Co., 1967), p. 146. Reprinted by permission.

The Intercostal Muscles

There are two sets of intercostal muscles: (1) the external intercostals, which assist the diaphragm during inhalation, and (2) the internal intercostals, which assist the abdominal muscles during exhalation. They, like the diaphragmatic and abdominal muscles, operate as opposing groups (agonist and antagonist). When one set is contracted, the other is relaxed, and vice versa.

There are eleven intercostal muscles on each side of the rib cage, occupying the exterior and interior space between each of the twelve ribs. This amounts to a combined total of forty-four individual muscles involved (see Figure 9-1).

These muscles fulfill an important function in breathing, by regulating the size of the rib cage. During inhalation, the external intercostals contract, causing the rib cage to expand outward, forward and downward. During exhalation, the internal intercostals do the contracting, which causes the rib cage to move in exactly the reverse directions: inward, backward and upward. Therefore, even though the diaphragm and the abdominal muscles are the primary muscles used in breathing, the intercostals are also significantly involved, and should not be ignored.

Normal Breathing Versus Forced Breathing

Breathing is a fundamental, natural process, which we all use constantly in order to stay alive. In this context we refer to it as normal breathing. But if we consider breathing as it is used in singing and wind playing, we call it forced breathing. Actually these two types of breathing are quite similar in their most basic function, as I will explain in the following discussion. Forced breathing is simply an amplification of the normal breathing process.

Normal inhalation is achieved mainly via contraction of the diaphragm and some of the lower external intercostal muscles. Forced inhalation, on the other hand, involves the use of a larger number of intercostal muscles in addition to other inspiratory muscles. This is automatically accompanied by a more extensive outward relaxation of the abdominal wall. Greater use of the intercostal and other inspiratory muscles allows the rib cage to expand more and thus increase the size of the chest cavity at the sides and the top. More extensive outward relaxation of the abdominal wall provides additional space in the abdominal cavity into which the diaphragm can descend, and thus increases the size of the chest cavity at its base. The result of all this is that the lungs are then able to accept up to three or more liters of additional air.

Normal exhalation is brought about mainly via relaxation of the diaphragm and some of the external intercostal muscles, this action exerting a natural weight or pressure on the lungs, which pushes the air out of the lungs. As such, normal exhalation is largely passive in nature and generally does not require any active participation of the expiratory muscles. Forced exhalation, on the other hand, is brought about mainly through contraction of the abdominal muscles which decreases the size of the abdominal cavity, thus causing the abdominal organs to move

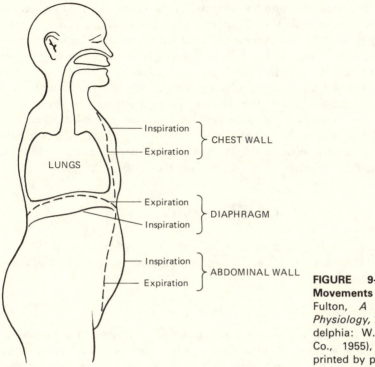

FIGURE 9-5 Breathing Movements John F. Fulton, *A Textbook of Physiology,* 17th ed. (Philadelphia: W. B. Saunders Co., 1955), p. 809. Reprinted by permission.

upward and exert pressure against the diaphragm. This forces the diaphragm higher into the chest. At the same time the internal intercostals and other expiratory muscles also are contracting, and decreasing the size of the chest cavity at the sides and top. Together these two actions result in maximal compression of the lungs (see Figure 9-5).

In Figure 9-5, note that both the chest wall and the abdominal wall move outward during inhalation and inward during exhalation.[3] The diaphragm descends during inhalation and ascends during exhalation. The degree of movement in each case depends upon the depth of breathing required or desired. In singing and wind playing, we simply breathe much more deeply than usual and expel a larger quantity of air at a faster speed than normal. Thus, forced breathing is merely an amplification of the normal breathing process.

However, this is *not* a full explanation of what happens physiologically during the process of breathing. We are still a long way from a complete understanding of this complex process, as physiologists who specialize in respiratory physiology are

---

[3]Although not illustrated in Figure 9-5, the chest wall also moves upward and forward during inhalation, and in the reverse direction during exhalation, of course. The diaphragm also moves forward as well as downward during inhalation. (For a more detailed illustration of this process, see Teal's *The Art of Saxophone Playing,* p. 32.)

among the first to admit. Breathing is a highly complex physiological function that is basically involuntary. This is certainly true of normal breathing, since we do it unconsciously most of the time, especially when we are asleep. Singing and wind playing, on the other hand, do require some degree of conscious involvement in order to initiate deeper inhalation and forced exhalation, but even here the actual physiological actions are basically involuntary. Our conscious involvement is, or at least should be, limited to focusing on the *goal* of deep breathing, not on individual muscles such as the diaphragm. As stated in Chapter Seven, physiological analysis of involuntary functions by the performer should be avoided. It only creates muscular tension and anxiety, both of which create additional performance problems. Instead we should focus on the general goal, not the details of the process.

THE ORAL CAVITY

Among the many different anatomical parts within the oral cavity, there are only four that are of direct concern to singers and wind players. These are the voice box, throat and the tongue.

The Voice Box

The voice box (larynx) is located at the base of the tongue and functions as the singer's musical instrument. Within the voice box are two vocal cords, which vibrate analogously with the brass player's lips or embouchure. Therefore, the voice box not only serves as the mechanism where vocal tone is produced; it is also the place where pitch is regulated. The term ''glottis,'' on the other hand, refers to the opening between the two vocal cords.

According to Kofler, the voice box and related muscles are controlled automatically by the breathing muscles during respiration: the slower the inhalation, the smaller the glottis; the faster the inhalation, the larger the glottis.[4] Holding one's breath, on the other hand, is made possible by automatic closing of the glottis when the breathing muscles are held firm. Once the breathing muscles relax, the glottis opens automatically, thus allowing the air to be expelled.[5]

This is in direct contradiction to what some voice teachers seem to believe, as evidenced by their written statements and teaching procedures. Such teachers suggest that the action of the voice box is not automatic, that it can and should be controlled by the performer. Recently, two brass-instrument authors have also entered this area of controversy by stating that the size of the airstream in brass playing is governed by the size of the glottis, thereby implying that the performer should somehow try to exert control over laryngeal action. Laryngeal action can be regulated by the performer, but not through direct conscious control over individual

---

[4]Leo Kofler, *The Art of Breathing as a Basis for Tone Production*, 7th rev. ed. (New York: Edgar S. Werner, 1897), p. 61.

[5]Ibid., p. 62.

muscle action. It is controlled indirectly, through the use of various vowel formations, which will be discussed in Chapter Eleven.

The Throat and the Tongue

According to Fillebrown, it is difficult to discuss tongue action without considering the throat at the same time. Physiologists support this view. The tongue and
the throat operate together, in an integrated fashion, because of their common
attachment to the hyoid bone. Because of this they are capable of only slight
movement independently of each other.[6] Here we have another example that indicates that the idea of conscious control over individual muscular function is virtually
impossible. If we add the fact that the tongue is probably the most complicated
muscle in the entire body, conscious control in this area seems still less feasible.

What has been stated regarding the voice box, the throat and the tongue
applies equally to the muscles of the embouchure. Attempts to control the tension
and function of individual muscles through direct, conscious means should generally be avoided. Indirect methods involving vowel formations and verbal imagery
are preferred, as will be discussed in Chapter Eleven.

SUMMARY

The most basic component of the tone-production mechanism for singers and wind
players is the breathing apparatus. While the lungs are the organs that contain the air
we need for performance, their function in the breathing process is essentially a
passive one. They depend almost entirely upon the action of the various breathing
muscles in order to operate. Understanding of breathing function, therefore, requires an understanding of the various muscles that activate inhalation and exhalation.

The primary muscles of inhalation are the diaphragm and the external intercostal muscles. When they contract, this creates a partial vacuum inside the lungs,
which causes external air to enter the lungs until the air pressure inside the lungs
becomes equal to the external atmospheric pressure. The primary muscles of exhalation are the abdominal and internal intercostal muscles. When they contract, the
air inside the lungs is expelled. The depth of inhalation and the pressure of the
airstream during exhalation is controlled by the number of muscles used at any
given moment. During musical performance we use a larger number of muscles
than we do during normal breathing. Breathing as used in musical performance is,
therefore, an amplification of the normal breathing process.

Despite the foregoing physiological explanation it is important to realize that
all breathing actions are basically involuntary and beyond our direct conscious
control. Even in musical performance our conscious control is limited to general

---

[6]Thomas Fillebrown, *Resonance in Singing and Speaking,* 3rd ed. (Boston: Oliver Ditson Co.,
1911), pp. 8, 9.

goals, such as depth of breathing, and does not include control of individual muscles such as the diaphragm. The same concept applies equally to direct control of the voice box, oral cavity and the embouchure. Our conscious control is limited to the use of indirect methods such as those involving various vowel formations and verbal imagery. Attempts to control physiological function of these components through conscious means should therefore be avoided.

chapter ten

principles, methods
and theories of breathing

The essence of all singing is tone, and breath is its lifegiving force.[1]
Breathing is fundamentally the most important aspect of playing *any* wind instrument.[2]

Without a doubt, breathing is vitally important to good tone production. The performer's breath has been aptly described as "fuel for the tone." Some refer to it as the "wind player's bow." It is in fact the source or generator that causes the vocal cords, brass embouchure and woodwind reeds to vibrate. Without air, obviously, there can be no vibration, and thus no sound. Also, the manner in which the performer uses breath directly affects intonation, articulation and diction, vibrato, dynamic level and intensity of the tone as well as phrasing, accents, and other aspects of musical expression. Correct breathing, therefore, is an essential requisite to good performance, since it affects practically every aspect of tone production and musical expression. On the other hand it is not necessarily the single most important aspect of singing and wind playing. Good tone production depends upon proper function of all parts of the tone production mechanism.

[1]Joyce Herman Allen, *The Technique of Modern Singing* (London: Sir Isaac Pittman and Sons, Ltd., 1935), p. 23.
[2]Arthur Hegvik, "An Interview with Anthony Gigliotti," *The Instrumentalist* (June 1970), 46. Reprinted by permission.

As stated in Chapter Nine, tone production is a very complex, highly integrated process involving various parts of the oral cavity and the vibration source (voice box, embouchure or reed) in addition to the breathing apparatus. Production of a good tone requires perfect timing and balance among all of these parts. If any single part of the mechanism fails to function properly, the timing and balance of all the others is upset. Therefore, correct breathing alone is not the answer to good tone production. At the same time we cannot deny that breathing is the primary basis for good tone production. Without good inhalation and exhalation function, good tone production is impossible. In fact, the source of most tone-production problems can be traced directly to the breathing apparatus, even when the most obvious problem symptoms appear elsewhere. This is why I am devoting a separate chapter to the subject of breathing.

This chapter is divided into three major sections. The first includes principles and methods of breathing recommended by this author. The next two are devoted to review and evaluation of selected breathing theories, the first part dealing with methods of inhalation, the second related to theories of exhalation and breath control.

PRINCIPLES AND METHODS

As stated in Chapter Nine, good breathing in singing and wind playing is essentially an amplification of the normal breathing process. It requires quicker, deeper inhalation and exhalation under pressure over a more extended period of time. The basic requisites for good breathing are: (1) to be able to move large amounts of air into the lungs during inhalation, and (2) to be able to move that same air out of the lungs properly during exhalation. Efficient movement of air, therefore, is the foundation of good breathing.

Inhalation

In order to achieve good, deep inhalation, the following criteria must be met:

1. There must be a fully open passageway (mainly an open throat and glottis) through which the air can move into the lungs without restriction.
2. The lungs must be free to expand in all directions to their fullest potential.

To open the throat and glottis, do the following:

1. Inhale using the syllable "oh."
2. Inhale through the mouth, not the nose.
3. Think of inhaling as in a yawn.
4. Think of sucking on a drinking straw.

To allow for maximal expansion of the lungs in all directions and help insure good breathing habits from the beginning, do the following:

1. Have students stand rather than sit during their lessons and in home practice, as recommended in Chapter Four.
2. Stress good, relaxed posture, as described in Chapter Four, including the use of movement as a means toward achieving it.
3. To develop kinesthetic awareness of how a deep, complete breath should feel, inhale several small breaths in rapid succession (without exhaling in between) until you can't take in any more air. You should feel maximal expansion of the rib cage as well as the abdominal area, sides and back.

Exhalation

In wind playing, the precise methods used during exhalation vary considerably, depending upon the type of instrument played and the mouthpiece and/or reed used. Even different makes and models of the same instrument will require somewhat different ratios of air volume, air speed and breath pressure, depending mainly on bore size, which affects internal resistance to the air. Add to this the differing ratios of air variables needed to perform in different registers as well as specific musical requirements of a given phrase such as dynamics and articulation, and we quickly find ourselves in a quagmire of complex performance variables. These variables will be covered in the next chapter. The following discussion, however, is limited to two general principles of breathing exhalation that we should aim for:

1. As in good inhalation, there must be a fully open passageway (mainly open throat and relaxed jaw) through which the air can move without restriction.
2. The rib cage must be free to move inward and downward while the diaphragm relaxes upward, in order to maintain a continuous flow of air from the lungs.

To keep the throat open and the jaw relaxed, do the following:

1. Exhale using the syllable "toh." If a brighter sound is desired, use a less open syllable like "to" or "tah."
2. Think of exhaling as in a yawn.
3. Think of trying to blow up a giant balloon.

To maintain a continuous flow of air from the lungs (called good breath support), do the following:

1. Stress good, relaxed posture, including the use of movement to achieve it.
2. Begin exhalation by using the natural weight of the breathing apparatus (natural recoil of the rib cage and lungs). Add abdominal pressure later, gradually, as needed. Avoid overt attempts to force the air out or hold it back. Let the breathing apparatus function as naturally as possible. Do this by focusing mainly on the musical-performance goal, not the physiological process.

3. To develop good breath control, practice crescendos and diminuendos in front of a strobe. The goal is to maintain good tone quality and consistent intonation throughout.

4. To locate the primary breath-support muscles of the abdomen from a kinesthetic standpoint, practice breath vibrato slowly as in "ha ha ha ha. . . ." Another method for locating these muscles is to simulate a series of coughs.

5. Perhaps most important, realize that the all-important prerequisite of good exhalation is good inhalation. There is no way you can produce a good tone if you do not have enough air to begin with. Good inhalation, therefore, is the first and foremost aspect of good breathing.

Nose Versus Mouth Inhalation

In meeting the criteria for good inhalation, the air should be inhaled through the mouth, not the nose. The reason for this is simply that mouth inhalation allows for much quicker intake of air. The passageways of the nose are smaller than that of the mouth. They are also filled with numerous tiny hairs, which further inhibit rapid air intake. While these tiny hairs serve an important function in filtering dust and other particles in the air, they also appreciably slow down the inhalation process.

A major concern among some wind players and teachers has to do with whether the air should be taken through the corners of the mouth or the bottom of the mouth by dropping the jaw. The argument for bottom-of-the-mouth inhalation is that it allows for the fastest inhalation. In addition, some argue that dropping the jaw during inhalation promotes a more relaxed, open throat in preparation for actual tone production. While bottom-of-the-mouth inhalation is possible and desirable for some instruments, it is impractical and therefore undesirable for others. So let us discuss each of the instruments separately.

"The flute player takes a breath by relaxing the lower jaw for a quick intake of air. This may be done with so little motion as to be hardly noticeable, and without disturbing the embouchure."[3]

The oboist, according to Colwell, should take in air through the corners of the mouth, with the center of the lips remaining on the reed, so as to not disturb the embouchure.[4] Sprenkle and Ledet, on the other hand, state: "The breath should be consciously taken in through the nose, but with the mouth open and relaxed. When a quick breath is required it should be taken through the mouth."[5]

Colwell recommends that the clarinetist breathe through the mouth corners. The bassoonist, however, can take the upper lip away from the reed while drawing a breath. Care should be taken that the lower lip and jaw retain their normal position, however, in order to maintain a stable embouchure.[6]

---

[3]Richard J. Colwell, *The Teaching of Instrumental Music,* © 1969, p. 106. Reprinted by permission of Prentice-Hall, Inc., Englewood Cliffs, N.J.

[4]Ibid., p. 107.

[5]Robert Sprenkle and David Ledet, *The Art of Oboe Playing* (© 1961 Summy-Birchard Music, Princeton, N.J. Used by Permission), p. 14.

[6]Richard J. Colwell, *The Teaching of Instrumental Music,* © 1969, p. 107. Reprinted by permission of Prentice-Hall, Inc., Englewood Cliffs, N.J.

Many saxophonists breathe similarly to clarinetists—through the corners of the mouth. An exception to this is suggested by Teal, who recommends that the jaw be dropped away from the reed, with the breath taken through the bottom of the mouth while the upper teeth remain anchored to the mouthpiece. This method, according to Teal, allows for larger, quicker intakes of air, since both the lips and throat are fully open.[7]

Trumpet players should inhale through the corners of the mouth, with the mouthpiece resting lightly against the lips. The same applies to the horn and all the other brass instruments.[8] Some brass players drop the jaw and inhale in much the same way that Teal recommends for the saxophone. However, this approach does not seem to meet the approval of most brass teachers.

In summary, most wind-instrument authorities recommend that breaths be taken through the corners of the mouth, since this allows for quicker, easier inhalation. Yet, if one has plenty of time to take a deep breath through the nose, there is no physical reason why this cannot also be done successfully. Some teachers insist that nose breathing be used by young flutists and brass players, especially when they perform in the upper range. This is so that the embouchure, once it is properly set, will not be disturbed. While use of this pedagogical crutch may have some validity in the beginning, under these particular circumstances, it probably should be discarded as soon as possible, like any other crutch.

In the case of singers, some teachers recommend inhalation through the nose rather than mouth inhalation since the latter tends to dry out the throat, which causes irritation and resultant huskiness of the voice. If such be the case, inhalation through the nose, whenever practical, has its obvious advantages. While a few vocal experts recommend nose breathing exclusively, most others recommend taking air in through both the nose and the mouth, the reason being that mouth inhalation allows for a quicker, deeper intake of air.

Vital Capacity

Every individual possesses a maximum potential for the intake of air into the lungs. This maximum potential is referred to as one's vital capacity (see Figure 10-1). During normal breathing we use only about 25 percent (one pint) of our vital capacity; this volume is called tidal air. During forced inhalation this means, theoretically, that an additional 75 percent (three pints) of air can be taken into the lungs; this is called the inspiratory reserve (also called complemental air by some physiologists). During forced exhalation this additional 75 percent of air volume is called the expiratory reserve (sometimes referred to as supplemental air).

In addition to the vital capacity, the lungs also contain residual air and minimal air, as seen in Figure 10-1, but neither of these can be inhaled or exhaled. Both

[7]Larry Teal, *The Art of Saxophone Playing* (© 1963 Summy-Birchard Music, Princeton, N.J. Used by permission.)

[8]Richard J. Colwell, *The Teaching of Instrumental Music,* © 1969, p. 108. Reprinted by permission of Prentice-Hall, Inc., Englewood Cliffs, N.J.

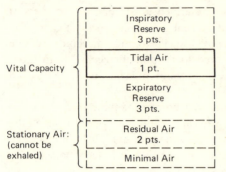

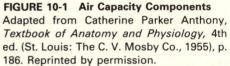

FIGURE 10-1   Air Capacity Components
Adapted from Catherine Parker Anthony, *Textbook of Anatomy and Physiology,* 4th ed. (St. Louis: The C. V. Mosby Co., 1955), p. 186. Reprinted by permission.

represent stationary air, which remains in the lungs and cannot be expelled even through maximal effort.[9] The function of residual air is to prevent the lungs from collapsing and to give them the vitality necessary for each new breath to be initiated easily and naturally, without undue effort. This, however, is in direct conflict with the written statements of some musician-authors, who advocate use of residual air by combining it with the tidal air in order to extend the length of the exhalation period. Actually, I suspect the problem is one of semantics. These authors really mean expiratory reserve, not residual air.

The vital capacity percentages and measurements cited earlier and specified in Figure 10-1 are, of course, broad generalizations. They are not absolute, since physical size and age directly affect each individual's actual vital capacity. The smaller one's physical size, the less one's vital capacity, and vice versa. The vital capacity of children and most women will therefore be proportionately less than that of large men. Teachers therefore should not expect youngsters to perform unusually long phrases in one breath, as a large adult can. On the other hand, youngsters can and should be expected to use good breath support and produce a good, full tone, albeit for a shorter period of time.

As the child grows older, vital capacity will of course increase, reaching a maximum at about age twenty. After that it begins gradually to decline. But we need to realize that the extent of one's vital capacity is not necessarily the key to good breath support. I know a professional brass low player in a major orchestra in this country who, even in his sixties, functions with only one lung, because of a respiratory problem experienced early in life. Despite his handicap, he produces excellent results. All of us have surely also known fine female instrumentalists, some of them quite small and/or young, whose breath capacity was inherently limited but who still managed to achieve good performance results. Consequently the development and use of one's total vital capacity is not in itself the answer to good breathing and breath support. Rather, it is a matter of "what you do with what you've got."

[9]Wallace O. Fenn, A. Bouhuys, and A. B. Craig, Jr., "Some Physiological Principles of Interest to Wind Instrument Players" (Unpublished paper presented during the Seminar on the Physiology of Breathing for Woodwind and Brass Instruments, Eastman School of Music, 1964), p. 1.

Increasing One's Vital Capacity

Despite the fact that physical size and age are the primary factors that determine the extent of one's vital capacity, it is possible to improve one's potential in this area through proper training. Like an athlete who is genuinely serious about improving one's skill in a given sport, the aspiring singer and wind player should be involved in a good exercise program designed to get the total body in good physical condition. The place to begin is with cardiovascular conditioning, running laps being the usual prescription. The serious athlete will also do various calesthenics for general muscular development as well as focus on exercises designed to develop specific skills. Singers and wind players should do likewise, with a particular focus on developing the breathing muscles.

Closely related to getting the body in good physical condition is the practice of good health habits as an aid toward the development of physical endurance. Since singing and wind playing require significant physical endurance, it should be obvious that good eating and sleeping habits are important for good performance.

It also seems logical that running laps is a good way to develop greater breathing capacity, especially for low brass players and others who require large quantities of air to play their instrument. Those musicians—trumpet players for example—whose instrument requires considerable breath pressure in the upper range might do well to consider doing exercises to strengthen the abdominal, chest and back muscles used to support the tone. Indeed, such exercises are often recommended by brass teachers in particular, and at least one trumpet-playing author outlines specific exercises designed for this purpose. But, as stated earlier, the extent of one's vital capacity is not necessarily the key to good breath support. Proper usage of the air available is far more important.

Regarding specific exercises to be practiced on the instrument, long tones have long been an integral part of almost every wind teacher's pedagogical repertoire, for a variety of reasons. One of these is to develop the tone-production mechanism, including the capacity for deep breathing and good breath support. Other breathing exercises designed to be practiced with the instrument are outlined next.

1. Take a breath, then play or sing a short tone. Do not exhale, but quickly take in more air and play another short note; inhale more air, and play a short note. Continue doing this until it is impossible for you to take in any more air. Then use all of the air in your lungs to play or sing as long a tone as you can at a consistent dynamic level. This kind of practice should, of course, be done in moderation, especially the first few days. Doing this too many times in succession can cause dizziness due to hyperventilation. Extension of the rib cage to this degree can also cause muscular soreness the next day.

2. Choose a scale, arpeggio or lip-slur exercise, vocalise or even a slow melody to be performed in one breath. Using a metronome, decide on a tempo at which you can comfortably play or sing the complete exercise without undue strain. Then move the metronome setting one notch slower and practice the exercise at that tempo for one week. Next week move it down one more notch, and the week after that, still another notch. This approach will help you focus on two worthy goals of good breathing: (1) taking big breaths and (2) learning how to conserve air and use it efficiently.

How Big Should Each Breath Be?

Should each breath be as deep as possible? No. One should inhale only the amount of air actually needed to perform a given musical phrase on a specific instrument. Taking a full, deep breath for a short phrase and having more than 50 percent of it left over is a waste of physical energy. It can also cause drowsiness when not enough carbon dioxide is expelled from the lungs. Secondly, the volume requirements for each wind instrument are different. The tuba, primarily because of its large-size bore, requires the most air volume. The oboe, primarily because of its small reed tip opening, requires the least. The problem faced by the oboist, therefore, is not usually one of insufficient air. Rather, the problem is how to get rid of excess unused air. Among brass instruments, the horn requires the least air volume. Air volume should not be confused with breath pressure, however. Both the oboe and horn require significant amounts of breath pressure.

Despite these variables, there are some general principles that can be applied to this area. According to Fillebrown, "It is a law of good singing that every phrase should end with the breath unexhausted."[10] Jacobs is more specific, saying that we should inhale enough air that we do not need to use the remaining one-third of our total vital capacity.[11] Compare the breath with a violin downbow. The strongest sound is most easily produced from the frog to about two-thirds of the way down. The last third of the bow toward the tip is the weakest in volume. Likewise, the "wind bow" is strongest and most easily controlled in its upper two-thirds. In the bottom third it is difficult to maintain a steady airflow. Repeated attempts to use one's total vital capacity also tend to create muscular-tension problems in various parts of the tone-production mechanism. Therefore, try to rely mainly on the upper two-thirds of the "wind bow" during performance. The real answer, in the final analysis, is to experiment and learn from playing experience.

Deciding When and Where to Breathe

The most obvious answer to the question of where to breathe is to breathe at the ends of phrases. To beginners this fact is not always obvious; consequently the teacher will need to provide appropriate verbal instructions and possibly write in breath marks in the music as well. As soon as possible, of course, beginners should be taught how to locate the ends of phrases and to write in breath marks themselves.

Normally, advanced players need not indicate breath marks at the end of each phrase; however, there still will be instances where the "right place" to breathe is not easily determined at first glance. Close examination may reveal that there is more than one acceptable place to take a breath, or there may be no logical place at

[10]Thomas Fillebrown, *Resonance in Singing and Speaking,* 3rd ed. (Boston: Oliver Ditson Co., 1911), p. 37.

[11]Based on a personal conversation with Arnold Jacobs.

all to breathe. In such cases the player will need to make decisions based upon alternatives such as the following:

1. Probably the best place to breathe in most cases is when there is a written rest in the music. On the other hand, avoid breathing during every rest if numerous written rests exist. Let actual physical and musical needs govern when you breathe in such cases.

2. If there are no written rests, breathe at the end of long tones. In other words, cheat on the length of a long tone, but do this only after having first considered the melodic and harmonic functions of the long tone in question. Indiscriminate interruption of the phrase can seriously disrupt continuity of the musical line and violate basic harmonic principles.

3. In fast passages of running eighth or sixteenth notes, there may literally be no time or place to breathe. Decide which notes are of secondary importance melodically and/or harmonically, and plan to leave out these notes. Use parentheses to indicate this and then breathe where the notes have been eliminated.

4. As a general rule, try to avoid breathing at the end of a measure, since this often interrupts the phrase at a point of strong hamonic tension leading to a cadential resolution. Instead, breathe after the first beat of the next measure.

5. Avoid breathing one or two notes before the end of a phrase. If the phrase is long and you know you probably cannot play it all in one breath, breathe during some earlier part of the phrase, preferably after a long tone.

6. Avoid breathing just before a climactic note or in the middle of a wide ascending intervallic leap. This robs the note or interval of its expressive essence. If you must breathe in the near vicinity of such an interval, decide whether taking a breath a note or two before, or a note or two afterward, would be best, keeping other musical factors in mind, of course.

The preceding six breathing alternatives are intended as compromises the player might use in solo performances. In large ensembles, where there is more than one person playing a part, staggered breathing is often recommended. To those unfamiliar with this term, it means simply that two players on the same part using the same music stand reach some kind of agreement beforehand as to how to alternate (stagger) their breathing so that neither player breathes in exactly the same place. One means for accomplishing this is to use two symbols such as a plus (+) and a small circle (○) written on the part to indicate where each player will breathe. Player number one uses the plus symbol; player number two uses the small circle. The result should be one of continuous sound with each player still being able to breathe at normal intervals.

Despite the inherent advantage of staggered breathing, care should still be taken that the suggestions given earlier for solo playing are not ignored entirely. If several players in a section breathe at the end of a measure, for example, the abnormal decrease in volume at this point will be not only noticeable but also quite undesirable musically. Staggered breathing should be done in such a way as to be imperceptible.

The major point is that deciding where to breathe is something that should be analyzed carefully. It is too important a matter to be left entirely to chance, except in those instances where the phrase outlines are very obvious. Like the string player who often must decide which bowing to use in a given passage, the wind player must decide how to deal with irregular breathing situations in performance. This is best accomplished in both instances by writing the appropriate bowing or breath mark directly into the part.

Playing Unusually Long Phrases

Even though the rate and depth of our breathing are normally determined by the physical needs of our bodies, an individual can increase or decrease both of these factors through an act of the will or programming of the brain. By hyperventilating the lungs—that is, by breathing rapidly and deeply for several seconds—the carbon-dioxide content of the blood can be decreased to below normal, which results in fewer motor impulses from the brain. If the degree of hyperventilation is brief and moderate, this form of abnormal breathing can be used to advantage by both athletes and musicians in certain situations. For example, swimmers often hyperventilate by taking several deep breaths just before diving into the water. Similarly, singers or wind players can take several deep breaths just prior to starting a long phrase, and thereby extend their ability to exhale over a longer period without the need to expel excessive carbon dioxide right away. On the other hand, if the degree of hyperventilation is excessive, "the body may become so alkaline (from lack of carbonic acid) that dizziness and tingling and eventually convulsions may result."[12] People are sometimes confused about this point, thinking the dizziness is caused by excessive oxygen intake rather than by insufficient carbon dioxide. Even though carbon dioxide is a waste product, the body needs a certain amount of it in order to maintain normal metabolic function.

This also explains what happens physiologically to beginning flutists who become dizzy during their first practice periods. Owing to the student's inability to create the necessary resistance to breath pressure with the embouchure, the breath is expelled very quickly, forcing the student to breathe more often than one should. In so doing, the carbon-dioxide content of the body is lowered to below normal, resulting in the negative effects of hyperventilation. We should realize, however, that

> there is no real possibility of developing convulsions during wind instrument playing. Overbreathing to this degree requires a great deal of voluntary effort and determination. Thus the metabolic needs of the body for breath control are taken care of automatically and the musical performer does not need to give it any particular attention.[13]

---

[12]Wallace O. Fenn, A. Bouhuys and A. B. Craig, Jr. "Some Physiological Principles of Interest to Wind Instrument Players" (Unpublished paper delivered at the 1963 Symposium on Breathing, Eastman School of Music), p. 2.

[13]Ibid.

Another form of abnormal breathing is hypoventilation, the opposite of hyperventilation. If we program the brain to stop all breathing by voluntarily holding our breath, this creates an excess of carbon dioxide in the body, which manifests itself visually by a reddening of the individual's face. This condition, as we all know, is not uncommon, especially among novice singers and wind players, who frequently run out of air toward the ends of phrases. The problem can be temporarily solved through moderate hyperventilation prior to starting a long phrase, assuming there is sufficient time beforehand to do so. Usually the source of the problem can be attributed to inefficient inhalation procedures. Lacking an adequate supply of air, the performer is obliged to expel every ounce of usable air in the lungs, beyond the point where the brain would normally have triggered a new breathing cycle to relieve the body of excess carbon dioxide. The solution lies in learning how to increase one's vital capacity so that it becomes unnecessary to use absolutely all of the air in the lungs.

Circular Breathing

A unique approach to breathing for wind players is one discussed by Kynaston and labeled "circular breathing." This type of breathing involves taking in air through the nose while simultaneously expelling air from the mouth, all without stopping the tone. Kynaston suggests that this technique can be useful to any wind performer in allowing one "to sustain extremely long phrases without breaking them in the middle or straining the last few notes. . . ."[14] He recommends that it be practiced initially as follows:

> Standing over a sink, fill your mouth with as much water as possible. Now breathe in and out through your nose and continue to do so as you expel the water in a small, slow, steady stream. Air can also be forced out of the mouth in the same way—without involving the body's breathing apparatus, thus allowing breathing in and out through the nose without any problem.[15]

Following this general explanation, Kynaston goes on to explain the procedure in several detailed steps. (For further information, read his entire article.)

Mental Imagery

As stated in Chapter Seven, a major problem with literal verbal instructions is that they often tend to confuse rather than help the student. This is especially true as regards breathing pedagogy. For this reason, the following list of imagery examples is provided as another means for communicating certain specific breathing concepts.

[14]Trent Kynaston, "Circular Breathing," *The Instrumentalist* (January 1973), 19.
[15]Ibid.

1. Imagine that you have just finished running about ten city blocks. What would your breathing be like? First of all, you would breathe through your mouth, not the nostrils, and your breathing would be very deep. You would also move large quantities of air in and out of the lungs. Your chest and abdominal areas would expand and contract much more than normal. Correct breathing in wind playing and singing is much like breathing after running or doing other strenuous physical activity. The only big difference is that the duration of the exhalation phase is much longer and under pressure. Both the chest and abdominal areas also expand simultaneously, not just the abdominal area alone, as so many teachers emphasize.

2. In wind playing and singing you should breathe in essentially the same way you do when you talk. Quick inhalation and slow exhalation are not unique to musical performance. We use both in ordinary speech, and most of us have used our breathing apparatus and voice mechanism in this manner unconsciously since we were at least three years old.

3. To achieve good breath support, think of blowing several feet past the mouthpiece.

4. To project the tone better, think of "placing" the sound in the last row of the balcony.

5. "In playing a long and forte passage think of inhaling a basketball and exhaling a rope. In playing a short and pianissimo passage, think of inhaling a tennis ball and exhaling a thread."[16] This concept not only relates to breathing and breath support. It also pertains to embouchure aperture size, as will be discussed in the next chapter.

The focus in each of the preceding examples was to use the imagination in applying the pedagogical principle of relating the known to the unknown. Being visually aware of breathing movements in the chest and abdominal areas is helpful, but most important is how it feels to move large quantities of air. Now we are talking about kinesthetic, or what some people simply refer to as muscle, memory. I remind you that kinesthetic sensitivity is an integral part of the body's built-in learning mechanism, which we discussed earlier. We don't have to learn it or acquire it; it is already there. We simply have to learn how to use it to our advantage. One of the best ways of approaching it is through psychological, not physiological, means—through the imagination.

Listed next are examples specifically intended to teach correct inhalation. The first three are taken from a list by Colwell.[17] Examples 4 through 7 are recommended by Jacobs.[18]

1. Imagine what it is like to step into a cold shower on a hot day. The result is a sudden gasp of air down deep.

2. Pretend you are taking an unmannerly slurp of soup.

3. "Inhale several short breaths in sequence. For instance, before playing a whole note, inhale on each of the four preceding counts."

4. Think of inhaling along the "bottom of the mouth."

[16]Philip Farkas, *The Art of French Horn Playing* (© 1956 Summy-Birchard Music, Princeton, N.J. Used by Permission), p. 60.

[17]Richard J. Colwell, *The Teaching of Instrumental Music,* © 1969, p. 105. Adapted by permission of Prentice-Hall, Inc., Englewood Cliffs, N.J.

[18]Based on a personal conversation with Arnold Jacobs.

5. "Suck in air past the lips."
6. "Suck in a big bubble."
7. Yawn as in "oh." The sound of friction as in "ee" should be avoided.

The following examples are designed for teaching proper exhalation. The first three are taken from Colwell.[19]

1. "Hiss in imitation of a tea-kettle."
2. "Blow up a toy balloon."
3. "Shout 'hey' in a loud voice."
4. Cough while holding your hands on your chest and abdomen.
5. Think of blowing out a match or a candle.

INHALATION THEORIES

Three basic theories of inhalation will now be discussed: upper-, middle- and lower-chest breathing; the Yoga Complete Breath and the Jacobs Complete Breath. Each theory will be evaluated on the basis of its physiological and pedagogical practicality.

Upper-, Middle- and Lower-Chest Breathing

Upper-chest breathing is also called "high breathing" by some authors and "clavicular breathing" by others, the latter name being derived from the clavicle, or collarbone. Basically it is a method of very shallow breathing similar to that used in a state of exhaustion or anger. It involves elevation of the shoulders and the collarbone accompanied by a drawing in of the abdomen. As Yogi Ramacharaka points out, upper-chest breathing is not only unhealthy but also very inefficient, since "a maximum amount of effort is used to obtain a minimum amount of breath."[20]

Middle-chest breathing is sometimes referred to as "mid breathing" and is also called "costal breathing," the latter term presumably derived from the intercostal muscles of the chest. While this breathing method is considered to be better than upper-chest breathing, it also involves some drawing in of the abdomen during inhalation and is, therefore, viewed as being inefficient physiologically.

Lower-chest breathing is known to musicians via a wide variety of terms: diaphragmatic, abdominal, deep breathing and the belly breath, to name a few.

[19]Richard J. Colwell, *The Teaching of Instrumental Music*, © 1969, p. 105. Adapted by permission of Prentice-Hall, Inc., Englewood Cliffs, N.J.

[20]Yogi Ramacharaka, *The Hindu-Yogi Science of Breath* (Bombay: D. B. Taraporevala Sons & Co., Private Ltd., © Yoga Publication Society, Jacksonville, Fla. 32211, 1960), p. 28. Reprinted by permission.

Yoga specialists refer to it simply as "low breathing." In this type of breathing, conscious emphasis is placed upon extreme expansion in the abdominal area during inhalation. The intent of this action is to allow the diaphragm to descend as low as possible, so that the lungs can accept a maximal amount of air. But does this really happen? In far too many cases it does not. In fact, it is possible for a student to expand the abdominal area outward without taking in any air at all. To prove this to yourself, do the following: holding your nostrils closed with the thumb and fore-finger and keeping your mouth closed, expand as much as you can in the abdominal area while viewing yourself in a full-length mirror. Even though you are easily able to execute the desired muscular behavior, the goal of deep inhalation is not accom-plished. Similarly, if the focus in teaching is on exterior muscle movement alone, there is no guarantee that adequate air will be drawn into the lungs. In fact I categorically recommend that such an approach to inhalation be avoided entirely.

Traditionally, however, diaphragmatic or abdominal breathing has been a popular method and continues to be so. Another approach to teaching it to students is to use the analogy of a baby breathing while lying on its back. "Note that only the abdominal area moves; the rest remains still," is a typical explanation provided by music teachers. It is true that the breathing movements of infants are largely di-aphragmatic, as explained in the following:

> In the infant the ribs are positioned nearly at right angles to the spine, and a movement of the ribs in either direction would decrease the volume of the thorax. For this reason, infantile breathing is largely abdominal. On assumption of an upright posture, the force of gravity and the rhythmic contractions of the diaphragm assist in giving the ribs the downward slant they attain in adult life. Elevation of the ribs will then increase the diameters of the chest.[21]

Based on the foregoing explanation, it is clear that abdominal breathing is not only the most efficient way for an infant to breathe; it is in fact the only way a young baby can breathe. In the case of older children and adults, however, the situation is changed, because of the downward slant of the rib cage. We are no longer able to breathe like an infant. Therefore, use of the baby-breathing analogy as a teaching technique is questionable, to say the least, and possibly even harmful. Nevertheless, some wind teachers in particular insist that the chest should not be actively involved during inhalation, claiming that its role should be a passive one, with primary attention given to full expansion in the abdominal area. Others, vocal experts especially, recommend that one concentrate equally, if not more so, upon expansion of the chest. Differing rationales are used to defend the latter approach, but one of the more popular arguments is that a "high chest" is important to good breath control. Another argument is that so-called good "chest tones" in singing depend upon a fully-expanded chest cavity in order to achieve good tonal resonance.

---

[21]John F. Fulton, *A Textbook of Physiology*, 17th ed. (Philadelphia: W. B. Saunders Co., 1955), p. 810. Reprinted by permission.

So there are two different concepts regarding the role of the chest during inhalation: in one, the chest should remain basically stationary; the other favors full, active chest expansion. Based on what respiratory physiologists tell us, however, both concepts are essentially wrong. According to Fenn, Bouhuys and Craig, forced breathing requires the participation of most, if not all, of the respiratory muscles. To inhale using the diaphragm alone without some participation of the chest and vice versa is physically impossible. Conversely, pressure exerted by the abdominal muscles during exhalation would expand the chest if the opposing chest muscles did not contract to balance the increased pressure.

> Likewise, an increase of pressure in the lung caused by collapse of the chest wall would merely depress the diaphragm unless the abdominal muscles exerted a counter-balancing pressure. The subject may think he is controlling his breathing by the diaphragm alone or the chest alone, but actually the control is much more widespread and complicated.[22]

Based upon this, we can say that good inhalation as well as exhalation require that both the chest and abdominal areas be actively involved. When one attempts to emphasize abdominal movement over chest action or vice versa, breathing efficiency is automatically reduced. In teaching, neither area alone should be stressed. Both are equally important.

Another related inhalation theory is one in which the student is told that the lungs should be filled from the bottom upward. For example, when you fill a glass with water, the water first goes to the bottom of the glass, which fills gradually to the top. This is how the lungs should be filled with air says the theory. Shallow chest inhalation is therefore wrong because it is like filling the water glass from the middle to the top while leaving the bottom half empty. While this is an interesting and seemingly logical analogy, it is also inaccurate physiologically. Fenn, Bouhuys and Craig point out that regardless of whether one attempts to use abdominal breathing or chest breathing, the air inhaled will be distributed "into *all* parts of the lungs more or less equally. Air inhaled by lowering the diaphragm does not go exclusively or mainly into the lower parts of the lung or vice versa."[23]

Therefore, an individual has no real control over how the air is distributed within the lungs; the only factor one can control directly during inhalation is the quantity of air taken in. While the water-glass analogy has perhaps served as an effective "psychological technique" for teaching deep inhalation to some students, I do not recommend it. There are better, more efficient ways to teach deep inhalation. They will be discussed in the next chapter.

---

[22]W. O. Fenn, A. Bouhuys, and A. B. Craig, Jr., "Some Physiological Principles of Interest to Wind Instrument Players" (unpublished paper presented during the Seminar on the Physiology of Breathing for Woodwind and Brass Instruments, Eastman School of Music, 1964), p. 1.

[23]Ibid., p. 1.

The Yoga Complete Breath

In essence, the Yoga Complete Breath is a combination of upper-, middle- and lower-chest breathing, each "succeeding the other rapidly in the order given, in a manner as to form one uniform, continuous, complete breath."[24] This approach to breathing is not entirely new to musicians, since it has already been discussed by several musician-authors. To insure accuracy in describing it, however, I quote directly from Ramacharaka:

> (1) Stand or sit erect. Breathing through the nostrils, inhale steadily, first filling the lower part of the lungs, which is accomplished by bringing into play the diaphragm, which descending exerts a gentle pressure on the abdominal organs, pushing forward the front walls of the abdomen. Then fill the middle part of the lungs, pushing out the lower ribs, breast-bone and chest. Then fill the higher portion of the lungs, protruding the upper chest, thus lifting the chest, including the upper six or seven pairs of ribs. In the final movement, the lower part of the abdomen will be slightly drawn in, which movement gives the lungs a support and also helps to fill the highest part of the lungs. [This process should not be viewed as three separate, distinct movements. Instead, there should be one continuous breathing action from the beginning to the end of inhalation. With practice, this type of inhalation can also be completed in about two seconds.]

> (2) Retain the breath a few seconds.

> (3) Exhale quite slowly, holding the chest in a firm position, and drawing the abdomen in a little and lifting in upward slowly as the air leaves the lungs. When the air is entirely exhaled, relax the chest and abdomen. A little practice will render this part of the exercise easy, and the movement once acquired will be afterwards performed almost automatically.[25]

Ramacharaka further states that "Yoga Complete Breathing includes all of the good points of High Breathing, Mid Breathing and Low Breathing, with the objectional features of each eliminated."[26] The entire breathing mechanism is fully utilized, including all parts of the lungs, ribs, and all of the breathing muscles. Based upon these facts it definitely appears to be superior to lower-chest or diaphragmatic breathing, since it allows for greater, more complete intake of air.

In addition to the Complete Breath, there are several other types of breathing used by Yogis. One of these is the Cleansing Breath, which reportedly is quite useful to singers and speakers after they have tired their respiratory organs through extended use. Other types include the Nerve Vitalizing Breath, Voice Breath, Retained Breath and several others. Those interested in further information on these topics are urged to read chapters X–XIII of Ramacharaka's book.

[24]Yogi Ramacharaka, *The Hindu-Yogi Science of Breath,* (Bombay: D. B. Iaraporevala Sons & Co., Private Ltd., © Yoga Publication Society, Jacksonville, Fla. 32211, 1960), p. 27. Reprinted by permission.

[25]Ibid., p. 28.

[26]Ibid., p. 31.

The Jacobs Complete Breath

To find a practicing professional musician who possesses an extensive knowledge of human physiology is rare, but fortunately we have such a person in Arnold Jacobs, an internationally recognized expert in breathing and wind-instrument pedagogy. According to Jacobs, the lower chest or diaphragmatic breath is only "half a breath." Consistent with the views of Ramacharaka and Fenn and his coauthors, you cannot achieve full lung capacity without also expanding the chest area to its maximal diameter. In view of these facts, the Yoga Complete Breath would seem to be the ideal solution, since it emphasizes using both the abdominal and chest areas. Jacobs disagrees. His main objection lies in the fact that the breathing process is initiated in the abdominal area.[27]

Let me explain why this causes a problem. All the muscles of the abdominal wall are attached to the lower ribs. When a concerted effort is made to push these muscles outward at the beginning of inhalation, this pulls downward on the lower ribs, which in turn inhibits the freedom of these ribs to move upward and outward, which is necessary in order to achieve maximal chest expansion. While it may be possible to attain maximal chest expansion later by drawing the lower part of the abdomen slightly inward, why compensate with an additional muscular movement later that seems unnecessary? Why not simply take a deep breath naturally, the way nature intended, by initiating movement in all parts of the breathing apparatus simultaneously? When this is done, both groups of breathing muscles (agonist and antagonist) are allowed to operate in a balanced, coordinated fashion providing for maximal breathing efficiency. This in turn eliminates wasted effort, which results when opposing muscles work against one another. Perhaps most important, this method allows for quicker intake of air, a major concern to all musicians.

For a better understanding of this, let us take a close look at what happens physiologically when a breath is taken in the manner advocated by Jacobs. First of all, the key factor is to expand both the rib cage and the abdominal area naturally and simultaneously. To accomplish this, the breastbone must rise gradually, accompanied by outward as well as upward movement of the rib cage, particularly in the area just above one's elbows. At the same time that the rib cage is expanding outward and upward, the abdominal muscles should be relaxing gradually outward, so that the contracting diaphragm can descend downward and thereby increase the size of the lower section of the chest cavity. In other words, rib-cage and abdominal-muscle action must be coordinated and balanced. When this goal is accomplished, the chest cavity is able to reach its maximal size with minimal use of body energy. This allows the lungs to expand to their maximum potential. The desirable end result, of course, is one of maximal inhalation with a minimum of effort.

Figure 10-2 is an illustration of how the Jacobs Complete Breath works. Note that the movement of the rib cage is compared to that of a handle on a water bucket. When the handle is raised (inhalation), it has to move outward and upward in order

---

[27]Based on a personal conversation with Arnold Jacobs.

FIGURE 10-2   Rib-cage Action

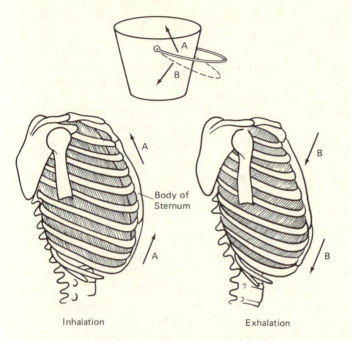

Inhalation   Exhalation

An adaptation of Plate 77 from *The Anatomy Coloring Book* by Wynn Kapit and Lawrence M. Elson. Copyright © 1977 by Wynn Kapit and Lawrence M. Elson. Reprinted by permission of Harper & Row, Publishers, Inc.

to reach the top (peak of inhalation). When the handle is lowered (exhalation), it moves outward and downward (point of rest).

THEORIES OF EXHALATION
AND BREATH CONTROL

During forced exhalation as used in singing and wind playing, there are three primary things a performer needs to be able to do:

1. Sustain a long tone or phrase with a continuous stream of air.
2. Vary air flow at will in order to perform accents, slow, short staccato, subito piano, sforzando and other nuances as well as alter the dynamic level and intensity of individual tones and phrases.
3. Regulate air volume and air pressure in accordance with the unique requirements of a given instrument and the register being used.

In discussing these functions, teachers sometimes discuss one or all of them collectively, using such terms as diaphragmatic support, breath support and breath control. Such synonymous usage is indeed unfortunate, since these terms do not really mean the same thing. To begin with, the term "diaphragmatic support" should not be used at all. As was pointed out in Chapter Nine, the diaphragm is relaxed during exhalation and thus is nonfunctional. The term "breath support," however, is a functional term but is limited mainly to the function described in item 1. Breath control, on the other hand, is the more encompassing term, and includes all three functions.

Breaking the Belt

"Breaking the belt," an exhalation theory quite popular in the first half of this century, involves conscious pushing of the abdominal area outward against the belt while performing. A major purpose of this method is to assist the brass player in particular in the production of upper-register tones. A survey of brass specialists by Bellamah in 1960 indicates, however, that this theory no longer enjoys popular support. Current general opinion of this method is reflected in a statement by one of Bellamah's respondees:

> Pushing the "gut" against the belt to ascend has caused more trumpet hernias than all other reasons combined. I have seen hundreds ruptured in this manner. I had 18 teachers and all stated that the lower extremities must be pushed out to ascend. I am sorry, but all 18 were wrong, as my life of teaching has proven.[28]

Reinhardt reinforces this by stating that breaking the belt "was wrong, is wrong, and always will be wrong!"[29] The bad effects of this method are: (1) the chest falls or contracts inward, (2) the throat area tightens when it should remain basically relaxed and (3) the lower extremities suffer from unnecessary pressure and strain, resulting in hemorrhoids, ruptures, hernias, and so on.[30] Nevertheless, Weast recommends what appears to be a modified use of breaking the belt when he describes proper exhalation as contracting the abdominal muscles "in and down, except around the waist, where the contraction is felt as a pressure pushing against the belt."[31] He admits that while many players are successful in applying pressure inward or upward at the waist, "greater compression can be secured on the Air Tube [a device used in his experiments] by forcing against the belt."[32] He does not explain how many persons were used in his experiments to reach this conclusion, nor does he indicate whether their method of exhalation, prior to the experiment, was one of inward or outward pressure against the belt.

[28]Joseph L. Bellamah, *Brass Facts: A Survey of Teaching and Playing Methods of Leading Brass Authorities* (San Antonio: Southern Music Co., 1960), p. 40. Reprinted by permission.

[29]Douglas S. Reinhardt, *The Encyclopedia of the Pivot System*, (New York: Charles Colin, 1964), p. 33. Reprinted by permission.

[30]Ibid., p. 24.

[31]Robert D. Weast, *Brass Performance: An Analytical Text* (New York: McGinnis and Marx, 1961; revised edition, 1965), p. 21. Reprinted by permission.

[32]Ibid.

Physiologically speaking, breaking the belt involves the use of isometric contraction, in which extreme tension exists but no movement takes place. The length of the muscle remains the same despite the presence of extreme tension. Isotonic muscle contraction, on the other hand, involves tension brought about by shortening the muscle between its points of attachment. Shortening of the muscle is what allows actual movement (physical action) to take place, which is the natural function of a muscle. With regard to breath regulation, isotonic contraction of the abdominal muscles is clearly preferred, since it allows the abdominal wall to move inward gradually and naturally, as nature intended. The only practical value of isometric contraction, on the other hand, appears to be that of body building. Continued use of specific isometric exercises is known to increase muscle size.

Another problem with breaking the belt is that it causes us to use a greater number of muscles than we need. When we contract more muscles than we need for a given tone-production task, excessive muscular tension automatically results, which not only wastes physical energy but also produces undesirable strain and pressure on the lower pelvic region. Instead we should allow the expiratory muscles maximal freedom to operate naturally. The related mental attitude here is to focus on the performance goal, not the process. In so doing we can help to avoid additional problems such as premature contraction of the chest cavity and excessive tension in the throat and other areas of the tone-production mechanism.

A Functional Theory of Breath Support

One of the most thorough discussions of breathing theory exists in a series of five articles by Stephen Maxym, former solo bassoonist with the Metropolitan Opera Association.[33] Although the terminology used in this discussion is essentially my own, some of the basic concepts, such as those regarding weight and pressure, were acquired through reading Maxym's articles some twenty years ago.

Good breath support depends upon two principal factors: natural weight and induced pressure. Natural weight refers to the natural force that the rib cage, diaphragm and other inspiratory muscles exert on the lungs as a result of their relaxation. The deeper the inhalation, the more natural weight there will be. (Some refer to this process as the natural recoil of the breathing apparatus.) Induced pressure, on the other hand, is the additional force that can be obtained in substantial quantity through contraction of the expiratory muscles (mainly the abdominal and internal intercostals). This muscular action has the effect of increasing weight even though it has no actual weight of its own.

The more natural weight there is, the less the amount of induced pressure needed. Excessive dependence upon induced pressure brings about excessive tension and less controlled support; therefore, the best type of breath support is one

---

[33]Stephen Maxym, "The Technique of Breathing for Wind Instruments," *Woodwind Magazine* (December 1952; January, February, March, April 1953). Reprinted by permission.

where the player can depend upon natural body weight as much as possible and on induced pressure as little as necessary. This type of breath is best achieved via the Jacobs Complete Breath method of inhalation.

Induced pressure is best achieved by allowing the abdominal muscles to contract inward, isotonically. This pushes the abdominal organs upward as well as downward, thereby exerting upward pressure on the diaphragm. Some teachers have thus determined that good breath support can be best achieved by consciously emphasizing this process. "Concentrate on pulling the abdomen in and lift the tone out" has been a common instructional directive. While this approach has some pedagogical value, at least from a psychological standpoint, care must be taken that it is not overdone. Excessive inward abdominal movement, initiated consciously, can be potentially as harmful as breaking the belt when basic rules of nature are violated. Generally speaking, the best approach remains that of focusing on the performance goal rather than on the process.

Air Suspension

During exhalation the general concern is to use one's air efficiently. A specific concern expressed by some musician-authors in this regard is that of finding a way to conserve and retain air in the lungs so that none of it is wasted. This alleged need for air conservation and retention is based on the belief that if one does not somehow consciously hold back the flow of air from the lungs, much of it will be quickly expelled, as is the case in normal exhalation. One approach designed to solve this alleged problem is that of air suspension, where the air is consciously held back (suspended) in order to insure that all of it is used efficiently.

The air suspension theory appears to be well over 100 years old. Manuel Garcia is said to have been among the first to use and recommend it. However, this belief has been seriously questioned by several of today's writers on the voice, though others continue to advocate and use it in their teaching. Interestingly, several prominent wind-instrument performer-teachers have recommended its use in wind playing in recent years. Some of their thoughts on the subject are given next.

Timm discusses the act of "holding the breath" or grasping control which he calls "suspension." "Suspension stops and sets the diaphragm and abdominal muscles so that they can control the pressure during . . . exhalation."[34] Gigliotti states that "the important thing during exhalation . . . is retention of the air as long as possible."[35] Do not think of blowing air through the instrument; think instead of singing through the instrument. To those teachers who advocate pulling the abdominal muscles inward during exhalation, Gigliotti suggests trying it both ways; he says you will definitely hear a difference. It will be quite obvious to everyone; it is not something so subtle that you must listen very carefully to be aware of it. It can be

[34]Everett L. Timm, *The Woodwinds: Performance and Instructional Techniques* (Boston: Allyn and Bacon, 1964), p. 4. Reprinted by permission.

[35]Arthur Hegvik, "An Interview with Anthony Gigliotti," *The Instrumentalist* (June, 1970), 40. Reprinted by permission.

described in many ways, but all mean the same thing—the tone will be much deeper, and it contains more of the fundamental and a wider spectrum of the overtone series. "I don't care what the equipment is—the clarinet, the mouthpiece, the reed—the results are *always* the same. You always get this same basic difference."[36]

This also applies to singers, claims Gigliotti. "You listen, you watch what they do, and it's the identical thing that takes place with a wind instrument."[37] In the same context Tosé states that breathing techniques for singers and wind players should be identical, his opinion based upon "a twenty year period of participation with the Chicago opera and the Lyric opera companies."[38]

While the air-suspension theory seems logical enough, it is by no means accepted by a majority of either singers or wind players. Stanley clearly states that the idea of a singer actually controlling the rate of expiration while singing is "fallacious."[39] Reid also refers to "the inherent fallacy of attempting to control the breath . . ."[40] Farkas is also clearly opposed to it (for brass players, at the very least), when he states that it is *wrong* to create resistance artificially by little or no pressure on the diaphragm, since this results in an uncontrolled, fluttery tone.[41] Taylor is still more adamant in his opposition to the air-suspension theory—he calls it "Opposed Muscular Action,"—as the following quote indicates: "The 'breath control' type of singer is never found in the ranks of the great artists. There is something utterly unnatural about this holding back of the breath, repugnant to every singer endowed with the right idea of forceful and dramatic delivery."[42]

Taylor uses the following explanation to justify his view: assume that the expiratory muscles must exert five units of tension while the inspiratory muscles counteract this with four units of tension. The resulting tension available is one unit. But the problem is that in order to use one unit, the performer has exerted a total of nine units, which amounts to a waste of eight units that could have been used more efficiently in other ways.[43]

I agree with Taylor and the others that the air being exhaled should not consciously be held back. Even though it may well be that artist singers and wind players do use some form of air suspension in their performance, I believe this to be largely an unconscious, involuntary function learned and achieved mainly as a result of trial-and-error practice. When attempts are made to bring this or any other

[36]Ibid., p. 50.

[37]Ibid., p. 50.

[38]Gabriel Tosé, *Artistic Clarinet: Technique and Study* (Norwalk, Cal: Highland Music Co., 1962), p. 61. Reprinted by permission.

[39]Douglas Stanley, *Singer's Manual* (Boston: Stanley Society, © 1950), Part I, p. 25.

[40]Cornelius L. Reid, *The Free Voice: A Guide to Natural Singing* (New York: Joseph Patelson Music House, Ltd., 1965), p. 162. Used by permission.

[41]Philip Farkas, *The Art of Brass Playing* (Rochester, N.Y.: Wind Music, Inc., 1962), p. 29. Reprinted by permission.

[42]David C. Taylor, *The Psychology of Singing* (New York: The Macmillan Co., 1908), p. 123.

[43]Ibid.

similar process under direct, conscious control, one negative side effect is that described above by Taylor—wasted effort and inefficiency due to opposing muscular action. An even greater problem is the excessive muscular tension itself, which is transferred to other parts of the tone-production mechanism, causing, for example, a tight, tense throat and/or pinched embouchure—unnecessary additional problems.

At this point I wish to discuss some of the arguments cited earlier by the advocates of air suspension. First of all, the example given of air escaping almost immediately once the inspiratory muscles relax is something that happens only during normal exhalation, where the glottis opens to allow free, unrestricted flow of air from the lungs. This is as it should be for normal breathing. In singing, however, the glottis (the opening between the vocal cords) decreases significantly in size in order to allow the vocal cords to vibrate, which creates a built-in resistance to the air not present in normal exhalation. In the case of wind players, breath resistance exists in the mouthpiece, reed or embouchure as well as in the instrument itself. Secondly, it is not the tensing of the diaphragm and abdominal muscles that holds in the air at the peak of inhalation, as implied by two of the authors. Rather, the involuntary closing of the glottis accomplishes this. Thirdly, as for the negative connotation accorded to the inward pulling of the abdominal muscles during exhalation: conscious thought that results in excessive inward pulling can be quite harmful because of the excessive muscular tension it can generate; but normal inward contraction of the abdominal wall is both natural and desirable, as was explained in Chapter Nine.

Concerning the broader concept of air suspension itself, it is quite obvious that the performance of slow staccato, spaced accents, and other similar nuances requires that the act of exhalation be suspended immediately. But again we should not try to exert conscious control over this physiological process. Our thoughts should be directed mainly toward the musical goal conceived within our musical ear and the attainment of that goal through regular trial-and-error practice. Through this means our body will eventually learn to use appropriate degrees of air suspension as needed, via The Natural Learning Process. For all of these reasons, I find the concept of air suspension not only a highly questionable pedagogical theory, but also one that should be avoided in order to prevent the negative side effects cited in this discussion.

Laryngeal Control

In 1855, Manuel Garcia invented the laryngoscope, a device he used to observe the action of the larynx through the open mouths of his singing pupils.[44] One of the most important things he noted was that the glottis went through various changes in size during vocal performance. Since that time the idea of training the

---

[44]Thomas Fillebrown, *Resonance in Singing and Speaking*, 3rd ed. (Boston: Oliver Ditson Co., 1911), p. 8.

larynx has become a topic of rather bitter controversy among many voice teachers. Some blame Garcia for starting it. Others, such as Fillebrown, insist that Garcia never mentioned the larynx, pharynx, glottis or any other vocal performance organ to his students. He was quite knowledgeable about all of these but used this information only to direct his own teaching.[45]

But the basic question that remains is whether one can or cannot consciously control the action of the larynx. Some vocal teachers believe that the larynx is under the direct control of the singer; others insist that the larynx is an involuntary mechanism, and that any effort made in trying to train it is not only a waste of time but can cause additional problems as well. More recently, a few wind teachers have also become concerned about laryngeal function and control. Their thoughts are discussed next.

Teal,[46] Schuller[47] and Farkas[48] all recommend that the larynx be used to control the passage of air through the windpipe. Farkas explains his theory as follows: there are four points of resistance that the horn player must contend with: (1) the horn and the mouthpiece, mainly the size of the mouthpiece bore, (2) lip aperture, (3) the base of the tongue "where the letter 'k' is formed" and (4) the larynx. Of these, the first two are basically fixed and cannot or should not be altered indiscriminately. The tongue and the larynx, on the other hand, can and should be altered in order to focus the tone properly, the more important of the two being the larynx. Somewhere between a completely closed and a completely open larynx exists the desired opening, which provides proper resistance for individual notes at given dynamic levels.[49] But since Farkas did not provide scientific evidence to support his theory, it remained for someone else to research this area. This was done in the mid-sixties, at Ohio State University, by William Carter. Let us briefly review Carter's article.[50]

Using X-ray photography, Carter analyzed several brass players and one flutist under four different playing conditions: (1) loud high note, (2) soft high note, (3) loud low note, and (4) soft low note. This resulted in the following conclusions relative to the brass players:

1. A definite variation in the glottis was noted. Glottis opening was smaller for soft tones than for loud tones.
2. There was no significant difference in glottis opening from the high to the low register.
3. Trombonists used glottis variation the most, horn players the least, with trumpet players being in the middle.

[45]Ibid., p. 9.

[46]Larry Teal, *The Art of Saxophone Playing* (© 1963 Summy-Birchard Music, Princeton, N.J. Used by Permission), p. 34.

[47]Gunther Schuller, *Horn Technique* (London: Oxford University Press, 1962), p. 22.

[48]Philip Farkas, *The Art of French Horn Playing* (© 1956 Summy-Birchard Music, Princeton, N.J. Used by Permission), p. 29.

[49]Ibid.

[50]William Carter, "The Role of the Glottis in Brass Playing," *The Instrumentalist* (December 1966), pp. 75–79. Reprinted by permission.

In the case of the flutist, the X-rays showed "the glottis to be almost completely closed under all conditions, the opening being only slightly larger for loud tones." I do not find this at all surprising, since we already know that flutists, lacking any appreciable resistance from the instrument itself, face a particular problem in easily and quickly running out of air. Maintaining a small embouchure aperture traditionally has been a solution to this problem. The foregoing appears to indicate that the glottis is also significantly involved in this task.

There seems little doubt, therefore, that glottis size does in fact vary somewhat during certain types of performance. But while all of this may be quite interesting, it still does not answer the most important question: can the performer exert any direct conscious control over the opening of the larynx? The answer is no. As with other parts of the tone-production mechanism, the larynx's basic mode of operation is involuntary, or automatic. When we focus our attention on it in a direct, conscious way, problems of muscular tension in the throat area are often created. Such problems usually manifest themselves in the production of tones that are thin, strained and otherwise deficient in quality.

In view of all this, so long as the larynx is functioning properly, why not simply leave it alone? Its basic mode of operation, like that of the heart and stomach, is involuntary. But if the larynx fails to function properly, especially in vocal performance, we cannot afford to ignore it, any more than we can ignore palpitations of the heart or painful indigestion. We have to find a way to relieve the source of its malfunction. The problem that remains, therefore, is not whether we can relieve it, but how.

Since the larynx's basic mode of operation is involuntary, some still insist that, like the eye and ear, it cannot be trained. Yet we know that all three of these, including the musical ear, *can* be trained successfully. The secret is to approach the task through indirect means. For example, if you want to make your heart beat faster and harder, you can achieve this by running or engaging in other strenuous cardiovascular activity. If you want to improve aural awareness of tone, intonation, phrasing, attacks and releases, practice in a dark room or with your eyes closed. To train the larynx, good voice teachers use exercises involving various combinations of vowels. The vowel "oh" is the least stimulating, the vowel "ee" the most stimulating. The actual movement of the larynx can be felt by placing the index finger on the Adam's apple while pronouncing the various vowel sounds. When saying "oh-ee," for example, the Adam's apple moves upward on the "ee."

Even though training the larynx through the use of vowels is appropriate for singers, does this have any relevance for wind players in the control of exhalation? Based upon Carter's research, cited earlier, we know that glottis size does in fact vary under certain performance conditions in wind playing. However, this does not necessarily mean that wind players should make any conscious efforts in this direction. Unlike the singer, whose physical instrument exists mainly in the larynx itself, the wind player's primary vibratory source is found either in the embouchure or the reed, not the larynx. Rather than concern themselves with controlling the size of the glottis, it is my opinion that wind players, like singers, should direct their attention instead toward maintaining proper tongue arch and throat opening through the use of proper vowel formations. In this way, the size and direction of the airstream can be varied as needed, before it reaches the vibrating embouchure or reed.

To conclude this discussion, the following suggestions are offered:

> Don't try to control the larynx; instead, listen to the sound of the air entering and leaving the lungs. It should sound the same during exhalation as it does during inhalation. The ideal tongue and throat position is achieved when whispering the syllable "oh."[51]

> . . . whenever sufficient breath is taken silently, it has been drawn correctly.[52]

> The proper position of the tongue will insure a proper position for the larynx. The less attention the larynx receives the better.[53]

SUMMARY
AND CONCLUSIONS

The basic prerequisites for good breathing are: (1) to move large amounts of air into the lungs during inhalation, and (2) to be able to move that same air out of the lungs properly during exhalation. The simplest way to achieve these is to inhale using the syllable "oh" and exhale using the syllable "toh." Beyond that, probably the less said about breathing procedure, the better. We should focus primarily on the performance goal, not on the physiological process, and simply allow ourselves to learn mainly via the Natural Learning Process. After all, breathing is a natural function. We shouldn't need to spend countless hours learning to do it, even in musical performance. As stated in Chapter Nine, forced breathing is simply an amplification of the normal breathing process. Specific instructions provided, if any, should be limited mainly to those involving mental imagery.

Unfortunately, musicians as a group have managed to develop a myriad of theories concerning both inhalation and exhalation control. Many of these not only fail to achieve the breathing objective desired; they create additional problems in tone production. I reviewed several of these in this chapter in order to expose them for what I consider them to really be: myths and pedagogical theories without scientific basis or validity. Learning to be a fine singer or wind player is challenging enough. As teachers, let us not be guilty of constructing additional roadblocks for our students. Let us try to make the process as simple, direct and efficient as possible. Inhale using the syllable "oh"; exhale using "toh."

---

[51]Based on a personal conversation with Arnold Jacobs.

[52]William Shakespeare, *Plain Words on Singing* (London: Putnam, 1924), p. 8.

[53]Thomas Fillebrown, *Resonance in Singing and Speaking,* 3rd ed. (Boston: Oliver Ditson Co., 1911), p. 9.

chapter eleven

regulation
of tone quality
and resonance

The primary factor influencing tone quality and resonance as well as intonation in both singing and wind-instrument playing is, of course, the breathing apparatus. Other important factors include the oral cavity, embouchure (wind players) and reeds (woodwind players), all of which will be discussed in this chapter.

THE ORAL CAVITY

The oral cavity consists of the voice box, throat and tongue. As stated in the previous two chapters, attempts to exert direct control over individual muscles in the oral cavity should be avoided. All operate automatically in an integrated fashion. But we can still train these muscles and thereby regulate the size and shape of the oral cavity through indirect means. We do this through the use of various vowels.

Performer Regulation of Oral
Cavity Size and Shape

Those who write on vocal matters generally classify the vowels used in singing into two categories: (1) fundamental vowels (sometimes also called "pure," "long" or "Latin" vowels) and (2) subordinate vowels. According to

Trusler and Ehret, "the vowels EE, AY, AH (farm), AW, OH, and $\overline{OO}$ are fundamental. All other vowels [EH, IH, Ŏ and UH] are subordinate because they are considered modifications of the fundamental sounds."[1] EH is derived from AY, for example, while IH is a modification of EE.[2] The long vowel II is generally not used, since it is considered to be a combination of AH and EE, a diphthong.

The fundamental and subordinate vowels, as just described, relate mainly to vocal diction. With regard to actual tone production, however, singers also use the vowels to regulate tone quality and resonance. One way this is accomplished is by varying the relative size of the mouth opening. Vowels that create a large mouth opening are logically labeled open vowels; those resulting in small mouth openings are called closed. Another way to regulate tone quality and resonance is to raise or lower the front, middle and back of the tongue and thereby alter the shape of the oral cavity. Vowels that cause the front (not the tip) of the tongue to be raised are called front vowels; those involving the middle and back of the tongue are called middle and back vowels respectively. "All front vowels are classified as bright, and back vowels are classified as dark."[3] For a better understanding of this entire area, see figures 11-1 and 11-2.

In Figure 11-1 notice that the front part of the tongue arches upward on EE, whereas in Figure 11-2 it is the back part of the tongue that is raised, especially on $\overline{OO}$. Both happen to be closed vowels, but $\overline{OO}$ produces a dark tone, while EE produces a bright one. Singers capitalize on this as a means of regulating resonance throughout the vocal range. As Trusler and Ehret point out, "A low pitch seeks large resonance cavities (throat, chest and mouth); a high pitch seeks small resonance cavities (head, nasal cavities)."[4] As a result of the many different tongue, lip and jaw positions possible through the use of different vowels and vowel combinations (diphthongs), the singer has at his or her disposal a built-in set of adjustable resonators. Through this means one is able to achieve the goal of mastering "evenness of resonance throughout all pitches in the vocal range."[5] (For more detailed discussions on this topic, I recommend Trusler and Ehret's volume and Vennard's *Singing: The Mechanism and Technic,* Chapter 6.)

Wind players regulate the size and shape of their oral cavity in much the same way that singers do—through the use of various vowel formations, the most common ones being "tee, tah, too or tu, and toh." Traditionally, wind players think of "tee" as producing the brightest sound, with "tah and too" aimed toward a progressively darker tone and "toh" being the darkest in quality. Some writers on wind-instrument playing understandably refer to this process as "voicing." I favor "toh," the darkest vowel, as a basic starting point for every wind instrument. I do

[1]Ivan Trusler and Walter Ehret, *Functional Lessons in Singing,* 2nd ed., © 1972, p. 84. Reprinted by permission of Prentice-Hall, Inc., Englewood Cliffs, N.J.
[2]Ibid.
[3]Ibid., pp. 24, 25.
[4]Ibid., p. 15.
[5]Ibid.

FIGURE 11-1   Front Vowels

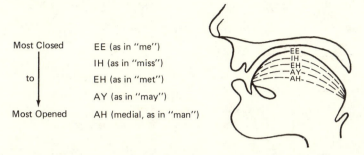

Most Closed   EE (as in "me")

                IH (as in "miss")

to   EH (as in "met")

                AY (as in "may")

Most Opened   AH (medial, as in "man")

Ivan Trusler and Walter Ehret, *Functional Lessons in Singing,* 2nd ed., © 1972, p. 84. Reprinted by permission of Prentice-Hall, Inc., Englewood Cliffs, N.J.

so because it tends to blend better with other instruments in ensemble. If you prefer a lighter, more brilliant sound, however, "too or tah" will probably be more to your liking.

To experience how the foregoing process works, do the following: place your hand immediately underneath your chin and, while alternately whispering "tee" and "toh," note the significant movement of the jaw. If you want students really to understand what you mean when you ask them to drop the jaw and open the throat, this method should get the concept across easily and quickly. In addition to being aware of jaw and throat position, ask students to listen to the sound of the air as they breathe in and out. Begin with "ee," a strong "white sound" caused by the friction and resistance of the small opening of the oral cavity. Progressing through "ah," "oo" and "oh," the sound of friction should be correspondingly less. In the "oh" position the air sound should be almost inaudible, thanks to the minimal resistance of the oral cavity.

Another function of vowels, especially in brass playing, is to assist in actual

FIGURE 11-2   Middle and Back Vowels

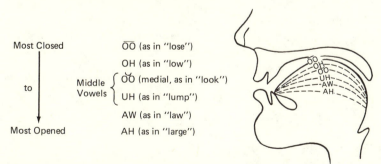

Most Closed   OO (as in "lose")

                OH (as in "low")

        Middle ⎰ OŎ (medial, as in "look")

to   Vowels ⎱ UH (as in "lump")

                AW (as in "law")

Most Opened   AH (as in "large")

Ivan Trusler and Walter Ehret, *Functional Lessons in Singing,* 2nd ed., © 1972, p. 94. Reprinted by permission of Prentice-Hall, Inc., Englewood Cliffs, N.J.

tone production in various playing ranges. Understanding this process first requires an understanding of the concepts of air volume and air speed in addition to breath pressure.

Air Volume, Air Speed and Breath Pressure

Air volume is synonymous with air quantity. Air speed, on the other hand, has to do with the velocity of the airstream. We regulate the ratio of air volume to air speed mainly by varying the size and shape of the oral cavity through the use of vowels. For example, it is possible to have maximal air volume with minimal air speed. Yawning is a perfect example of this. Conversely, it is possible to have minimal air volume and maximal air speed. Whistling is a good example in this instance. In both of these cases air volume and air speed work in opposition to each other.

It is important that we not confuse air speed with breath pressure, which is regulated mainly by the expiratory muscles. Breath pressure has to do with breath support, which influences both air volume and air speed. The greater the breath pressure (breath support), the greater the combined air-volume and air-speed ratio we have to work with. In blowing out the candles on a birthday cake, for example, we use maximal air volume and air speed along with maximal breath pressure. In this instance air volume and air speed work together as a unit supported by increased breath pressure from the lungs.

The main components that regulate the size and shape of the oral cavity and thus the ratio of air volume to air speed are the tongue and throat, which in turn control the size and shape of the glottis. The more we arch the tongue, the more closed the throat will be and the smaller the opening between the vocal cords. Thus, as with water flowing through a small water pipe, we will have created a situation where we have minimal air volume accompanied by relatively fast air speed. The more we flatten the base of the tongue, the more round and open the throat and the larger the glottis opening. This brings about increased air volume with relatively slower air speed.

Proper regulation of air volume and air speed is important to wind players in its effects on intonation, tone quality and tone production, as stated earlier. The precise ratio required between air volume and air speed depends upon the instrument played and the position of a given tone within that instrument's playing range. Ultimately this means that the ratio must be somewhat different for every note on every instrument, so that detailed scientific analysis of such a complex subject would be of no practical value. However, a review of some general factors related to this subject can be helpful.

General Factors Influencing Air-Volume–Air-Speed Ratio

There are two general factors influencing air volume and air speed in wind playing that will be discussed here: instrument-bore size and playing range. Embouchure tension and reed resistance will be discussed separately later in this chapter.

Among wind instruments the tuba requires the greatest air volume and relatively less air speed, because of its large bore size. The oboe requires the least air volume, mainly because of its small tip opening. Smaller-bore instruments like the trumpet require significantly greater air speed than the tuba and relatively less air volume. Thus bore size is a major factor that determines the general air-volume–air-speed requirements on any given instrument. But the problem with bore size does not end here. Different makes and even different models of a given instrument must be considered, since bore sizes will often be somewhat different. Obviously such variance in bore size directly affects not only the playing resistance but also the resulting quality of tone the player is able to produce.

Another important factor is playing range. The lower one plays on any given instrument, the more air volume and the less air speed will be required. Conversely, the higher one plays, the more air speed and the less air volume required. To achieve the necessary air speed in the upper register, especially in upper brass playing, increased breath pressure is also required. Consequently the goal in all cases is to achieve the proper ratio between air volume, air speed and breath pressure, depending on the specific note being played on a given instrument. An incorrect ratio will result in a poor tone at best. At worst the player may not be able to get the tone to "speak" at all.

To help achieve the proper air-volume–air-speed ratio, some brass instrument teachers recommend the use of "too" in the lowest register, "ta" in the middle register and "tee" in the upper. What happens when these vowels are used is that the tongue moves from a relatively flat position in the lowest register toward a progressively more arched position through the middle and upper registers. Altering the tongue level in this manner is accompanied by related movement in the throat, which alters the size and direction of the airstream from the lungs as it flows through the mouth. This combined action allows the player to produce notes in all registers with greater ease and without overworking the breathing apparatus and embouchure to produce the correct pitch.

While this procedure may be helpful to some advanced players, I do not recommend teaching it to the typical public-school brass player. The reason is that most of them already play with a throat that is too closed and a tongue that is arched too high. What such students need instead is instruction on how to open up and develop more efficient methods of inhalation. They should then concentrate specifically on using more air speed and breath pressure to produce the upper notes while practicing lip slurs. A helpful cue is to tell them that they are blowing air at twenty-five miles per hour, figuratively speaking. To produce the upper note, suggest that they think of blowing at fifty miles per hour. Beyond that, I might suggest that they use the pivot system, to a conservative degree. The pivot system involves raising the bell of the instrument slightly in the lower register, lowering it when playing in the upper register. This helps to redirect the airstream in such a way that it aids tone production in each of these extreme registers.

Still another use of vowel formations is found among saxophonists in the production of "high notes" (harmonics) above and beyond the traditional playing range. According to Runyon, " 'high notes' require increased air speed. Use the vowel formation 'ee' to achieve this."[6] In addition, the lower jaw should be extended slightly.

Starting and Stopping the Tone

In addition to its function of varying the size and shape of the oral cavity, the tongue in wind playing is also directly involved in starting the tone (some prefer the phrase "releasing the tone"). In fast staccato performance, the tongue is also used to end the tone. For a detailed discussion of this, see pages 146–158 in *Instrumental Music Pedagogy*.

Proper use of the tongue in starting the tone requires good coordination and timing between several related physiological functions, including body rhythm in breathing, application of breath support and embouchure preparation. In ensemble performance I recommend that players be trained to begin inhalation with the syllable "oh" at the precise moment when the conductor's preparatory beat begins its upward movement, and exhaling on the downbeat with "toh." Inhalation before the preparatory beat will result in the player's having to hold the air back until the downbeat is finally given. This usually causes excessive muscular tension in the throat and embouchure. "Oh" on the preparatory beat followed immediately by "toh" on the downbeat will go a long way toward establishing good body coordination and timing of the initial attack.

FUNCTION OF THE
EMBOUCHURE

As with other parts of the tone-production mechanism, attempts to regulate the embouchure muscles through direct conscious means should generally be avoided. Our efforts to train these muscles should be confined mainly to use of indirect methods. Again I recommend the use of vowels and syllables as a basic approach to embouchure formation. In each of the following, I also recommend that players observe themselves in a mirror while forming the embouchure.

Basic Embouchure Formation

Oboe, clarinet, trumpet and horn players should use the vowel "e" to pull the chin down and the syllable "em" to firm the upper lip. In cases where there is a tendency to pull the corners too far back, as in a smile, I recommend "oo" to bring the corners in. In addition to "ee-em-oo" I recommend that clarinetists also contract what I call the "snarling muscles" on either side of the nose. The snarling muscles are ones we use in trying to reposition eyeglasses that have slipped down below the bridge of the nose.

---

[6]Santy Runyon, "High Notes for Saxophone," *The Instrumentalist* (December, 1974), p. 56. Reprinted by permission.

For low brasses, saxophones, bassoon and low clarinets, I recommend the normal tonguing syllable "toh." For saxophones and all low reeds, the alternate syllable "voh" has proved to be more successful in some cases. Regarding the flute, the corners of the mouth should be pulled back and down, as in a sardonic smile. Then, with the lips together, blow them apart gently, as in "pooh," being careful that the mouth corners do not move inward to form a pucker. Another suggestion for flute and the brasses is to think of blowing bubbles. Again care must be taken that the corners remain firm and back and the lips do not form an extreme pucker.

Ultimately, however, the primary goal in all embouchure formation is to discover the right amount of tension needed in the muscles surrounding the lips. The lips themselves need to be firm but not overly tense. To achieve this goal, the traditional solution has been to practice long tones, lip slurs, scales and arpeggios. This solution, of course, continues to be a valid one even today.

In trying to produce notes in the upper range in brass playing, student players traditionally assume that the most important thing to do is tighten the lips. This is true up to a point, but what is needed even more is a faster stream of air. In teaching upper-range tone production I recommend that the student concentrate mainly on increased breath support, which produces increased breath pressure inside the oral cavity in order to achieve greater air speed. With increased breath pressure inside the oral cavity, the embouchure muscles will respond automatically with increased tension to prevent the cheeks from puffing out and the lips from allowing air to escape from the corners of the mouth. In this way the embouchure assumes a reactive function. The prime initiator or active component is the breathing apparatus, which is the way it should be.

This problem also applies to many novice flutists. To produce tones in their third octave, they rely mainly upon excessive embouchure tension, with a minimal use of breath support. They, like the errant brass players described earlier, need to be reminded frequently that they play *wind* instruments, not *lip* instruments!

A specific technique used by some teachers in trying to get students to use more air speed and breath pressure in the upper range is to tell them simply to blow harder. An even better technique in my opinion is a psychological one described earlier. Tell students they are blowing at twenty-five miles per hour, and to think of blowing at a speed of fifty, seventy-five or even one hundred miles per hour if necessary.

Jaw Position

A critical factor related to all wind instruments is the position of the jaw, which controls the position of the chin and ultimately the vertical positioning of the lower lip in relation to the upper lip. If the jaw is down and back, the airstream is directed downward. As the jaw is moved forward, the airstream is directed increasingly higher. Clarinetists generally play with the jaw in a forward position. Tenor saxophonists and bassoonists in particular play with the jaw far down and back. Flutists play with the jaw back in the lowest register and move it progressively forward as they ascend in the playing range. The usual recommendation for brass players is that the jaw be moved forward until the lips are even vertically. This allows the airstream to be directed straight ahead. In upper-register brass playing, some teachers recommend that the player think of "spitting a hair off the tongue" in an upward, not downward, direction. This is commonly referred to as "up-stream" embouchure. Not all brass players favor this embouchure type, however. Some prefer the "down-stream" kind, where the airstream is directed downward.

Lip Aperture

Closely related to embouchure tension is the matter of lip aperture (opening between the lips). In brass and flute playing, the greater the lip tension, the smaller the aperture. The less lip tension there is, the larger the aperture.

Lip-aperture size affects air volume and air speed to a degree. The smaller the aperture, the greater the air speed and the smaller the air volume. Conversely, the larger the aperture, the greater the air volume and the smaller the air speed. In upper-register brass playing, increased air speed and decreased air volume are needed, and thus a smaller aperture. The reverse is needed for low-register playing. Also, loud tones require a larger aperture and soft tones a smaller aperture, owing to changes in breath pressure. Ultimately every tone at every different dynamic level requires a different-size aperture.

In view of these facts it should be obvious that direct conscious control over aperture size in a performance situation is impossible. If the teacher suspects that problems in tone production are caused by improper aperture size, having the student play on the mouthpiece alone or, preferably, on a mouthpiece visualizer may help expose the problem. The ultimate solution lies, however, in prescribing the same practice assignments recommended earlier—long tones, lip slurs, scales and arpeggios. Results will thus be achieved mainly via evaluation by the musical ear combined with trial-and-error practice as it relates to The Natural Learning Process.

PRINCIPLES OF REED
FUNCTION AND
ADJUSTMENT

Reeds have long been a source of frustration for reed players and nonreed players alike. Even though the complexity of reed structure and function has been overly exaggerated in my opinion, and in some cases almost shrouded in mystery and even secrecy, the fact remains that it is an area that requires specialized knowledge and ability. In the case of double reeds in particular, the source of a great majority of performance problems is one of faulty reeds. The purpose of this discussion, there-fore, is to provide the nonreed player with general information that can be under-stood and used immediately. I will try to make the information as simple, direct and concise as possible.

What is a Good Reed?

A good reed should meet five basic performance criteria:

1. It blows freely and with good resonance.
2. It has good pitch and tonal stability.
3. It is playable at all dynamic levels (pp through ff) throughout the playing range.
4. It responds well to the attack in all registers, even when playing pianissimo.
5. It feels comfortable to the player.

No reed will meet all of these criteria without the need for at least some minor, if not major, adjustments; but some reeds can never be made to play satisfactorily. Poor-quality cane and/or poor design are the usual reasons for this. Aside from looking at the cane and avoiding that which is obviously green and therefore inadequately cured, one's only real control over cane quality it to limit one's purchases to known reputable brands or distributors, particularly in the case of double reeds. In terms of reed design, however, some basic information can be helpful.

1. All reeds should possess a good heart (center section), a thin tip and generally be tapered (thinner) at the sides. However, there are some oboists who prefer thick sides as well as a strong heart, with a kind of trough between the sides and the heart.
2. When looking at the tip head-on, double reeds should have a tip opening that looks like ⊂⊃, not ◁▷. (The latter is too open, making soft dynamics difficult if not impossible.)
3. When observed under a light, single reeds should have a conical shape. Be sure that the sides are not excessively thin. Thin sides tend to create a very bright, nasal tone, thereby making it difficult to achieve good ensemble blend within a clarinet or saxophone section.

Assuming you have good quality cane with good basic design, you are ready to make some basic adjustments.

Single-Reed Adjustments

The three most basic adjustments necessary for single reeds are:

1. The reed must be perfectly flat on the bottom. It must not be warped. We can check for this by—
    a. holding our hand over the bottom opening of the mouthpiece and sucking all of the air out through the top end. If the reed is flat, the reed will "stick" against the mouthpiece for at least two seconds before "popping" away. A warped reed will leak air around the sides and not stick to the mouthpiece.
    b. laying a wet reed against a piece of glass, turning the glass over and searching for air bubbles. Air bubbles on one or both sides indicate reed warpage. Warped reeds can be sanded with 400A silicon carbide paper to flatten them out. To prevent sanding away a tip that is already quite thin, put a piece of Scotch tape on the underside.

2. If a reed is too soft, use a reed clipper.
3. To increase the life of a good reed, gently sand both the top and bottom sides with 400A silicon carbide paper to waterproof it. Silicon carbide paper can be purchased at most hardware stores. It is commonly used for automobile body sanding prior to the application of new paint.

Double-Reed Adjustments

There are four basic adjustments necessary for double reeds.

1. Check for air leaks around the sides. We do this by covering the bottom end of reed and blowing air through the tip. If an oboe reed is leaking, use fishskin. If a bassoon reed is leaking, thin down the sides with a good, sharp reed knife.
2. If the reed blows hard, and response in soft dynamics is poor, begin by thinning down the tip on both sides with a reed knife. This is especially necessary in the case of new reeds in the process of being broken in.
3. If the reed for bassoon does not fit properly onto the bocal, ream out the butt of the reed.
4. If the tip of an oboe reed is too closed, squeeze the reed tube with pliers (top and bottom). On the bassoon, squeeze the second wire (top and bottom).

Checking for Proper Reed Resistance

In most cases, reeds will tend to be too soft. To determine whether this is so, play a crescendo on a tone of minimal resistance (a tone that uses an open fingering). If the reed closes up at the peak of the crescendo or before, it is soft and needs to be clipped at the tip. Another check for reed softness is to play an upper-register scale and listen carefully for pitch and tonal stability. Using appropriate embouchure tension, let the reed function on its own. A soft reed in this register will usually produce a ''flabby'' tone and sound flat in pitch.

After clipping a soft reed, check for response to the attack in pianissimo. The tip may now need to be thinned down somewhat to bring the reed back into proper balance. This will be particularly necessary in the case of double reeds.

Other Suggestions

In order to perform the foregoing reed adjustments you need the following equipment:

1. Oboe and Bassoon placques, clarinet and saxophone reed clippers
2. Top-quality reed knife and sharpening stone—don't skimp here!
3. Round rasp and steel punch to use as mandrels on bassoon and oboe, respectively
4. Fish or goldbeater's skin
5. 400A Silicon Carbide paper
6. Long-nose pliers
7. Reed glass for clarinet and saxophone about one-half inch wider on all sides than the size of the reed. Have some made at a store that sells plate glass.

In conclusion, I recommend the following:

1. Keep reeds in a reed case or reed holder to protect them.
2. Buy a top-quality reed knife and keep it sharp.
3. Be sure reeds are sufficiently wet before you attempt to play them or adjust them. Double reeds should be soaked in water for at least five minutes.
4. For further details on reed function and adjustment, see pages 91–97 of *Instrumental Music Pedagogy*.

CENTERING THE TONE

With regard to string playing, Kievman states that ''the first order of business in musical performance is to deliver good intonation. If a particular passage is out-of-tune, neither technique, tone, nor interpretation will have appeal for the listener.''[7] In wind playing, good intonation is equally important, of course, but the solution to intonation problems involves more than mere physical adjustment of the pitch. It requires development of a good, centered tone first, which then makes it possible to play the instrument in tune with itself. Wind players who consistently play above or below tonal center can never achieve good intonation, nor can they achieve acceptable tonal quality. Unique acoustical and design factors inherent in wind instruments preclude this possibility. Tone quality and intonation in wind playing are, therefore, inseparable. Consequently, the first order of business in wind playing is to produce a good, centered tone. Once this is achieved, the majority of one's intonation problems will disappear automatically.

A centered tone is one that represents the maximal resonance qualities of a given wind instrument. It includes the presence of those overtones, in appropriate quantity and intensity, that create a tone characteristic of that instrument. Such a tone will possess just the right amount of richness and brilliance without being harsh or dull. A centered tone is perhaps best described as one that has a good ring to it.

If you haven't realized it by now, let me point out that there is a direct relationship between oral-cavity function and tone centering. The same is equally true with regard to breath support, embouchure tension and reed resistance. The main difference between this discussion and the ones preceding it is that in directing our attention to tone centering we are focusing on a specific musical goal rather than the individual components of the process. In so doing we are able to meet the objectives of teaching-learning theory outlined in parts I and II of this text.

General Procedures

The first requisite for producing a good, centered tone is to have a good mental conception of the tone one hopes to produce. This is best achieved through listening, singing and imitation, as described in Chapter Seven. This allows us to

[7]Louis Kievman, ''Improving String Intonation,'' *The Instrumentalist* (December 1976), p. 72.

focus on the performance goal, not on control of the physiological process. The only exception lies in the area of kinesthetic sensation. Good tone centering and intonation require developing a knowledge of ''how it feels'' as well as how it sounds. In some respects I believe kinesthetic sensitivity is even more important than aural sensitivity. (See pp. 114–119 of Kohut, *Instrumental Music Pedagogy,* for further details.)

The most prevalent problem in tone production among wind players is that of playing above tonal center. The tone is thin, nasal in quality and sharp in pitch, especially in the upper register. To solve this problem begin by using the syllable ''toh'' to separate the teeth, lower the tongue, open the throat and glottis and drop the jaw. Try to feel the vibrations in the instrument itself when the tone is well-centered and resonating at its maximum potential. Beyond that, the following specific aids are recommended according to instrument family.

Specific Aids for Brass Players

1. Play the lowest open-valve or first-position tone (second partial) normally written for the particular brass instrument. Through lipping alone, begin by playing the note one-half step flat, then play it on center, then one-half step sharp. The purpose is for the player to experience through direct means how all three variations sound and feel, aurally and kinesthetically.
2. Practice buzzing specific pitches immediately afterward on the mouthpiece. The student needs to be made aware that vibration frequency of the lips should correspond with the specific pitch desired when actually playing the instrument. The instrument simply amplifies and colors the sound produced by the lips.
3. In the case of persistent above-center (pinched) playing, insert a piece of cork between the back teeth to help keep the teeth separated and the jaw down. Try to maintain as much of an ''oh'' position as possible in the oral cavity. Do this by first buzzing the mouthpiece alone, then with the entire instrument.
4. Most problems of playing below tonal center will be experienced by euphonium and tuba players. The usual source of the problem is lack of sufficient air because of poor methods of inhalation.

Specific Aids for Woodwind Players

Achieving a centered tone on the woodwinds requires the use of correct embouchure tension and being able to use it consistently through kinesthetic recall. In the case of the flute, the following notes (Example 11-1) should be played to help establish correct embouchure tension and determine proper angle of the air stream.

The goal of Example 11-1 is to get the C tonally centered (focused) and in

EXAMPLE 11-1   Flute Exercise

EXAMPLE 11-2   Oboe Exercise

tune with the A and the B. Many students play with too little lower lip covering the embouchure hole or with the jaw too far back. Appropriate adjustments through trial-and-error experimentation should be made until the tonal and intonational goal is achieved. This exercise should also be practiced during warm-up of each practice period until kinesthetic memory for correct tone centering is firmly established.

While correct embouchure tension is important for the oboe, having just the right amount of reed inside the mouth is equally important. Owing to the inherent resistance of the reed to air volume because of its small opening, many novice oboists take the easy way out by inserting far too much reed in the mouth. The result is an uncontrolled, strident tone and pitch that is very sharp on third-space C. To help solve this problem, Example 11-2 is recommended.

The goal of Example 11-2 is to get the C tonally centered and in tune with the A and the B. This will require taking a minimal amount of reed into the mouth. For the player who consistently has played with too much reed in the mouth, the change involved may seem very extreme. One will feel that there is no reed in the mouth at all. But if the tone is centered and the pitch of the C is in tune, the amount of reed in the mouth should be correct.

Good tone centering and intonation on the oboe is of course greatly dependent upon the quality of the reed, particularly with regard to its resistance, which directly affects both pitch and tonal stability. The same is equally true with regard to all of the other reed instruments. There is no way a reed player can achieve good tone quality and good intonation with a reed that lacks sufficient resistance to breath pressure and embouchure tension. Using strong enough reeds is essential; consequently, you may now wish to quickly review the related, earlier discussion on reed resistance. An additional technique for checking the strength of a double reed not mentioned earlier is to listen to the pitch of its "crow." A good oboe reed should crow a third-space C. A good bassoon reed should crow an E♭ above the bass clef.

Identifying correct embouchure tension for clarinets and saxophones is outlined in examples 11-3 and 11-4. All of the pitches listed are concert pitch to be produced on the mouthpiece alone. (For more details see pages 56–58 and 99–109 of *Instrumental Music Pedagogy*.

EXAMPLE 11-3   Clarinet Family

B♭ Sop.   E♭ Alto   B♭ Bass   E♭ Contra   B♭ Contra

**EXAMPLE 11-4   Saxophone
Family**

E♭ Alto   B♭ Tenor   E♭ Bar.

SUMMARY

To train the muscles of the oral cavity we should avoid attempts to exert direct conscious control. We should instead train the muscles through indirect means, specifically the use of various vowels. Singers use the fundamental vowels EE, AY, AH, AW, OH and $\overline{OO}$ as well as the subordinate vowels EH, IH, $\widetilde{OO}$ and UH. The purpose of these vowels from the standpoint of tone production is to achieve good tonal resonance. Wind players use the sounds tee, tah, too or tu and toh. "Tee" is considered to be the most closed and produces the brightest tone. "Toh" is the most open and produces the darkest sound. The ratio of air volume and air speed is directly affected by the vowel used. An open vowel helps create a large air volume moving at a relatively slow speed. A closed vowel helps to produce a fast air speed with minimal air volume. The higher the pitch for a wind player, the less air volume needed and the greater the air speed required. Both air volume and air speed can be increased collectively through the use of additional breath pressure. Additional breath pressure is needed mainly when performing at louder dynamic levels and in upper registers, the latter being a special need in the case of brass players.

Basic formation of the embouchure is likewise best achieved through the use of various vowel formations and syllables, with different formations and syllables for each instrument. Jaw position is also an important factor relative to tone production, but again the precise placement varies for each instrument, with the exception of the brasses, where the general rule is to move the jaw forward until the lips are even vertically. Lip aperture in brass and flute playing is also an important factor, but its size and shape is not easily controlled from a conscious standpoint. This is not normally a matter of great concern, since any problems experienced in this area are usually symptoms of problems created by improper use of the expiratory muscles. Both too little and too much breath pressure can cause the aperture to be pinched, thus creating a thin, nasal, sharp pitch.

A reed player cannot achieve good tone quality and good intonation if the reed lacks sufficient resistance to breath pressure and embouchure tension. Other factors, such as dynamic control, resonance and responsiveness to the attack in all registers, are largely dependent on reed quality. Therefore, a knowledge of basic reed function and adjustment is absolutely essential for anyone charged with the responsibility of teaching reed players.

The primary means for achieving both good tone quality and intonation on wind instruments is to focus on proper centering of the tone. A centered tone is one that represents the maximal resonance qualities of a given instrument.

The first requisite for producing a good, centered tone is· to have a good mental conception of the tone one hopes to produce. Good tone centering also requires development of kinesthetic sensitivity, which may be even more important than aural sensitivity. Specific methods for proper kinesthetic development include various techniques unique to each instrument. All of them involve what is basically unconscious adjustment and readjustment of all the parts of the tone-production mechanism in response to focusing on a specific tonal goal. Through this means performers are able to use their natural learning capacities, as nature intended.

chapter twelve

tone-production problems:
causes and solutions

The focus of this chapter will be on wind-instrument tone production problems. (An excellent related discussion of vocal tone production already exists in Trusler and Ehret's *Functional Lessons in Singing*.) First will be a brief review of the general principles of tone-production diagnosis. Then general performance problems common to most of the wind instruments will be considered. Next there will be a discussion of problems unique to individual instruments and specific instrument families. The chapter ends with a discussion about audiovisual-kinesthetic teaching aids especially recommended for remedial teaching and learning.

DIAGNOSTIC PRINCIPLES

As stated in Chapter Nine, the tone-production mechanism is highly integrated in its function, requiring delicate balance and coordination among all of its parts. This means that any change made in one part of the mechanism automatically requires compensatory changes in the rest of the mechanism in order to maintain balance and coordination within the integrated whole. In brass playing, for example, if we identify a thin, bright, sharp tone and begin by asking the student to open up extensively, as in "oh," this often results initially in the tone's going below center and the pitch's becoming flat. To compensate for the greater air volume and decreased air speed created through use of a more open throat, we now need to increase the breath pressure from the lungs. This in turn increases the loudness of the tone. As a counterbalance, we need to decrease the size of the lip aperture so as to decrease air volume and increase air speed. This brings about less tonal loudness and greater tonal intensity. Therefore, it may appear at first that the player controls pitch, tonal resonance or some other factor mainly with one component such as the embouchure, but the ultimate source of control is far more widespread and complicated than it seems. Ultimately every act we perform involves the entire body to a greater or lesser degree. Human function is a highly integrated process, which cannot realistically be divided into separate, isolated functions. The whole is more than the sum of its parts.

To illustrate the foregoing problem a bit differently, the tone-production mechanism consists of three basic elements: (1) the generator, (2) the vibration source, and (3) resonance. The performer's breath is the generator. The vocal cords serve as the vibration source for the singer, while the embouchure fills this role for the brass player, and the reed does so for the reed player. The oral and nasal cavities serve as the primary resonators for the singer, while the instrument itself is the wind player's primary resonator. The size and shape of the oral cavity are also believed to affect resonance in wind playing, at least indirectly, but this topic has not been as widely discussed in written form.

The ultimate goal in performance is to learn to coordinate all three of these basic elements so that artistic performance is possible. For example, if a brass player's generator (breath) is insufficient, this immediately puts an added burden on the other two elements, especially the vibration source (embouchure). Symptoms likely to result are a small, pinched aperture, along with excessive mouthpiece pressure, as an alternate means to "squeaking out" a sound. If the tone produced sounds dull and flat in pitch, the player may also tighten the throat and raise the jaw to bring up the pitch. It should be obvious, therefore, that proper balance between all three elements is critical. Tone production involves numerous minute adjustments of give and take, a careful balancing and timing of all parts of the mechanism.

The highly integrated operation of the tone-production mechanism, therefore, makes accurate diagnosis a real challenge. It is all too easy, for example, to blame a thin, bright, sharp tone on what appears to be an overly tense embouchure, when the real source of the problem lies with insufficient inhalation or even improper tongue arch and throat position. Like a physician, the teacher must learn to accurately diagnose and correct the source of the problem rather than merely treating the symptoms.

How can a wind or vocal teacher accomplish this when it is not possible to view the body's internal function? As explained in Chapter Eight, the main answer lies in listening to the performance results and making a logical deduction based upon diagnostic teaching experience. Since voluntary control of perceptual-motor function is impractical, corrections are usually best achieved through indirect means such as mental imagery and the use of vowel formations to help control glottis, tongue and throat position. When these approaches fail to achieve adequate results, I recommend practicing with the mouthpiece and/or reed alone. Often this allows the teacher to evaluate the operation of the breathing apparatus, oral cavity and embouchure and/or reed more easily, which permits a more accurate diagnosis of the real source of the performance problem. For brass players, use of a mouthpiece visualizer is also highly recommended.

Once a specific problem is identified through these means, I recommend that prescribed exercises also be practiced at home with the mouthpiece and/or reed alone. Continuing to practice with the entire instrument will only serve to reinforce existing bad habits. Remember that to get rid of bad habits we have to stop using the old habit and replace it with a new one. This is usually best achieved in more severe cases by changing the playing environment. Practicing with the mouthpiece and/or reed alone is one way of achieving this, to a degree. In certain cases it may be necessary to do some of one's practice *completely* away from the instrument, including the mouthpiece and reed, and focus on the use of various audiovisual-kinesthetic teaching aids, as will be discussed later in this chapter.

GENERAL PROBLEMS

Next I will discuss those problems common to either all or a large majority of the wind instruments. Through identifying similarities, making direct comparisons and otherwise relating groups of instruments to one another, I hope to make it easier for you to remember the various causes of and solutions to specific performance problems when dealing with heterogeneous technique classes and full-ensemble rehearsal situations.

The Thin, Bright, Sharp Tone

The most prevalent problem among wind players is the production of a thin, bright tone played above tonal center and sharp in pitch. With brass players the major source of this problem usually lies in lack of proper breath pressure due to inadequate inhalation. To compensate for this lack of air, the player often creates artificial resistance to breath pressure by decreasing either the size of the oral cavity (closing the throat and using a high tongue arch) and/or decreasing the size of the lip aperture (pinched embouchure). It is all too easy in such a case to diagnose either the oral cavity or the embouchure as being the primary source of the problem. Instead, the place to start is to work on inhaling a larger quantity of air, so that good breath support becomes possible. This in turn should allow the player to open up both the oral cavity and the lip aperture in response to the increased flow of air. If not, the teacher will also need to work separately on the oral cavity and/or the embouchure until proper balance among all three components is achieved.

In connection with this, I remind you that the tendency to produce a thin, pinched sound increases, the higher the range we play. Lacking adequate air speed and breath pressure in order to properly produce upper register tones, flutists and brass players in particular acquire the faulty habit of forcing the tone out through excessive closing of the lip aperture. ("Do we play *wind* instruments or *lip* instruments?") The correct solution instead is to focus primarily on increased breath pressure to meet the need for greater air speed as one ascends in the range and let embouchure tension and related aperture size largely take care of themselves. Let embouchure tension increase reactive to increased breath pressure inside the mouth, not the reverse.

In the case of reed players, however, lack of breath pressure is less likely to be the main problem. Instead, the difficulty will usually involve a soft reed. Soft reeds encourage minimal use of air, which causes the tone to fall below center and the pitch to go flat. The astute reed player with a good ear hears this and quickly learns to improve both tone and intonation somewhat by biting the reed. In the process, however, the tone thins out and the pitch goes sharp, resulting in a negative resolution to the original problem. The real solution, therefore, lies in adjusting the reed until it is of proper strength. Such a reed will provide just the right amount of resistance to breath pressure and thus make it possible to achieve both good tone and intonation.

Occasionally the source of a tight, pinched tone may be the use of excessive breath pressure. Brass players who try to break the belt while blowing, sometimes create excessive breath pressure, which the throat and the embouchure try to hold back by tensing and closing up. If not this, then the radiation of muscular tension from the isometric contraction of the expiratory muscles will cause excessive tension in the throat and embouchure. A key factor in both of these situations, therefore, is to *move* sufficient air into the lungs, as in "oh," and exhale it freely and naturally, as in "toh." Focus on the goal, not the process.

Excessive breath pressure can also be a problem for reed players, but for a different reason. If the reed is too soft, it will shut when a certain degree of breath pressure is applied. When this happens, especially to younger players, the assumption is that the reed is too hard because it is "hard to blow." In this instance the problem is that the reed is so soft that it cannot handle good, solid breath pressure. The solution, of course, is to change to a harder reed, not to a softer one.

Excessive breath pressure is seldom, if ever, a problem for the flutist. The flutist's prime concern usually is one of having enough air and learning to regulate its expulsion properly, through controlling the size of the lip aperture. If the aperture is too large, the air will, of course, escape very quickly. Therefore, a well-developed embouchure is important in creating just the right amount of resistance to breath pressure so that all of one's air is used efficiently, and not wasted. A good flute embouchure is developed, of course, mainly through judicious practice of long tones.

Having enough air is seldom a problem for the oboist. Rather, the problem is that of having too much air and trying to find ways to get rid of the excess. Therefore, oboe players and, to a lesser degree, bassoonists must learn to expel all their unused air before taking a new breath. Otherwise, muscular tension and even drowsiness, caused by excessive amounts of carbon dioxide retained in the lungs, may occur.

The Dull, Lifeless, Flat Tone

Among the brasses, euphonium and tuba players are the ones most likely to produce a dull, lifeless tone that is below center and flat in pitch. When an entire section plays this way in an ensemble, the result is what is traditionally referred to as a "muddy" sound. Since these large-bore instruments require maximal air volume, the usual source of the problem will be lack of sufficient air, owing to shallow inhalation coupled with an embouchure that is too relaxed. Students need to experience how it feels to *move* larger quantities of air with increased pressure *through* the horn. Most important always is that they have a vivid mental conception of the type of tone they should be trying to produce. This in itself will often solve most problems in this area.

A dull, lifeless tone and especially a flat pitch is also a frequent problem with beginning clarinetists and oboe players. Unlike the low conical brasses, however, the main problem lies in the use of a very soft reed. Since such a reed promotes shallow breathing and an excessively relaxed embouchure, the result is the same. The solution is to change to a harder reed. For beginning clarinetists I recommend nothing less than a number 3 strength. Saxophonists and bass clarinetists should use at least a number 2 or 2½. Anything less than these minimum levels will only retard good breathing and embouchure development, both of which are essential for good tone and pitch control.

In the case of the oboist, soft reeds are only one reason why the pitch may be very flat. Another equally important factor has to do with the small size of the reed-tip opening, which will admit only a very small quantity of air. In coping with this unique problem, student oboists often develop the bad habit of taking shallow breaths accompanied by use of minimal breath pressure. The result, of course, is a poor tone and very flat intonation, especially if the reed is also very soft. Good tone production on the oboe requires lots of good, consistent breath pressure throughout the playing range combined with a reed that is hard enough to withstand the pressure of air from the lungs. Breath pressure should be strong and constant even in pianissimo. In oboe playing, dynamics are controlled by the lips, not the breathing apparatus, through what Sprenkle and Ledet call "lip diminuendo." (For further details see page 24 in *The Art of Oboe Playing* by Robert Sprenkle and David Ledet.)

Common Breathing Errors

The most common physical source of breathing errors is poor posture. As stated in chapters Four and Eleven, poor posture upsets normal body balance, which results in excessive muscular tension. The most common symptoms of poor posture are: (1) slouching in the chair, (2) slumping forward in the chair, and (3) holding the arms tightly against the sides of the body. Less common errors, which .might easily be overlooked, are: (1) undue stretching of the neck, (2) excessive raising of the shoulders and chest and (3) pulling the chin down against the neck. All of these create excessive muscular tension and should be eliminated.

The basic solution to all of these problems is the same as that recommended in Chapter Four. Have students stand during lessons and home practice, and also have them move about while playing, to relax the larger muscles of the body. Later, when sitting, body position should be the same as when standing, from the hips upward.

Throat-Tension Problems

Shallow chest inhalation and use of excessive breath pressure are usually the main causes of throat-tension problems. If performers have too little air, they learn to tighten the throat in order to make the oral passageway smaller and thus artificially make the air supply last longer. When too much breath pressure enters the oral cavity, the throat also tightens, in order to hold some of it back. The result is isometric muscular opposition between the expiratory muscles and the throat, which is, of course, a terrible waste of muscular energy.

The most common symptom of throat tension is that of grunting or similar strained sounds emanating from the throat area. Other symptoms are a fast, uncontrolled tremolo, swollen throat muscles, weak low register, pinched upper register, sluggish tonguing and difficulty in slurring (ascending leaps in particular).[1]

A good many of the foregoing problems are sometimes directly the fault of the teacher rather than the student. Recommending reeds that are too hard or allowing brass students to use large-bore instruments before their embouchure and breathing muscles are ready can create considerable tension in the throat. The same applies to premature upper-register brass playing. Train the embouchure muscles gradually. Don't ask for too much too soon.

One of the worst kind of throat-tension problems exists when the performer inhales long before it is necessary and then locks the glottis shut while waiting to start the tone. The symptoms of this are easy to see and hear even at a distance. The student inhales and raises the shoulders, then lets the shoulders fall and the abdomen jut outward suddenly. When the tone starts, it will have an explosive beginning. To solve this, use the "oh-toh" exercise related to the conductor's preparatory and downbeat, which was discussed in Chapter Eight.

For severe problems, a remedial technique for relaxing the throat as well as the jaw is to prescribe slow practice of jaw vibrato. This approach is recommended mainly for those instruments that commonly use the jaw type of vibrato: the brasses and single reeds. Another method utilizing the concept of mental imagery is one recommended by Spencer: Think of exhaling warm air onto a pair of eyeglasses for cleaning.[2]

---

[1]William Spencer, *The Art of Bassoon Playing* (© 1958 Summy-Birchard Music, Princeton, N.J. Used by Permission), p. 46.

[2]Ibid., p. 47.

Embouchure Problems

Probably the most common embouchure problem among brass players and flutists is excessive embouchure tension. Among reed players, however, this problem manifests itself in the form of biting the reed. Basic diagnosis is the same for both woodwinds and brasses: have the student play for you on the mouthpiece and/or reed alone. If the pitch produced is consistently above the pitch desired, the embouchure is too tight. Practice daily on the mouthpiece alone until the desired pitch can be produced easily and naturally, at will.

Probably the most common cause of excessive embouchure tension among brass players and flutists is lack of sufficient breath pressure. Another common cause among brass players is physical fatigue, particularly the type caused by excessive high-register playing. Usual symptoms in this instance are a pinched aperture, upper-lip numbness due to excessive mouthpiece pressure, excessive curling of the lower lip and "clenched teeth" (jaw raised too high) accompanied by a tense throat. The solution is obvious. Avoid playing beyond the point of fatigue, and limit performance time in the upper register in relation to the degree of one's embouchure development.

Among reed players, the main cause of biting is the use of a reed that is too soft. With such a reed that is lacking both pitch and tonal stability, players soon discover they can raise the pitch and focus the tone somewhat better by biting. In so doing, however, the pitch is usually raised too high and the tone thins out. The preferred solution is to increase reed strength gradually, until reed resistance is compatible with good breath pressure and proper embouchure tension. A proper-strength reed will provide good pitch and tonal stability without any need for biting.

Tonguing Problems

Probably the most frequent tonguing problem is that of a heavy tongue, which causes an explosive attack. One cause of this may be premature inhalation, as discussed earlier. Another cause is using too large a surface of the tongue; here the solution is to use a lighter syllable like "doh" instead of "toh" or at worst "thoh." In the case of severe tonguing problems deeply engrained through hours of practice and performance, the only solution may be to stop using the tongue entirely for an extended period, as long as two or three months in some instances. The idea behind this approach is to apply the remedial teaching principle of going from one extreme to the other, as discussed in Chapter Eight. By discarding the old habit through lack of use, a new one can be learned later to replace it.

On reed instruments, a specific method for eliminating a heavy tongue is to use the "hiss-sound" approach as a remedial technique. (For specific details read pages 149–154 in *Instrumental Music Pedagogy.*)

Some problems in tonguing are really problems of articulation, which involve various combinations of slurred and tongued notes. Such problems can best be worked out by first working with the mouthpiece and/or reed alone. Next, using a single pitch for all notes, play the articulations on the instrument. Then play the passage as written.

SPECIFIC PROBLEMS

A unique characteristic of reed instruments is the variety and richness of their tonal color, particularly in ensemble performance. In the hands of good performers this characteristic can be a great asset, but in the hands of novices it can be a real liability. Tone is frequently thin, nasal, above center and sharp in pitch, with minimal dynamic range. The major problem is usually that of a soft reed. Beyond that, tone-production problems on reed instruments may be due to one or more of the following:

Oboe

1. Strident, wild tone, sharp in pitch caused by too much reed in the mouth. Use A, B, C exercise (see Example 11-2) to determine proper reed placement.
2. Tone is still strident, perhaps even "honky." Reed tip is too open. Gently pinch the blades together at the tip and hold together for several seconds to decrease size of opening.
3. Reed responds poorly except when played at a loud dynamic level. Reed is too hard and should be thinned at the tip, also on the sides if necessary.
4. Tone is very thin and bright, and volume is minimal. Tip opening is too small. First check to see if inside of reed is dirty. Clean with a pipe cleaner as needed. If tip opening is still too small (smaller than one millimeter), it can be increased by gently squeezing the *center* of the winding (top and bottom) with long-nose pliers. (Squeezing the *sides* in the center of the winding, on the other hand, will decrease tip-opening size.)
5. Tone lacks center, and the pitch (particularly in upper register) is flat. Caused by soft reed (insufficient heart). Buy harder-strength reeds or find a new and better reed source. Sometimes cutting off the reed tip and reworking the tip will improve the reed. More often, however, the resultant improvement will be so small that is not really worth the time and effort.
6. Tone sounds thin, pinched and sharp, in upper register in particular. Caused by biting, usually encouraged by soft reeds that sound flat and produce a "wild" tone as described in number 5. Solution is to use stronger reeds, less smile and more pucker, as in "oh" in the embouchure. Practice trying to produce a third-space C on the reed alone to develop proper physical feel for correct embouchure tension and correct voicing of the oral cavity.

Bassoon

*1. Tone is honky and response is poor, especially in the upper register. Tip is too open. Squeeze sides of the second (middle) wire with long-nose pliers.

*2. Tone is very thin and bright, plays with minimal volume, and response is poor, especially in the bottom register. Tip opening is too small. Squeeze top and bottom of second wire.

---

*Tip opening can also be varied by adjusting the first wire. However, the assumption here is that the first wire is already properly adjusted (in an egg shape) for optimum tone color and intonation level. Thus it should normally be left alone, with primary adjustment confined to the second wire. If the first wire is not properly adjusted, squeezing the sides will make the tone darker, and higher in pitch. Squeezing the top and bottom of the first wire will make the tone brighter and the pitch flatter.

3. Tone lacks focus, and the pitch of E♮ and E♭ in the staff in particular is quite flat. Reed is too soft. Use a harder reed.

4. Reed responds poorly in general except when played at a loud dynamic level. Reed is too hard and should be thinned at the tip, also on the sides if necessary.

5. Tone sounds thin and sharp, particularly in the upper register. Player is biting, usually encouraged by soft reeds. Use a stronger reed, think ''voh'' to drop the jaw, and practice trying to produce an E♭ above the staff on the reed alone.

Clarinet

1. Unfocused, flabby tone and flat pitch. Reed is too soft. Clip with reed clipper if very soft. Sand tip with 400A silicon carbide paper if it feels only slightly soft for the player.

2. Tone lacks center, and the pitch, particularly in the upper clarion register, is flat. Reed is too soft. Adjust as in number 1.

3. Tone sounds thin, pinched and sharp in upper registers. Caused by biting, usually encouraged by soft reeds, which sound flat and produce a wild tone as described in number 2. Use stronger reeds, less smile and more pucker, as in ''oh,'' in the embouchure. Practice trying to produce a Concert C above the staff with the mouthpiece alone, to develop proper kinesthetic feel for correct embouchure tension and voicing of the oral cavity.

4. Tone is generally thin and stuffy. Clarinet may be held too far away from the body, causing too much lip tissue to cover the reed. Bring clarinet toward the body, so that first ligature screw *almost* touches the chin.

5. Reed sounds airy and harsh. First check for reed warpage by giving the reed and mouthpiece the suction test. Sand bottom of the reed with silicon carbide paper if it is in fact warped. If this doesn't solve the problem, the top side of the reed needs scraping. Unless you are already knowledgeable about such aspects of reed adjustment, you would do better by simply changing to a softer reed and adjusting it as needed.

6. Heavy tongue. Use hiss-sound exercise to eliminate excessive tongue pressure.

Saxophone

1. Tight, pinched tone and excessive sharpness in pitch, especially in the upper range. Player is biting. Try to produce A above the staff with the mouthpiece alone.

2. If the foregoing procedure does not break the biting habit, push the mouthpiece onto the neckpipe as far as it will go and force the player to open up and lip down to extreme. Introducing jaw vibrato can also help unlock the jaw.

3. Stuffy, airy tone. Reed is too hard. Use a number 2 to 2½ strength reed.

4. Unfocused, flabby tone and flat pitch, especially in upper range. Reed is too soft. Use reed clipper or silicon carbide paper as described under Clarinet, number 1.

5. Heavy tongue. Work on hiss-sound exercise.

Flute

The most common problem experienced by flute beginners is that of a tone that is excessively windy, lacks tonal focus and has little carrying power. This is usually the result of a lip aperture that is too large, which is the direct result of a weak, undeveloped embouchure. There is no simple, immediate solution to this problem. It requires continued practice of long tones over a period of several weeks or even months, until the embouchure muscles are strong enough to control aperture size at will throughout an extended playing period.

1. Another cause of windy tone is improper covering of the embouchure hole by the lower lip and improper placement of the embouchure plate in relation to the lower lip. The embouchure plate should hug the lower lip from below, not crush down on the lip from above. One-fourth to one-third of the embouchure hole should be covered by the lower lip. Use the A, B, C exercise (Example 11-1) to check for a centered, resonant tone and thereby insure correct lip placement and alignment.

2. Player cannot sustain a long tone in the second octave; pitch keeps dropping to the octave below. Jaw is too far back, thus causing the airstream to be directed too far down into the embouchure hole rather than horizontally across it. Move jaw forward for upper octave as a temporary solution. Practice harmonics through at least the sixth partial for a more long-term solution.

3. Another solution to the foregoing problem for the young player is to practice ascending octave slurs slowly, with primary emphasis on increased breath support for the top note, as in "tah hah." Contract the abdominal muscles inward quickly as you aim for the upper octave. "Lift the tone out." This inward abdominal action should be clearly visible several feet away.

4. Bright, strident tone, sharp pitch in the upper register. This is usually caused by a pinched embouchure coupled with a lack of adequate breath support. Use more air and relax the embouchure. Think of producing the tone with the breath, not the lips. "Wind instrument, not lip instrument!"

5. Dull, unfocused tone and flat pitch in lower register. Aperture is too large and airstream is not concentrated. Firm the upper lip and think of blowing downward into the embouchure hole.

6. Pitch at the ends of phrases goes quite flat. Requires good breath support coupled with slight lifting of player's head to prevent instrument from going flat in pianissimo, as it naturally wants to do. In extreme cases, breath pressure can be maintained above a normal pianissimo level while the right hand gradually pushes the foot of the flute away from the body. As a result of the latter, air is directed toward the inside corner of the embouchure hole, which gradually decreases tonal volume without causing the pitch to go flat.

Brass-Instrument Problems

Problems common to all of the brasses are outlined next:

1. Related to jaw position is what brass players often refer to as clenched teeth. This simply means that the jaw is too high, causing the oral cavity to be too closed. To drop the jaw, think "toh," or even "voh." For students who have extreme difficulty in this area I recommend placing a piece of cork (of the proper thickness for the instrument concerned) between the back teeth and having the student play while the cork is in place.

2. Excessive mouthpiece pressure causes embouchure fatigue. It is also a "cheap" way to produce high notes, but this only creates more endurance problems. The white ring remaining on the lips just after the mouthpiece is first taken away is the telltale sign of excessive mouthpiece pressure.

3. In order to play in the upper range, there needs to be a slight decrease in the size of the oral cavity, which is inevitably accompanied by some upward movement of the jaw. The tendency is, of course, to overdo this process, sometimes to the point where the lower lip curls in under the upper lip. To check for this problem use a mouthpiece visualizer. If the lower lip is in fact curling in, push the jaw forward until both lips are even.

Special Problems on the Horn

The typical student horn player's tone sounds very bright, above center and quite sharp in pitch. Solve by:

1. Checking right-hand position in the bell and adjusting as needed to properly darken the sound.
2. If tone is still bright and pitch is noticeably sharp, have player open the throat, as in "toh."
3. Once the tone is sufficiently dark and tone is centered, then use second-line G for tuning the main tuning slide on the F side of the horn. Use first space open F for tuning the B♭ side of the horn.
4. With the aid of a strobe, adjust valve slides on both sides of the horn.
5. Go back and recheck all of the valve slides by playing second-line G♯ through third-space C. (The fingerings for these notes are exactly the same on both sides of the horn.) Alternate by playing G♯ on the F side, then on the B♭ side. Next play A on the F side, then on the B♭ side, and so on, through third-space C. Pitches should be the same on both sides of the horn. If they are not, adjust slides accordingly until they are.

AUDIOVISUAL-KINESTHETIC
TEACHING AIDS

All of the teaching aids to be discussed next represent forms of augmented feedback. They are especially designed to aid the player faced with problems in remedial learning. However, they can also be used in developmental training where deemed appropriate. Each is intended to focus on a specific isolated technique related to tone production.

Plastic Pipe

For students experiencing severe problems in opening the oral cavity both during inhalation and while playing, probably the most helpful aid is a plastic pipe about one inch in diameter and six inches long, which can be purchased at a hardware store. The student simply inserts the pipe between the teeth, breathes in and out through the pipe and focuses in on two aspects of kinesthetic sensation: (1) how it feels to move large quantities of air in and out of the lungs, and (2) how it feels to have the oral cavity relaxed and open and the teeth far apart. Then try to inhale and exhale in the same way without use of the pipe. Finally, do this while playing a tone on the instrument.

Plastic Bag

For students who do not seem to be able to inhale reasonably large quantities of air for whatever reason, I recommend use of a plastic bag with a capacity of about five liters, which can be purchased in a grocery store. If a regular plastic bag is not readily available, even a large bread bag will do. Then follow this procedure:

1. Blow air into the bag until it is completely full. Use two breaths, more if needed.
2. Then try to inhale all of the air from the bag with a single inhalation. By watching the bag you will actually *see* how much air you are inhaling. Try to remember how it feels to inhale this much air.
3. Then exhale all the air back into the bag while watching the bag and tuning in to related kinesthetic sensations.
4. Finally, try to duplicate these steps without using the bag. Focus on kinesthetic sensation.

In using both the plastic pipe and plastic bag, care must be taken not to hyperventilate or hypoventilate. One minute's practice at any one time should be the maximum.

Party Favor

Either at a birthday or New Year's Eve party, each of us has surely seen (and probably used) the kind of party favor that uncurls straight out when you blow into it and curls back up once you stop blowing into it. So long as breath pressure remains constant, the favor remains uncurled. Once breath pressure is decreased, the favor begins gradually to curl back up. This device, therefore, can be used to help the student experience the feeling of increased abdominal support for the air as the air in the lungs is used up.

In order for this to be functional, you need to get the largest-size party favor available and then poke a small hole in the end so that some of the air can escape and thus approximate the feeling of air going into an instrument.

Other Possibilities

All of us are familiar with the use of video and sound-tape recording as effective tools for evaluation *after* performance. Not so common is the use of these tools for evaluation *during* performance. In the case of video taping, there is no reason why a monitor couldn't be easily set up to make this possible. I would suspect that seeing oneself during the act of performance should be especially helpful to string players as well as conducting and vocal students concerned with dramatic visual effect. They could make appropriate changes immediately, rather than waiting until after seeing their tape.

Receiving instantaneous aural feedback presents something of a problem, as it would require the use of earphones to monitor one's performance. This would prevent use of normal aural feedback, since the ears are occupied with hearing the recorded version. This might create some miscues between kinesthetic sensation related to the live versus recorded versions, especially if the quality of the recorded version were to be tonally inferior. Still, these problems surely could be worked out—if in fact they are potentially troublesome.

Use of both video and sound recording as described here could result in another major step toward self-instruction. This would further limit the role of the teacher to serving primarily as a superior performance model and as a motivator. In my opinion, this would be a positive step forward in both teaching and learning.

epilogue

In preparing this text I have tried to cover the subject as thoroughly and comprehensively as I could and at the same time make the discussions as practical as possible. In order to be thorough, I considered it essential to devote significant time and space to the behavioral and biological sciences. Some readers may still question the practicality of doing this. The basic reason is the same as that cited in the introduction; real human knowledge cannot be divided up effectively into separate, discrete disciplines and still be accurately understood. Also, I believe one cannot really understand the rudiments of a subject without also having some knowledge of its complexity; that is, too little knowledge can be dangerous. Yet some readers may still wonder why the scope of this particular text wasn't limited strictly to musical performance and pedagogy. Why not have the teacher in training simply enroll in physiology and psychology courses in order to obtain a basic background in these disciplines?

In theory this seems like a most logical course of action. In practice, however, this approach seldom works. First of all, one is rarely able to cover the field of human physiology in a one-semester course. Usually one must take at least two life science courses, and much of the material covered is irrelevant to the immediate practical needs and interests of the typical musical performer and teacher in training. The topic of breathing, for example, is often not covered until the second semester, and even then the primary focus is usually on normal breathing, not forced breathing. The same general pattern usually exists in the area of psychology. One usually takes a general introductory course in psychology, followed by one course in educational psychology. In educational psychology, primary emphasis is traditionally placed on Western concepts of learning and cognitive learning theory. Perceptual-motor learning receives comparatively less attention, and Eastern psychology is still generally ignored. Thus, one has to decide whether the process is really worth all of the time and effort expended by the student. In the majority of cases, I do not believe that it is.

But even if it were possible to take courses in physiology and psychology that were designed specifically with the musician in mind, one must face the even bigger problem of bridging the gap between psychophysiological theory and actual practice. Traditionally, educators appear to assume that students are able to take isolated information from several discrete courses in their required curriculum and combine it at some point into a coherent, unified whole, thus making it functional and applicable to real-life situations. Unfortunately, this doesn't happen very often. The pieces are never put together; they remain separate and isolated because they are not related to specific practical situations, nor are they applied to actual performing experience. Like leaves on a tree that die in autumn and fall to the ground, these isolated bits of knowledge are soon forgotten because they were never clearly understood or applied in direct, concrete ways.

Therefore, it is my strong hope that this text will fill a unique need by serving as a comprehensive treatise that includes the broad as well as the specific aspects of the subject. I have tried to relate general psychological and physiological principles to specific performance situations where possible. Applying these principles to actual performance experience, however, is something that must necessarily be left up to the reader and/or the instructor in charge of teaching the students who use this text.

In writing a general text of this type I recognize that I take a special risk—that of being criticized for delving into nonmusical disciplines, in which I am not a specialist. There are some who believe that specialized subjects should be dealt with only by specialists in those fields, claiming that others should leave such subjects alone because their knowledge is superficial and incomplete. While this may sometimes be the case, there is still a great need for generalists who can help us all to maintain a realistic perspective on the "big picture" as it relates to human knowledge in general. Even more importantly, we need generalists who can get past the rigid rules and structural confinements of individual disciplines and help us find alternate solutions to some of our most basic problems. Too often we find specialists who are so locked in to the dogma of their respective disciplines that they cannot break out and see possibilities beyond it. In this connection a quote from Maltz seems particularly appropriate:

> Any breakthrough in science is likely to come from outside the system . . . Pasteur was not an M.D. The Wright brothers were not aeronautical engineers but bicycle mechanics. Einstein, properly speaking, was not a physicist but a mathematician. Yet

his findings in mathematics completely turned upside down all the pet theories in physics. Madame Curie was not an M.D. but a physicist, yet she made important contributions to medical science.[1]

I might also add that Maltz was not a trained psychologist but a plastic surgeon. Yet he wrote one of the best, most practical books on human psychology that we have today, particularly as it relates to the development of positive self-image. Thus the need for generalists who are able to think creatively continues and probably always will. A primary goal of education, therefore, should be to develop generalists of this type. How is this to be done? Suzuki provides us with a good clue when he quotes Albert Einstein: "It [the optics of motion] occurred to me by intuition. And music is the driving force behind this intuition. My parents had me study the violin from the time I was six. My new discovery is the result of musical perception."[2]

When I first read these lines, some ten years ago, I was immediately struck by the idea that herein lies possibly one of the best arguments for inclusion of music in the schools. If a creative scientist with the stature of Einstein believes so strongly in the value of musical training, who can deny its rightful place as an integral part of general education? Over the years I have discussed this concept with several non-music professionals, all of whom studied music seriously as youngsters and some of whom considered majoring in music at one time. The general consensus is that Einstein was correct. The freedom of expression experienced through musical performance can help one maintain a more open, free-thinking mind, which includes the faculty of intuition as a key element in the creative-thinking process. While it would be inappropriate to use my informal survey of a very limited population as sufficient to establish my theory as fact, I do believe it is worthy of a formal research study.

In this text I do not pretend to have arrived at the final answer on how to teach performance skills to music students or anyone else. Many questions remain to be answered; new, more specific and accurate information in the future will no doubt replace current theories and beliefs. On the other hand, I hope that this treatise represents a worthy starting point from which others may launch further study and research. As music educators, I'm sure we share the same basic goal—to search for improved methods of instruction that will make it possible for a greater number of students to experience the thrills of musical performance more quickly and in greater depth. If this text helps our profession to better meet this goal even to a limited degree, I will feel amply rewarded for the time and effort expended in writing it.

---

[1]From the book, *Psycho-Cybernetics* by Maxwell Maltz © 1960 by Prentice-Hall, Inc. Published by Prentice-Hall, Inc., Englewood Cliffs, N.J. 07632.

[2]*Nurtured by Love* © 1969 by Shinichi Suzuki. Reprinted by permission of Exposition Press, Smithtown, N.Y., p. 90.

REFERENCES

ANATOMY
AND PHYSIOLOGY

ANTHONY, CATHERINE PARKER, and NORMA JANE KOLTHOFF, *Textbook of Anatomy and Physiology* (8th ed.), pp. 46, 47, 113–163, 362–388. St. Louis: The C.V. Mosby Company, 1971.

CRITCHLEY, MACDONALD, and R. A. HENSON, eds., *Music and the Brain: Studies in the Neurology of Music*, Chapter 5. Springfield, Ill.: Charles C. Thomas, 1977.

ECCLES, JOHN C., *The Understanding of the Brain*. New York: McGraw-Hill Book Co., 1973.

EVANS, WILLIAM F., *Anatomy and Physiology: The Basic Principles*, pp. 153–158; Chapter 10. Englewood Cliffs, N.J.: Prentice-Hall, Inc., 1971.

EYZAGUIRRE, CARLOS, and SALVATORE J. FIDONE, *Physiology of the Nervous System* (2nd ed.). Chicago: Year Book Medical Publishers, 1975.

FULTON, JOHN F., ed., *A Textbook of Physiology* (17th ed.), pp. 806–818. Philadelphia: W.B. Saunders Co., 1955.

GRAY, HENRY, ed. CHARLES MAYO GOSS, *Anatomy of the Human Body* (27th ed.), pp. 446–467, 1167–1205. Philadelphia: Lea & Febiger, 1959.

GUYTON, ARTHUR C., *Function of the Human Body* (2nd ed.). Philadelphia: W.B. Saunders Co., 1964.

MACKENZIE, WILLIAM COLIN, *The Action of Muscles*, Chapter XV. New York: Paul B. Hoeber, 1921.

MILLER, MARJORIE A., and LUTIE C. LEAVELL, *Kimber-Gray-Stackpole's Anatomy and Physiology* (16th ed.), Chapter 19; pp. 369–398. New York: The Macmillan Co., 1972.

RANSON, STEPHEN WALTER, rev. SAM LILLARD CLARK, *The Anatomy of the Nervous System: Its Development and Function* (10th ed.). Philadelphia: W.B. Saunders Co., 1959.

TAYLOR, DAVID C., *The Psychology of Singing*. New York: The Macmillan Co., 1908. (Discusson of muscles, pp. 240–246, is recommended.)

ZEMLIN, WILLARD R., *Speech and Hearing Science: Anatomy and Physiology*. Englewood Cliffs, N.J.: Prentice-Hall, Inc., 1968, Chapters 2 and 3.

BREATHING

BLOOMER, HENRY HARLAN, *The Diaphragmatic Factor in Respiration*. Unpublished doctoral dissertation, University of Michigan, 1933.

CARD, ROBERT E., *A Study of Clavicular, Intercostal, and Diaphragmatic Breathing in Relationship to the Control of the Breath in Expiration*. Unpublished doctoral dissertation, Detroit Institute of Musical Art, 1942.

COLWELL, RICHARD J., *The Teaching of Instrumental Music*. New York: Appleton-Century-Crofts, 1969.

EISENSON, JON, "Diaphragmatic Breathing," *The Clarinet*, 23, pp. 21, 24, 25; *24*, pp. 21, 22.

FREEMAN, RUTH, "Problems of Breath Control," *Symphony*, VI (May 1952), 9.

GIBSON, DARYL J., *A Textbook for Trumpet*, pp. 5–12. Minneapolis: Schmitt, Hall and McCreary, 1962.

HEGVIK, ARTHUR, "An Interview with Anthony Gigliotti," *The Instrumentalist* (June 1970), 45–53.

HUTTON, CHARLES L., JR., *A Survey of Research Pertaining to the Singing Voice*. Unpublished Master's thesis, Department of Speech, University of Pittsburgh, 1951.

KOFLER, LEO, *The Art of Breathing as a Basis for Tone-Production* (7th rev. ed.). New York: Edgar S. Werner & Co., 1897. Pp. 61–63 contain an excellent discussion on the influence of the larynx.

MAXYM, STEPHEN, "The Technique of Breathing for Wind Instrumentalists," *Woodwind* (December 1952; January, February, March and April 1953).

RAMACHARAKA, YOGI, *The Hindu-Yogi Science of Breath*. Bombay: D. B. Taraporevala Sons & Co., Private Ltd., Copyright L. N. Fowler & Co., Ltd., 1960.

REINHARDT, DONALD S., *The Encyclopedia of the Pivot System*. New York: Charles Colin, 1964.

SAUTTER, FRED, "Yogi Exercises Bring Positive Results in Breath Control," *The Getzen Gazette* (April 1970), 1, 2.

SMITH, DOUGLAS, "The Diaphragm: Teacher's Pedagogical Pet," *The Instrumentalist* (March 1966), 87, 88.

STANLEY, DOUGLAS, *Singer's Manual*, Vol. 2. Boston: Stanley Society, © 1950. On breath pressure.

TOSÉ, GABRIEL, *Artistic Clarinet: Technique and Study*. Hollywood: Highland Music Co., 1962.

WEAST, ROBERT D., *Brass Performance: An Analytical Text*, pp. 19–30. New York: McGinnis and Marx, 1961.

CREATIVITY

BLAKESLEE, THOMAS R., *The Right Brain: A New Understanding of the Unconscious Mind and Its Creative Powers*. Garden City, N.Y.: Anchor Press/Doubleday, 1980. Chapters 3 and 5 are especially recommended.

GHISELIN, BREWSTER, ed., *The Creative Process: A Symposium*. Berkeley: University of California Press, 1952.

MASLOW, ABRAHAM H., *The Farther Reaches of Human Nature*. New York: The Viking Press, 1971.

WALLAS, G., *The Art of Thought*. London: C.A. Watts, 1945.

EDUCATIONAL PHILOSOPHY

LEONHARD, CHARLES, and ROBERT HOUSE, *Foundations and Principles of Music Education*. New York: McGraw-Hill Book Company, 1959.

MURSELL, JAMES L. *Education for Musical Growth*. Boston: Ginn and Company, 1948.

REIMER, BENNETT, *A Philosophy of Music Education*. Englewood Cliffs, N.J.: Prentice-Hall, Inc., 1970.

SUZUKI, SHINICHI, *Nurtured by Love*. New York: Exposition Press, 1969.

WHITEHEAD, ALFRED NORTH, *The Aims of Education*. New York: The Macmillan Co., 1929.

LEARNING THEORY

ADAMS, J. A., "Motor Skills," *Annual Review of Psychology*, 15 (1964), 181–202.

BARKER, SARAH, *The Alexander Technique*. New York: Bantam Books, Inc., 1978.

BRUNER, JEROME S., *The Process of Education*. New York: Random House, 1963.

CRATTY, BRYANT J., *Movement Behavior and Motor Learning* (2nd ed.). Philadelphia: Lea and Febiger, 1967.

GALLWEY, W. TIMOTHY, *The Inner Game of Tennis*. New York: Random House, 1974.

GALLWEY, W. TIMOTHY, *Inner Tennis: Playing the Game*. New York: Random House, 1976.

HILGARD, ERNEST R., and GORDON H. BOWER, *Theories of Learning* (4th ed.). Englewood Cliffs, N.J.: Prentice-Hall, Inc., 1975.

HOLDING, D. H., *Principles of Training*. London: Pergamon Press Ltd., 1965.

NIDEFFER, ROBERT M., *The Inner Athlete: Mind Plus Muscle of Winning*. New York: Thomas Y. Crowell Publishers, 1976.

NIDEFFER, ROBERT M., and ROGER C. SHARPE, *A.C.T., Attention Control Training: How to Get Control of Your Mind Through Total Concentration*. New York: Wyden Books, 1978. Chapters 1 and 6 are especially recommended.

PITTENGER, OWEN, E., and THOMAS C. GOODING, *Learning Theories in Educational Practice: An Integration of Psychological Theory and Educational Philosophy*. New York: John Wiley & Sons, Inc., 1971.

SAGE, GEORGE HARVEY, *Introduction to Motor Behavior: A Neuropsychological Approach*. Reading, Mass.: Addison-Wesley Pub. Co., 1977.

STELMACH, GEORGE E., ed., *Motor Control: Issues and Trends*. New York: Academic Press, 1976.

SUZUKI, SHINICHI, *Nurtured by Love*. New York: Exposition Press, 1969.

THORPE, LEWIS P., "Learning Theory and Music Teaching," *Basic Concepts in Music Education,* 57th Yearbook, pp. 163–194. Chicago: National Society for the Study of Education, 1958.

TEACHING TECHNIQUES—
INSTRUMENTAL

BELLAMAH, JOSEPH L., *Brass Facts: A Survey of Teaching and Playing Methods of Leading Brass Authorities.* San Antonio: Southern Music Co., 1960.

COLWELL, RICHARD J., *The Teaching of Instrumental Music.* New York: Appleton-Century-Crofts, 1969.

DUERKSON, GEORGE L., *Teaching Instrumental Music.* Washington, D.C.: Music Educator's National Conference, 1972.

GALAMIAN, IVAN, *Principles of Violin Playing and Teaching.* Englewood Cliffs, N.J.: Prentice-Hall, Inc., 1962.

GREEN, ELIZABETH A. H., *Teaching Stringed Instruments in Classes.* Englewood Cliffs, N.J.: Prentice-Hall, Inc.

FARKAS, PHILIP, *The Art of Brass Playing. A Treatise on the Formation and Use of the Brass Player's Embouchure.* Bloomington, Ind.: Brass Publications, 1962.

FARKAS, PHILIP, *The Art of French Horn Playing: A Treatise on the Problems and Techniques of French Horn Playing.* Evanston, Ill.: Summy-Birchard Co., 1956.

HOLZ, EMIL A., and ROGER E. JACOBI, *Teaching Band Instruments to Beginners.* Englewood Cliffs, N.J.: Prentice-Hall, Inc., 1966.

HUNT, NORMAN J., *Guide to Teaching Brass Instruments.* Dubuque, Ia.: Wm. C. Brown Publishers, 1968.

KOHUT, DANIEL L., *Instrumental Music Pedagogy, Teaching Techniques for School Band and Orchestra Directors.* Englewood Cliffs, N.J.: Prentice-Hall Inc., 1973.

POLNAUER, FREDRICK F., "Bio-Mechanics: A New Approach to Music Education," *Journal of the Franklin Institute,* no. 4 (1952), 297.

REINHARDT, DONALD S., *The Encyclopedia of the Pivot System.* New York: Charles Colin, 1964.

ROLLAND, PAUL, and MARLA MUTSCHLER, *The Teaching of Action in String Playing.* Urbana, Ill.: Illinois String Research Associates, 1974.

SPENCER, WILLIAM G., *The Art of Bassoon Playing.* Evanston, Ill.: Summy-Birchard Co., 1958.

SPRENKLE, ROBERT, and DAVID LEDET, *The Art of Oboe Playing.* Evanston, Ill.: Summy-Birchard Co., 1961.

STEIN, KEITH, *The Art of Clarinet Playing.* Evanston, Ill.: Summy-Birchard Co., 1958.

TEAL, LARRY, *The Art of Saxophone Playing.* Evanston, Ill.: Summy-Birchard Co., 1963.

WESTPHAL, FREDERICK W., *Guide to Teaching Woodwinds: Flute, Oboe, Clarinet, Bassoon, Saxophone.* Dubuque, Ia.: Wm. C. Brown Publishers, 1962.

TEACHING TECHNIQUES—
VOCAL

ALLEN, JOYCE HERMAN, *The Technique of Modern Singing.* London: Sir Isaac Pittman and Sons, Ltd., 1935.

APPELMAN, D. RALPH, *The Science of Vocal Pedagogy: Theory and Application.* Bloomington, Ind.: Indiana University Press, 1967.

CANTERBURY, LEWIS B., *The Singing Method of Manuel Garcia.* Chicago: Lewis B. Canterbury, n.d.

CHADBOURNE, NORMA JEAN, and E. THOMAS A. CHADBOURNE, *Singers Manual,* parts I–X. White Plains, N.Y.: Chadbourne Conservatory of Vocal Arts, 1950–1954.

FILLEBROWN, THOMAS, *Resonance in Singing and Speaking* (3rd ed.). Boston: Oliver Ditson Co., 1911.

GOVICH, BRUCE MICHAEL. *Vocal Science for Teachers of Singing.* Unpublished University of Illinois doctoral thesis, 1967.

HUTTON, CHARLES L., JR., *A Survey of the Research Pertaining to the Singing Voice: 1925–1950.* Unpublished Master's thesis, Department of Speech, University of Pittsburgh, 1951.

JONES, FRANK P., "Voice Production as a Function of Head Balance in Singers," *Journal of Psychology,* 82 (November 1972), 209–215.

REID, CORNELIUS L., *The Free Voice: A Guide to Natural Singing.* New York: Coleman-Ross Co., Inc., 1965.

ROMA, LISA, *The Science and Art of Singing.* New York: G. Schirmer, Inc., 1956.

SHAKESPEARE, WILLIAM, *Plain Words on Singing.* London: Putnam, 1924.

SUNDBERG, JOHAN, "The Acoustics of the Singing Voice," *Scientific American,* 236, no. 3 (March 1977), 82–91.

TAYLOR, DAVID C., *The Psychology of Singing.* New York: The Macmillan Co., 1908. The discussion of muscles, pp. 240–246, is especially recommended.

TETRAZZINI, LUISA, *How to Sing.* New York: George H. Doran Co., 1923.

TRUSLER, IVAN, and WALTER EHRET, *Functional Lessons in Singing* (2nd ed.). Englewood Cliffs, N.J.: Prentice-Hall, Inc., 1972.

VENNARD, WILLIAM, *Singing: The Mechanism and the Technic.* Los Angeles: William Vennard, 1964.

WESTERMAN, KENNETH N., *Emergent Voice.* Ann Arbor: Dr. Kenneth N. Westerman, 1947.

PSYCHOLOGY

BANDURA, A., *Principles of Behavior Modification.* New York: Holt, Rinehart and Winston, 1969.

Biofeedback and Self-Control 1972: An Aldine Annual of the Regulation of Bodily Processes and Consciousness. Chicago: Aldine Publishing Co., 1973.

BIRCH, DAVID, and JOSEPH VEROFF, *Motivation: A Study of Action.* Belmont, Cal.: Brooks/Cole Publishing Co., 1974.

BLAKESLEE, THOMAS R., *The Right Brain: A New Understanding of the Unconscious Brain and Its Powers.* Garden City, N.Y.: Anchor Press/Doubleday, 1980.

BRANDEN, NATHANIEL, *The Psychology of Self-Esteem.* New York: Bantam Books, Inc., 1967. Part II is especially recommended.

FITTS, PAUL M., and MICHAEL I. POSNER, *Human Performance.* Belmont, Cal.: Brooks/Cole Publishing Co., 1967.

HART, HORNELL, *Autoconditioning: The New Way to a Successful Life.* Englewood Cliffs, N.J.: Prentice-Hall, Inc., 1979.

HILTS, PHILIP J., *Behavior Mod.* New York: Harper's Magazine Press, 1974.

KRUMBOLTZ, JOHN D., and HELEN BRANDHORST KRUMBOLTZ, *Changing Children's Behavior.* Englewood Cliffs, N.J.: Prentice-Hall, Inc., 1972.

MADSEN, CLIFFORD K., R. DOUGLAS GREER, and CHARLES H. MADSEN, eds., *Research in Music Behavior*. New York: Teachers College Press, Teachers College, Columbia University, 1975.

MALTZ, MAXWELL, *Psycho-Cybernetics*. New York: Pocket Books, 1960.

MASLOW, ABRAHAM H., *The Farther Reaches of Human Nature*. New York: The Viking Press, 1971.

MASLOW, ABRAHAM H., "The Theory of Human Motivation," *Psychological Review*, 50, 370–396.

MAY, ROLLO, *Psychology and the Human Dilemma*. Princeton, N.J.: D. Van Nostrand Co., Inc., 1966.

MILHOLLAN, FRANK, and BILL E. FORISHA, *From Skinner to Rogers: Contrasting Approaches to Education*. Lincoln, Neb.: Professional Educators Publications, Inc., 1972.

NARANJO, CLAUDIO, and ROBERT E. ORNSTEIN, *On the Psychology of Meditation*. New York: The Viking Press, 1971.

ORNSTEIN, ROBERT E., ed., *The Nature of Human Consciousness: A Book of Readings*. San Francisco: W.H. Freeman & Co., 1973. Parts III and VI are especially recommended.

ORNSTEIN, ROBERT E., *The Psychology of Consciousness*. New York: Penguin Books, 1972.

ROGERS, CARL R., *Freedom to Learn*. Columbus, Oh.: Charles E. Merrill Publishing Co., 1969.

SCHMITT, SR. CECILIA, *Rapport and Success: Human Relations in Music Education*. Philadelphia: Dorrance & Co., 1976.

SKINNER, B. F., *Science and Human Behavior*. New York: The Macmillan Co., 1953.

ORAL CAVITY

CARTER, WILLIAM, "The Role of the Glottis in Brass Playing," *The Instrumentalist* (December 1966), 75–79.

MEIDT, JOSEPH ALEXIS, "A Cinefluorographic Investigation of Oral Adjustments for Various Aspects of Brass Instrument Performance." Unpublished doctoral dissertation, University of Iowa, 1967.

PUNT, NORMAN A., *The Singer's and Actor's Throat* (2nd rev. ed.). London: William Heinemann Medical Books Ltd., 1967.

RICHTMEYER, LORIN CAROL, "A Definitive Analysis of Brass Embouchure Abnormalities Including Recommended Remedial Techniques." Unpublished doctoral dissertation, Michigan State University, 1966.

RUNYON, SANTY, "High Notes for Saxophone," *The Instrumentalist* (December 1974), 56.

TETZLAFF, DANIEL, "The Transparent Man," *The Instrumentalist* (March 1969), 81.

THE WHOLE VERSUS
THE PARTS

BRIGGS, G. E., and W. J. BRAGDEN, "The Effect of Component Practice on Performance of a Lever-Positioning Skill," *Journal of Experimental Psychology*, 48, 375–380.

KNAPP, B. N., *Skill in Sport*. London: Routledge, 1963.

NAYLOR, J. C., and G. E. BRIGGS,   "Effects of Task Complexity and Task Organization on the Relative Efficiency of Part and Whole Methods," *Journal of Experimental Psychology,* 65, 217–224.

O'BRIEN, C. C.,   "Part and Whole Methods in the Memorization of Music," *Journal of Educational Psychology,* 34, 552–560.

index